MAKING
MOVIES

Also by John Russo

SCARE TACTICS: The Art, Craft, and
Trade Secrets of Writing, Producing, and Directing
Chillers and Thrillers

HOW TO MAKE YOUR OWN FEATURE MOVIE
FOR TEN THOUSAND DOLLARS OR MORE

VOODOO DAWN

MAKING MOVIES

MOVIES

THE INSIDE GUIDE TO INDEPENDENT MOVIE PRODUCTION

John Russo

A DELL TRADE PAPERBACK

A DELL TRADE PAPERBACK

Published by
Dell Publishing
a division of
Bantam Doubleday Dell Publishing Group, Inc.
1540 Broadway
New York, New York 10036

Simultaneously published as a hardcover by Delacorte Press and a trade paperback by Dell Publishing in 1989.

Designed by Rhea Braunstein

ISBN: 0-440-50046-X

Printed in the United States of America

Published simultaneously in Canada

March 1989

10   9

BVG

Acknowledgments

SPECIAL THANKS are due to the film people who allowed me to interview them so that their valuable experiences and insights could become part of this book. They are (in alphabetical order) Lizzie Borden, Rick Catizone, Tobe Hooper, Christopher Lewis, Linda Lewis, Joseph Pytka, Sam Raimi, George A. Romero, Monty Ross, Tom Savini, Dick Smith, Oliver Stone, and Russell W. Streiner.

I edited the interviews, eliminating my own questions, so the information truly has the flavor of a personal dialogue with the reader. Most of the interviewees were extremely busy, immersed in current projects, so it was very kind of them to take time out to co-host this trip through the magical world of making movies.

My appreciation also to my wife, Mary Lou, and daughter, Julie, for remaining cheerful and cooperative while I took long hours, days, and months away from them to do the writing.

And deep gratitude to my editor, Jody Rein, and agents, Athos Demetriou and Bruce Kaufman, whose help was invaluable.

Contents

PART VII: GOING ON TO BIGGER THINGS

Author's Note
Movie Magic

MOVIES AFFECT large masses of people—as art, as entertainment, as a method of wide-scale dissemination of fact and opinion. Making movies offers a means of involving the mind and body in creating something that will have a direct and powerful effect on those who see and hear it.

Because modern communication is the lifeblood of our culture, many persons nowadays feel a need to know how motion pictures are made and marketed. More and more people have jobs that require them to produce film, to supervise production, or at least to be knowledgeable enough to effectively employ the talents and services of motion picture specialists. If you are a critic writing about film, an advertising exec who recognizes the merits of film in selling products, services, and ideas, a home-movie enthusiast, a film investor, or simply an enjoyer of films, this book will enlighten and entertain you.

It was written primarily for those who have a consuming desire to *make* movies. But it is also for everybody who aspires to a deeper and broader understanding of the art and craft behind "movie magic."

JOHN RUSSO

Preview
The Adventure of Making Movies

MOVIE-MAKING is a craft, a business, and an adventure. It offers a creative challenge, an opportunity to work with attractive, talented, dynamic people, and a chance to make a lot of money. It can be frustrating. It is seldom boring. It is thrilling, fascinating, demanding, hard work.

This book will tell you how to have fun and make money while making sure that your cinematic creations are seen by millions of people. Using my own experiences and the experiences of other successful filmmakers, I'll teach you what we had to learn the hard way and help pave your way to success in a tough, competitive, exciting industry.

Sometimes getting there can seem like an impossible dream. But I want to put some flesh on your dream. I want to clothe it in reality. I want to show you how to get from where you are now to where you *want* to be as a professional filmmaker.

Right now you may feel like you're at the bottom looking up. The ladder seems almost too high to climb. You don't know how to get your foot on the first rung. But I know that wherever you happen to be in your career, however unreachable your aspirations may seem to be, you can climb higher. I can help you take that first step. I will teach you how to make the right moves and avoid most of the pitfalls; I hope to help you reach your goal.

Making it in the film business takes talent, drive, ambition, expertise, initiative, salesmanship, persistence, and luck. Talent and luck are perhaps the *least* important ingredients. You have to be endowed with at least a modicum of talent, or no one can help you get off the ground. But, remember, there are many talented failures. Most of them would have been "luckier" if they had been diligent and persistent enough to fully develop and properly channel their talents and abilities.

Learning how to make a good movie is only half the battle. You must know how to sell it and promote it and hang on to your fair share of the profits. You must know how to deal with agents and distributors and be able to participate wisely in the entire marketing process, from negotiating and signing a deal to raking in the cash.

I have designed this book to help you whether you want to make your way into the studio system or to produce your own low-budget movie and see it become a hit. Reading this book will raise your level of understanding and help you perfect your talent. It will demonstrate clearly how you can go about writing, financing, producing, and directing full-length theatrical motion pictures with a *realistic* shot at worldwide distribution. I hope it will make it easier for you to make money making movies.

In the pages that follow, George Romero and I tell you how we went from making TV spots together to making the classic horror film, *Night of the Living Dead.* Then Monty Ross *(School Daze; She's Gotta Have It)* talks about how he and Spike Lee started from scratch and took their own special path to enormous success. We help you see why now is the time for you to make *your* start. We intend to inspire you to launch your own career.

But first you have to learn the fundamentals, so I next acquaint you with basic filmmaking equipment. I give you tips and pointers that will help you make your films look so professional that you might be able to land commercial jobs. You'll see how you can make an excellent living, should you choose to stay in the advertising world for a while—and to prove this point, you'll hear from Joe Pytka and Russ Streiner, two filmmakers who have hit the top in that world.

Whether you're working in the commercial or the theatrical end of the business, you must understand how to collaborate with the tricksters of the trade: the animators, makeup experts and special-effects wizards. That's why I introduce you to Rick Catizone *(Creepshow),* Dick Smith *(Amadeus),* and Tom Savini *(Friday the 13th).*

With all this information (and a whole lot of practice) under your belt, you'll be chomping at the bit to try your first feature movie. I take you step by step through that process, from scripting, casting and shooting to screening a finished print. And getting it sold.

Lizzie Borden *(Working Girls)* and Sam Raimi *(The Evil Dead)* will fully explain how they went about raising money outside of the Hollywood system, then making and selling their own first features. If you're afraid that the money-raising part will be your own biggest stumbling block, you'll be highly interested in what Christopher and Linda Lewis *(Blood Cult; The Ripper)* have to say about their successful ventures into the made-for-home-video market.

You'll learn herein that making and selling a picture doesn't end your odyssey or your obligations. You need to know how to properly deliver what you've sold, so that the distributor won't break the contract. You have to contribute to the promotion and publicizing of the picture, making sure it won't flop when it hits the screen. I'll teach you how to do all this effectively, and also how to follow up and police playdates and boxoffice reports so your share of the money doesn't elude you.

If you make one hit movie, you'll want to make more. You won't want to be a one-shot wonder—a person who makes one fluke hit and then fades out of sight. Tobe Hooper *(Texas Chainsaw Massacre; Poltergeist; Invaders from Mars)* will join Oliver Stone *(Salvador; Platoon; Wall Street)* in helping me help you go on to bigger and better things.

No one can guarantee that you will be able to realize your dreams, but if you have the talent and the drive, this book will help you overcome major obstacles. It will answer many of the questions that are extremely important to the filmmaker anxious to make his mark in the industry:

How can I best learn the basic techniques of movie-making? Once I succeed in learning them, how do I make use of them?

Who will hire me? Will I have to start at the bottom? What *is* the bottom, and how long will I stay there?

Can I make a living even if I don't hit it big?

Can I make TV commercials as a sideline while I work for a chance to do my own feature film?

Should I work as a free-lancer or start my own company?

How do independent features get financed? How are they sold? Is the home video market a golden opportunity?

How do I negotiate a distribution contract? If I have a successful picture in distribution, how much of the money do I get to keep?

If I have a major or even a minor hit, does financing additional pictures become easier? Would the Hollywood studios become interested in my work? How did the big-name producers and directors get where they are?

The answers to these questions are not easy ones. They have been bought and paid for in sweat and disappointment and sometimes triumph by the filmmakers in this book. And now they're yours for the reading.

PART I

THE DREAM

"American independent films have never been stronger. Production is down in Europe. The traditional directors we used to depend on have either died or stopped making films, so there is no constant source of product. In the next three or four years, I think the American independent filmmaker is going to be quite a powerful person."

TOM BERNARD, Orion Classics

"The great Hollywood empire that ruled American tastes for more than half a century lies in dust, its tyrannical moguls dead or deposed, its back lots empty, its sound stages still, its ranks diminished or in disarray. But out of the ruins of the city of dreams a new film industry is rising."

Newsweek

1

How I Got Bitten by
the Movie Bug

I'VE BEEN WORKING in the film business for more than twenty years, getting pictures made, sold, and distributed. I learned from scratch, cutting my teeth on TV commercials, industrial films, political spots, and documentaries, then going on to write, produce, or direct a half-dozen money-making feature movies, starting with the horror classic *Night of the Living Dead* and extending currently to *The Majorettes,* a thriller in worldwide release through Vestron Video and Manson International Pictures. I've also had thirteen novels published, some based on my own screenplays.

TEAMING UP WITH GEORGE ROMERO

My life would have been considerably different if I hadn't met George Romero. We were both eighteen years old then, and George had already been severely bitten by the movie bug. He was wilder about movies than anybody I've ever known. He got hooked as a kid, loafing in his father's New York art studio, surrounded by lavish banners, standees, and posters created for the premieres of major motion pictures.

On his first day in Pittsburgh, having come here to start his freshman year at Carnegie Institute of Technology (now Carnegie-Mellon University), George bumped into my friend Rudy Ricci. They were both enrolled as fine arts majors, both loaded with the flamboyant kind of talent that doesn't take well to formal surroundings, so neither paid much attention in class. Rudy daydreamed about becoming an actor or writer, and George filled his sketch pads with splendid charcoal renderings of scenes from *Ben-Hur* and *Viva Zapata!*—epic movies he wished he could have directed.

While Rudy and George were skipping classes at Carnegie Tech, I was attending West Virginia University. On my first Christmas vacation, Rudy told me I had to meet his great new pal, so we drove to George's off-campus apartment. Rudy honked the horn of his '55 Plymouth convertible, and George came out wearing a huge sombrero, a drooping crepe mustachio, and a silver pistola, like one of Zapata's bandidos. We drove to a Dairy Queen and shook up the girl behind the counter, who slammed the window and didn't want to make us any milk shakes. The same Christmas vacation, George covered the walls of Rudy's bedroom with a mural of ancient Rome as seen from Laurence Olivier's balcony in *Spartacus*. I thought the artwork was wonderful, but Rudy's mother wasn't exactly thrilled. She didn't try to stop the project, though. When George was around, you could count on some crazy, creative things happening, over and above anyone's objections.

Almost six and a half feet tall, George is an amiable giant with a dimpled smile, sharp perceptions, and persuasive charm. He was a favorite in college; he could act, paint, write, and draw hilarious cartoons. He could mimic people and do funny voices. He could eat a large pizza at one sitting, folding it in two as if it were a sandwich. At age fifteen, he had been arrested for throwing a body from the roof of an apartment building. The "body" was a mannequin he was using in a movie. The cops told him to "grow up"—but the movie bug's bite had rendered him incapable of following their stern advice.

Luckily, I wasn't going to college in Pittsburgh, or he would have talked me into cutting classes with him and Rudy to make 8-millimeter flicks about bumbling spies and inept detectives—imitations of Peter Sellers that exhibited a crude flair despite their derivative nature. I got to laugh at these fabulous farces on weekends away from WVU instead of flunking out helping to produce them.

Through George and Rudy I met Ray Laine and Russell Streiner, who were both studying to be actors. We were all around the same age, all fearful of going to work in corporation land after we graduated from the various schools we were attending. I was majoring in English education but had started writing a novel in my spare time, hoping that if it got published I'd never have to go to work for anybody.

As graduation loomed nearer, with its threat of dull, mundane jobs, George kept saying that if we all banded together and made a full-length theatrical movie we'd have a shot at becoming rich, famous, and independent. He insisted that such a movie could be made cheaply. He said he had learned a lot about professional film equipment and production techniques by working one summer as a gofer (gofer this, gofer that) on the set of *Bell, Book and Candle*, starring Kim Novak and Ernie Kovacs. It impressed us that he could bandy those big stars' names around. He also told us that his father had connections with movie distributors, and we didn't ask if the connections went any deeper than making banners for the distributors' movies.

ZANY FUN AND EARLY STRUGGLES

While I was finishing my senior year in college, George Romero, Rudy Ricci, Russ Streiner, and Ray Laine borrowed $2,000 from George's uncle and formed a company called Ram Productions, fully intending to produce a full-length feature movie. They bought a 16-millimeter Bolex camera and some boxes of film, and whenever I was around, they enlisted me to work crew, run errands, and appear as an extra. Somehow this flick, a series of comic vignettes under the title *Expostulations,* actually got shot on a measly two thousand bucks, but it lacked a soundtrack.

George and Russ hoped they might raise enough cash to finish *Expostulations* by making commercial films for a while. The resources behind their new pipe dream amounted to only the Bolex camera, a couple of clumsy, antiquated movie lights, and five hundred bucks loaned to them by Rudy Ricci's cousin Richard. They formed a brand-new company called The Latent Image, Inc.—a latent image being one that has been photographed but not developed.

Everything about the new company was latent. George and Russ rented a shabby storefront flat for $50 a month and furnished it with a few sticks of Goodwill furniture. When winter came around, they couldn't afford to turn on the heat, so they had to chip ice out of the commode bowl before they could flush it. They ate, slept, worked, and played at "the studio." Every once in a while they'd land a "big job" taking pictures of a baby or a wedding or a funeral.

One day when they were "flush" from one of these "major gigs" they bought a hockey game and a pet monkey. When there wasn't any film work, which was 98 percent of the time, George and Russ would sit inside the storefront window playing hockey, intensely absorbed in pulling levers to make the tin players swat at the felt puck and teaching the monkey to play, too. Sometimes they would borrow money to feed the monkey or take him to the vet. Other times all three—George, Russ, and the monkey—went for days without eating.

When I got drafted into the army, Rudy Ricci drove me down to the studio to say good-bye to Russ and George, and Rudy brought them a six-pack of Pepsi and a bag of popcorn, which they greedily devoured while playing hockey; it was their only meal that day. They shook my hand and told me that if they were a success in the movie business by the time I got discharged, I should come to work with them. My stints as a grip on *Expostulations* had been enough to get me bitten by the movie bug, so I dearly hoped their offer would come true. I dreamed about it during my two years with Uncle Sam even though the dream should have seemed utterly irrational after I had watched them share popcorn with their monkey.

While I was slogging around Fort Bragg with a gun on my shoulder, a fellow named Larry Anderson brought George and Russ their first "big job." It was a commercial for Buhl Planetarium that required them to film a spaceship landing on the moon. There was a ton of money to work with—$1,600. Luckily, they didn't have to actually *go* to the moon. All they had to do was create a mock-up of the moon's surface on a tabletop, build a realistic-looking miniature spaceship, animate it, and film the "landing." Russ and George refused to believe they couldn't do all this on sixteen hundred bucks, which was a princely sum compared to the $25 they had gleaned for their last series of baby pictures.

Fortunately, Rudy Ricci's brother Mark, who was majoring in math and science at Carnegie Tech, with some friends had built his own radio-controlled rockets large enough and sophisticated enough to shoot a mile or more into the air with live mice in the nose cones. Mark's aid was donated to the Buhl project. George did all the backdrops and related artwork. Russ molded the craters of the moon out of clay. The spot was wildly successful. The lunar landing effect turned out as well as most such depictions in "B" science fiction movies of that period. Larry Anderson was so impressed that he quit his advertising job and joined Russ and George as a partner in The Latent Image.

They had lost money on the job. But it made getting additional work a little easier, because now they had a showpiece. They also had Larry's expertise and contacts with some of the Pittsburgh ad agencies.

By the time I got out of the army The Latent Image was starting to grow— due partly to a $30,000 loan cosigned by George's uncle. The company had moved into an impressive new studio. Russ's brother Gary and Larry's wife, Jeannie, had joined the staff. So had Vince Survinski, a World War II vet who, to everyone's amazement and glee, had sold his money-making roller rink to buy into The Latent Image to the tune of $10,000.

I was overjoyed when George asked me to join the outfit, but I didn't even know how to thread a projector. George said that he could train a monkey to thread a projector or push a camera button, but a monkey couldn't be as creative as he hoped I would be.

Thus inspired, I set out to learn the ropes and catch up to the others. I worked first as a grip, later as a cameraman-editor, and then as a producer and director. Over my five years at The Latent Image I helped make short films, long films, and in-between films. Films about catsup, corporation presidents, pickles, paint, soda pop, political candidates, and beer.

When I started, I was getting paid $325 per month, and Russ and George were each getting $400—theoretically. In truth, we often were broke for months at a time, sleeping on the studio floor, borrowing from friends, relatives, and finance companies, and busting hump on every low-budget job that came in. We hoped that doing good work on small jobs would help us land

A MAGNIFICENT ACHIEVEMENT
IN
MOTION PICTURES

George Romero's campy painting for a Latent Image flier, based on the one-sheet for *Ben-Hur*. The reverse side contains copy that I wrote, telling how Julius Caesar could have impressed the Roman senators and avoided assassination by letting The Latent Image film his conquest of Gaul.

bigger gigs, but this rarely happened. Clients counted on us to make purses out of sows' ears, but when they had real money to spend they ran away to New York or Hollywood.

COMMERCIAL SUCCESS

A tremendous amount of commercial film production is contracted out of Pittsburgh (it ranks third in the nation in corporate headquarters), and we were being tossed some of the scraps. At the time about twenty movie companies were listed in the local Yellow Pages, but most of the films being made by the older, more established outfits were dry and predictable. So there was an opening for mavericks like us to make a name for ourselves with snappier scripts, more fluid camera techniques, and jazzier editing.

Once we snatched a job away from one of our stodgier competitors we

The Latent Image crew on a camera setup designed to show off the city of Pittsburgh. George Romero is behind the camera, and I'm using the light meter.
Photo by Cramer Riblett.

worked on it with zest and intensity. We sweated the tiniest detail. If we were grinding out a ten-second spot for three hundred bucks, we tried to make it the best $300 spot ever. We eventually started to win some awards—gold and silver medals from international film festivals where our low-budget stuff was outshining other people's films with budgets ten times as high.

We became known as a bunch of young, creative maniacs, Bohemians with cameras. We were fiercely proud of our work. We had amazing drive and esprit de corps that made us feel we were on a roll, bound to hit it big someday.

Our goal was to use commercial filmmaking as a springboard into features, and even though the struggle was often bitter and frustrating, we thought it was our most viable choice. The Hollywood system appeared too tough to crack. We didn't want to go out there and take low-level jobs in the major studios with the vague hope that somebody higher up would eventually notice us and help us climb the rungs.

Rather than waiting for someone else to give us the chance to make movies, we stayed on our own turf and carved out a place for ourselves. Whenever we had any extra cash, instead of drawing higher salaries, we plowed it into more movie equipment. Within a few years we owned lights, cameras, recorders, projectors, editing tables, and mixing facilities. Then we bought a secondhand 35-millimeter Arriflex, and the time to make our first theatrical movie had arrived.

OUR "MONSTER FLICK" BECOMES A HORROR CLASSIC

One week after we picked up that camera we decided to make a "monster flick." It took us a while to figure out what kind of monsters we would create. We made a couple of false starts, at one point fooling around with a script for a sci-fi comedy starring some weird creatures that resembled gobs of over-cooked spaghetti. But finally we thought up the flesh-eating zombies in *Night of the Living Dead.*

We kicked in our own cash (mostly borrowed) to get the camera rolling and called upon our friends and associates not only to buy a bit of stock in our movie but also to work as grips, actors, extras, cooks, caterers, costumers, makeup artists, set builders, and prop gatherers. The camaraderie and know-how that we had developed over the years of cranking out commercial films carried us through our first feature with high-spirited energy and verve. We were all pulling together in one clearly defined direction, with George Romero as the indispensable ringleader.

We all wore many hats; we each had to do many jobs and handle them well. I helped write, finance, film, and edit the picture. I made props and built sets. In between working crew and loading magazines, I played the part of a ghoul who got stabbed in the head with a tire iron. I was narrowly missed by flying shrapnel while focusing my camera on a truck being blown up by TNT and nitroglycerin. At one point in the shooting schedule I volunteered to be set on fire with gasoline—without an asbestos suit, because the production couldn't afford it—to add realism to a sequence in which ghouls were being bombarded with Molotov cocktails.

I was lucky not to be killed doing some of these things, and I wouldn't recommend them to everybody who's trying to survive and get ahead in the business. But my experiences do point up the fact that sometimes, especially when you're struggling along on a ridiculously low budget, you have to be willing and able to do just about anything and everything to make a good movie.

We never had any doubt that we were making a very good movie, but none of us could have predicted the enormous success that it would achieve. Years after we made it, George Romero said, "That film was shot over a period of about nine months, with great breaks in between to come back and do a pickle commercial or something, which was distressing. After we got some footage in the can, people started coming around saying, 'Hey, that looks like a movie!' And we said, 'Well, that's what it *is!*' "

Made on a budget of $114,000, *Night of the Living Dead* has grossed more

A rare marquee shot commemorating the thrills and anxieties of opening night.

than $50 million worldwide. Critics call it a classic, one of the greatest horror movies ever produced. It has been in constant release since 1968, always playing somewhere, in theaters or on TV, in the United States or abroad. Videocassettes of it still sell phenomenally, in the original black-and-white version and in color, created by the new color-conversion process. Over the years the picture somehow has retained its impact, its raw power. *Night of the Living Dead* goes on scaring people, giving them goose bumps, making them afraid to go to sleep.

By giving millions of people nightmares, we latched on to our piece of the dream.

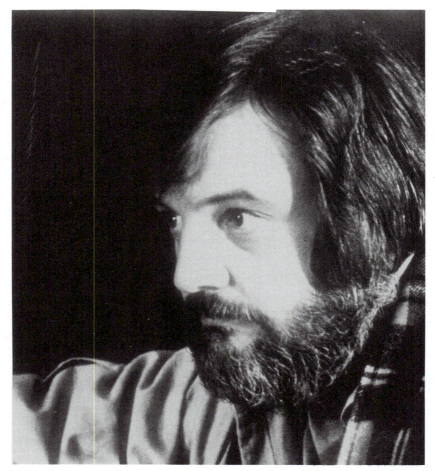

George A. Romero. *Photo courtesy of Imagine, Inc.*

After **George Romero** and I worked together on *Night of the Living Dead* and *The Affair,* he made three more low-budget movies: *Jack's Wife, The Crazies,* and *Martin.* Even though the box office grosses on these films were disappointing, they earned critical praise and demonstrated craftsmanship, intelligence, and creativity, so projects kept coming, 'til George hit it big once again with *Dawn of the Dead.* Independently financed, produced, and distributed, it grossed over $40 million. George next experimented with a philosophical blend of the modern with the ancient in *Knightriders,* a movie about armored warriors on motorcycles, then came back to horror with *Creepshow* and *Day of the Dead.* His current project is *Monkey Shines,* a $6 million psychological thriller for Orion.

2

George A. Romero
Doing It from the Heart

★ You know, if I had a magic crystal ball when I started out and could have seen all the setbacks I was going to suffer, and knew what I know now—I'd still make movies. In fact, I'd go back and do it all over again right now. I love what I do. But I'd sure have changed the way I handled things! We thought we were on top when *Night of the Living Dead* made money right out of the gate. I remember I went to see it at a drive-in with the co-producers, Russell Streiner and Karl Hardman and one of the actresses, Marilyn Eastman. It was like a picnic for us—the very fact that *our* film was playing there! It suddenly became a real movie for us.

But if we had any dreams of becoming rich, they didn't come true at that point. We got ripped off because we did not know how to negotiate the right kind of contract. But the notoriety of *Night of the Living Dead* at least made it possible for us to raise money for a second picture.

The second feature I directed, *The Affair,* with John Russo and Russ Streiner as co-producers, opened in a few places and just never caught on. The distributor was too small to have any clout. He just folded his hand . . . he never even tried. We had tried to follow up our success in horror with a romantic comedy, and I think it was a major mistake strategically. Had we made something like *Return of the Living Dead* at that time, maybe we'd all still be together.

The Affair was such a big disappointment that it helped cause our original group to fall apart. I stuck with The Latent Image, but most of the others left the company. I stopped doing commercials and concentrated on features because I made a connection with a brokerage that was going to finance three pictures. It was a big mainstream brokerage, all of its principals were heavy hitters, and they gave us a letter of credit so we borrowed money from the bank and started to make *Jack's Wife*. I still like the story—about an upper-middle-class lady who gets involved in witchcraft—but I never got enough money to do the film properly. The brokerage went belly-up right in the middle of production, and I personally borrowed money, and ended up about $600,000 in the hole. So the film didn't turn out exactly the way I wanted it to, but I give it an "A" for effort. I still have a warm spot in my heart for it. It's doing well on home video, under the title, *Season of the Witch*.

Even though I was in heavy debt, I remained passionate about making feature movies. It was what I really wanted to do with my life. I had lost interest in doing little TV spots and industrial films and keeping track of all the paperwork, materials, film elements, taxes and so forth on a jillion little piss-ant productions. I kept chasing feature projects, seeing them as a way of bringing in big chunks of money, and finally I landed *The Crazies*—a $275,000 project. That was 1971. So I had made four features in three years, but it took me a few more years to finally get out of debt. All of my older films were distributed inadequately, then sat around till 1980 or so, when I was told by my reps that we couldn't get distribution deals because the stuff was too dated. But the moment we unloaded the whole inventory for peanuts, home video cassettes started to appear in the stores. This includes my vampire film, *Martin,* and the final irony about that one is that about a month after we got rid of it some big legitimate theater producer decided to do it as a musical. I don't have any share of the royalties, but my name is splashed all over the ads and posters. So I profit from the publicity and that's all.

But, as I say, if I had it to do all over again, even knowing the pitfalls and the disappointments, I'd still go ahead and try to make feature movies, because that's always been my dream. The misadventures were just detours, good learning experiences. They happened because I didn't pay enough attention to the business aspects. I depended on other people who were supposed to be competent and left it in their hands. But now I'm totally involved in the whole thing, and I know I have to be, because I'm utterly on my own. In 1987 I folded The Latent Image and resigned from Laurel Entertainment—the company we set up to produce movies such as *Creepshow* and the syndicated TV series, *Tales from the Darkside*.

I wrote the pilot show, "Trick or Treat," for *Tales from the Darkside*, but the idea of doing a show for syndication came from a fellow in Los Angeles who had been a network exec and knew the syndication business, and he told us that there'd be a big market for a horror series with my name on it, if we could produce it cheaply enough. At first I was against it because I didn't think there was enough money in it to do the job well and still have money left over to make a profit. Laurel was committing to do 23 episodes for $2,300,000, and I said not to do it because I was appalled at the notion of trying to make 23 half-hour shows for a hundred thousand apiece—the networks can easily spend a million dollars on an hour-long show. I thought we'd end up in debt again. Six hours of material for just over two million dollars! But it wound up that Laurel took the deal, and it was very important to the company's financial life, and in that sense I was wrong. But I say anyway that after four years they've made *24 hours* of material for about eight million bucks, and the amount of effort and energy that it took would've made twelve or fifteen feature movies, each with a shot at enormous boxoffice profits. It all keeps coming back to my passion for making theatrical features.

All my features have been independent productions, although Warner Brothers picked up *Creepshow* after we already had it finished. My psychological-suspense movie, *Monkey Shines,* was made for an independent, Charles Evans in New York, who also did *Tootsie.* His brother Robert did a lot of big movies like *Love Story, Cotton Club,* and so on. By working independently, I've had some hassles, but I've also had some opportunities to work creatively with pretty decent budgets, in the seven to ten million-dollar range.

That I've been able to keep working is a testament to the fact that there has always been an audience for the fantastic. Ever since primitive man sat around a fire and wondered what lightning was, there has been a craving for fantasy. I think it's a much larger audience than Hollywood believes it to be. But there's no real recipe for satisfying an audience. You can't just throw in twenty minutes of blood, twenty minutes of nudity, or twenty minutes of violent action. People try that all the time and fail miserably.

CRACKING INTO THE BUSINESS

Most young people always want to know how they can crack into the business. I guess I would still do it pretty much the same way, outside the system. I mean, the mainstream industry attracts a certain kind of personality, and if you're the type of person who likes to work for IBM as opposed to opening your own business, then you're probably better off taking the studio route or joining one of the unions or finding some specialty that you can work in whether it's lighting or writing or editing. But if you don't have that mentality, if you're the kind of guy who'd rather open your own candy store or your own burger joint and do it your way, about all you can do is try to get as much experience as possible. The producers and distributors aren't out there specifically to beat you, they're out to benefit themselves, and if you can show them a way that they can benefit by working with *you,* then you'll find some way to skin the cat.

The only thing you can do is do the work. It's the only way you're gonna get experience. I often advise people to just sort of work around, try to get credits, work in public TV, wherever—just get around it for a while, try to get your hands on the hardware, even volunteer your services for a couple of years, if it comes down to that—just to get in, get a foothold somewhere. But then eventually, when you think you have the strength, go do it on your own.

The worst that can happen is you'll wind up in debt, but even that teaches you something. I could've gotten out of my own debt situation by bankrupting. I just didn't do it. And I developed important allies in my career when they saw that I didn't simply fold.

LOOKING AHEAD

I have so many things I'm looking forward to, at any given moment. Movies I dream about making. I'd love to do Stephen King's *The Stand*. Laurel Entertainment still has the film rights and I have some rights in it, too, so I might get a chance to do it one day. I'd love to try it.

I've always wanted to do *Tarzan of the Apes*. My own special way! Everyone gets to do that but me! I've also developed a project called *Copperhead,* in cooperation with Marvel Comics. Each project is like a new baby that's born. Until it happens, you can't think of it in anything but abstract terms. But when it happens, it suddenly becomes real and you fall in love with it.

It's tough for me to say what might be the greatest movie I could ever work on, but I know I'm always looking forward to the *next* movie with a great deal of excitement and anticipation. In a board game that I like to play, called *Careers,* the careers that provide the most joy all have to do with the arts and self-expression. Those are the things that make you feel the most useful. I mean, that's the stuff that comes from your heart.

3

Golden Opportunities for Today's Maverick Filmmakers

"THE UNDERGROUND has become the overground. They're already a major creative reality, and by the end of the decade, in my view, they will be a major financial reality," says David Puttnam, producer of *Chariots of Fire* and *The Killing Fields. Newsweek* adds, "The day of the American independent movie is at hand."

What happened? Why do things suddenly look so good for new filmmakers?

The marketplace has changed drastically in recent years, creating an unprecedented demand for independently produced movies. One reason for this is the "VCR Revolution"—the fifty million American homes that now house videocassette recorders and playback systems. A second factor is the boom in television syndication and cable broadcasting; in the last ten years the number of independent stations has more than doubled, and they all need product. However, the tremendous rise in Hollywood production costs makes it almost impossible for the major studios to produce enough films just when hundreds more are needed.

THE VCR REVOLUTION

Buyers and renters of videotapes are voracious consumers of motion picture product. The Video Software Dealers Association (VSDA) has a membership of about 30,000 stores. Each store carries an average of 3,500 titles. The jacket prices average about $29 per title. Each title will rent anywhere from 30 to 80 times, for an average of $2.40 per rental. We're talking here about a $2 billion business that's still growing by leaps and bounds.

In 1986, 50 percent of American households owned VCRs, and they're still selling at a rate of twelve million a year. Soon almost every household will include a VCR. There's already a tremendous market for home video entertainment, and suppliers can't keep up with the rapidly increasing demand.

It wasn't long ago that films played first in theaters, garnering their major income at the box office and reaping the huge publicity value of a national theatrical release, thereby ensuring a substantial ancillary, or secondary, income from videotape sales. But now home video is leaping from a mop-up business into a first-run business. Instead of looking solely toward acquisitions of already released movies to fill their product pipelines, cassette distributors are bankrolling hundreds of feature films out of their own pockets. These movies are being budgeted at anywhere from $50,000 each (generally made and distributed by smaller companies specializing in "low-end" product) to $5 million or more per film (produced and distributed by the larger home video firms, which are also setting up their own theatrical and foreign distribution arms).

Vestron Video has established a made-for-video film unit under the name Lightning Pictures, which is expected to crank out about forty films a year budgeted at around $1 million apiece. And Prism Entertainment Corporation is also trying to beat the high cost of acquisitions by getting directly involved in production. Barry Collier, president of Prism, says that instead of spending $6 million on a movie, he'd sooner produce thirty made-for-video films, knowing that if he sells just ten thousand units per release he'll pull in $15 million.

Almost all the home video companies are getting into the act, making their own movies or paying to have them made. Most production deals are made with established filmmakers, but often the home video distributors will take a chance on fresh talent. The VCR revolution has taken a great deal of the risk out of film financing because of the tremendous consumer demand. It has also opened a world of opportunity for new, creative filmmakers.

TV SYNDICATION AND CABLE MARKETS

Since 1978, the number of independent television stations has grown from 93 to more than 200—and they're all hungry for programming. Also, a fourth TV network, Fox Broadcasting Corporation, has joined ABC, NBC, and CBS in the scramble for Nielsen ratings. The networks are much healthier than they were several years ago, when they were losing large numbers of viewers to pay TV. Consumers have a wider choice of programs to watch and are watching more often than they used to.

The networks don't usually buy independently made movies for prime-time screening; instead they produce their own Movies of the Week and so on. But if an independent picture performs well in its theatrical release, it can land a network sale of anywhere from $250,000 to several million dollars. Failing this, a feature can still reap tremendous profits in syndication, which is the process of leasing screening rights to the television channels on a per-station basis. Even a "B" picture, if it doesn't contain nudity or excessive violence, can earn $250,000 to $500,000 in syndication.

The movie-oriented cable channels—like HBO, Cinemax, and Showtime—buy movies already completed and also make deals to have movies produced. A few years ago the cable channels didn't have to develop expensive programming because subscribers were won over by the opportunity to see uncensored Hollywood movies in their own homes, but today people can have the same opportunity by renting videocassettes. So the cable giants have been forced to meet the VCR revolution head-on. It is expected that 60 percent of American households will have cable by 1990—and this mass audience will consume more and more movies.

Furthermore, there is now encouraging evidence that, instead of hurting ticket sales, the home video craze has started to increase the public's appetite for quality theatrical releases. According to *Boxoffice* magazine, towns with cable have a higher movie attendance than similar towns without it. Apparently, exposure to quality movies on cable whets the appetites of many viewers, giving them an urge to go out and see the "real thing" on a big screen.

HOLLYWOOD NEEDS HELP MEETING THE DEMAND

The average cost of making a movie in Hollywood has risen from $3 million in 1976 to 20 million in 1988. Ironically, the boom in the ancillary markets has helped drive budgets up to this wildly exorbitant level. For a time, studio executives liked to believe that big-budget pictures that didn't succeed at the box office would always be bailed out by cable, syndication, and videocassette sales. Sometimes this notion turned out to be painfully foolhardy.

Despite this view, on average only one out of every ten Hollywood films can be considered a hit. All the rest lose money, while the few box office smashes earn millions. So the studios, in their "cautious" moods, have developed the habit of going for home runs, and this causes their pictures to fall more and more into a "proven" formula. That's why we're seeing so many pictures aimed at the huge teen-age audience. Some of these pictures have been accused of pandering to low-level tastes, delivering little more than unrealistic sex, silly jokes, or gratuitous gore. Regardless of content, once a picture hits, it can spawn big-budget sequels ad infinitum—or ad nauseam.

At the same time, studio execs still seem to feel the only other way to make a big splash is to pour the bucks into a single bathtub. Hollywood producers have been lavishing money on dazzling special effects, costumes and props, and they've been granting multi-million-dollar contracts to star actors, actresses, producers and directors who are supposed to be guaranteed box office draws.

Because Hollywood is spending more per picture, it must cut down on the number of pictures made. Meanwhile, more theaters have been built and many older ones have been converted to multiplexes. So there are more screens to fill, and when they're glutted with a fairly poor selection of Hollywood films (as they often are), moviegoers will try something they might not have tried ordinarily. Then, if they find out they like it, word of mouth spreads, potentially transforming a well-made independent movie that doesn't fit the studio mold into a "sleeper"—a surprise hit.

MOVIES ARE BEING MADE EVERYWHERE

When we made *Night of the Living Dead,* most people were sure that Pittsburgh was a good place to make iron and steel but not motion pictures. They didn't believe a "real movie" could be made anywhere but in Hollywood or New York.

Oh, how things have changed! Many major motion pictures have been filmed in Pittsburgh in recent years—Hollywood features such as *The Deer Hunter, Gung Ho!, Flashdance, Mrs. Soffel, Rappin',* and *Lady Beware.* TV movies such as *Fighting Back, Death Penalty,* and *Silent Witness.* And George Romero's big-budget pictures: *Day of the Dead, Knightriders, Creepshow,* and *Monkey Shines.*

What is happening in Pittsburgh is happening all over the United States. Hollywood companies are going outside of Hollywood to do their filming, and independent movie companies are springing up in "unlikely" places. Vestron Entertainment is headquartered in Stamford, Connecticut. Rock music superstar Prince has built a $10 million video/audio/film production studio in a suburb of Minneapolis. Sam Raimi operates out of Detroit, Michigan. Independent companies have been set up in Dallas, Houston, Miami, Tulsa, and San Francisco.

So, the move away from Hollywood is taking place on two important levels:

1. Independents based in Hollywood are choosing not to work within the studio system. Sometimes big-name directors and producers are bankrolled by relatively small distribution companies, and sometimes these heavy hitters make financing and distribution deals with the major studios. But in either case, they insist on a large measure of creative control, and they often film on locations far from Hollywood so they can avoid high studio overhead charges and exorbitant union wages. Oliver Stone shot *Platoon* in the Philippines, with a cast of relatively unknown actors, on a budget of $6 million. Robert Redford made *Ordinary People* in Vermont for $6 million. John Sayles's

> "What we decided was that films can be made anywhere in the country now. Hollywood and New York are not the film centers anymore. And if you have an inventive attitude, you can make a successful movie. If you're a young filmmaker, you can certainly go out there and for a reasonable amount of money, anywhere in the country, make a movie. That was our point with *Blood Cult*. We know it's not an award winner, but it's a financial success."
>
> Linda Lewis
> The Entertainment Group

movie *Matewan* was shot in West Virginia on a budget of $4 million—less than one fourth of the average Hollywood budget.

2. People who aren't "big names" are electing to go out and raise money just about any way they can and make their movies on budgets of $300,000 or less. Then they find a distributor. Or they win a major festival. And suddenly their names aren't "little" anymore.

Frustrated by the status quo for black actors in Hollywood, Robert Townsend used money he had made acting in *American Flyers* and *A Soldier's Story* to begin shooting his own movie, the satirical comedy *Hollywood Shuffle*. He even ran up $40,000 on his credit cards to pay for filmstock, props, sets, and costumes. He managed to finish shooting his movie in fourteen days on a total budget of $100,000. Then he sold it to the Samuel Goldwyn Company and watched it gross over $3 million.

Joel and Ethan Coen, two brothers from Minneapolis, made 8-millimeter movies while they were kids, then studied film in college. Businessmen in their hometown came up with enough cash for them to make *Blood Simple,* a sly, suspenseful murder story that critics found "maliciously entertaining." So did lots of theatergoers. The Coens then got $5 million from Twentieth Century–Fox to write, produce, and direct *Raising Arizona,* which turned out to be a smash-hit comedy.

Nowadays many filmmakers are going it on their own as mavericks, like Robert Townsend and the Coen brothers. They've made the same kind of choice that my friends and I made years ago when we produced *Night of the Living Dead*. Like us, they're carving out their own turf. You can carve out your own turf as a filmmaker, too. In the next chapter, Monty Ross *(School Daze, She's Gotta Have It)* will help show you the way.

Monty Ross. *Photo by Carol Wiggins.*

Monty Ross was production manager on Spike Lee's *She's Gotta Have It* and co-producer for Spike on *School Daze,* a $6 million movie for Columbia Pictures. Unable to crack into the Hollywood system, they worked their way around it—by making a hit movie on a shoestring.

4

Monty Ross
From Student Film
to Studio Film

Teaming Up with Spike Lee

★ Spike and I got together in college. In our junior year, he and I and some other friends put together a small feature that we took around to different campuses. It was a Super 8-millimeter film; Spike wrote the script, and I acted in it; that was our start as mass communications majors. Spike finally went to NYU film school, and in his third year he called me and asked if I'd like to read for a gangster film he was doing for his student thesis, *Joe's Bed-Stuy Barber Shop: We Cut Heads*. I acted in it; it won "Best Student Film of 1982" from the Academy of Motion Picture Arts and Sciences, and *that* was our start in the movie business. It was a sixty-minute film in 16-millimeter color, and it has since been translated into four different languages and has played in major film festivals across the country.

The way it got financed was that Spike asked his grandmother for money, got some private donations, got some money from the Brooklyn Delta Sigma Theta sorority . . . just local contributions. When it was finished, a faculty member suggested that he submit it to the academy; Spike's winning the award was announced during the Academy Awards of 1982, and it was even on *Entertainment Tonight*. It brought notoriety, but not money. It was a signature piece for Spike in that he could show that he had done some work that had credibility. It was very helpful to us. A lot of people in Brooklyn saw the film and could see that there was talent there.

I've known Spike for ten years, and we've established a business as well as a personal relationship. I don't try to infringe on his artistic ability, and he has called on me to fill a number of positions because we just didn't have the money to pay a big staff. He never *gave* me any position; I had to audition to act in his films; I had to prove myself as production manager and co-producer. So I never got these positions just because I was his friend. The same goes for his father, his brother, his sister, and whomever else he includes as his friends and working partners. He wants a film family, which is really what it's all about, but at the same time he doesn't want people there just because they're his friends. We've had some setbacks and we've learned a lot, and sometimes friendships don't always hold up and you have to move on; you hope people understand that.

We had to sacrifice because we weren't the type of people who wanted to work at the lower-level jobs. We had the talent for producing and the talent for administration on my side, and on Spike's side the talent for putting together and going out and shooting a film. I got most of my administrative experience in college, at Clark College in Atlanta, Georgia. A lot of the college productions didn't have anybody who wanted to take care of the administrative work, because they all wanted to be actors. But I would volunteer to work behind the scenes and learn how things are put together. As a result my drama teacher, Joan Lewis, took me under her wing and let me handle checks, invoices, purchase orders, ordering equipment and so on. I took some courses in administration, and there are still more I have to take.

Spike completed a film in each of his three years of graduate study at NYU, which most students do not manage to accomplish. The press had recognized him, and he had been given certain accolades—so here we were with a choice to make. And we decided not to go and get the nine-to-five jobs, not to go after the Mercedeses, the nice houses and condominiums. We decided we were going to sacrifice and get the things we really wanted. No matter how hard it was, that was what we were determined to do.

THE MAKING OF *SHE'S GOTTA HAVE IT*

Essentially, *She's Gotta Have It* came out of a script that Spike wanted to do earlier, called *The Messenger;* we had to abort that project because the producer pulled out at the last minute, after we were in preproduction about eight weeks. It was a much bigger project than *She's Gotta Have It.* When it fell through, we took the rest of the year off to write a new script. I wasn't living in New York at the time, so I went back to Atlanta and worked in the theater, with some other jobs on the side, 'til Spike got the script together and told me he wanted me to come back and be a part of it. We had been working like that, making one film at a time and doing whatever it took to survive between times.

Spike said he wanted to do a script that had material that a whole lot of people would want to see, but although it dealt with sex, he didn't want to do it in a Hollywood fashion, like a *Porky's.* He wanted to do something that was very well done on a topic that a lot of people never knew existed in the black community; that is, the sexual revolution not only touched the white community, but it touched the black community, and he wanted a look with a contemporary point of view at relationships within the community.

He did a lot of interviews, compiled a lot of research. He talked to therapists. He carefully considered the type of music that should accompany the piece. And when I got the script, I knew it was a good story. I'm finding in my own relationships that there are women who want the kind of free-spirited life-style that the heroine of our movie had.

Spike originally had gotten a grant that he was to use for *The Messenger,* and he got permission to switch that money to *She's Gotta Have It.* And a friend came through with his life savings. It all amounted to only $22,000, and we used it to shoot for twelve days. Then we got on the phone and asked our school friends for donations, and they sent in fifties and tens and twenties and so on. And we had everything so calculated that if $50 came in, we knew exactly where it had to go, whether it was toward meals for the cast or whatever. We were very cost-effective on that film. We had to rent the equipment. We made some deferment deals, but we paid the crew off up front.

A BIDDING WAR IS LAUNCHED

We were lucky to have a very good producer's rep, John Pierson, who was an investor in *She's Gotta Have It;* he took that film to the San Francisco Film Festival, and it was a hit. So Orion Pictures, Samuel Goldwyn Company, and Island Pictures—which distributed *Kiss of the Spider Woman*—saw our film, and there was a bidding war. We finally went with Island Pictures. And we became their number one priority; sometimes you can land a distributor only to have him put you on the back burner, but fortunately that didn't happen in our case. We didn't have to handle the advertising and promotion of our picture ourselves, but we did assist Island with the black press and the black community.

SCHOOL DAZE FOR COLUMBIA ON $6 MILLION

I served as co-producer on *School Daze,* which was released February 12, 1988. It's about a weekend college homecoming at a fictitious college in the South. The story takes place over three days, and the lead character is using the homecoming as a platform to talk about apartheid and divestment of the school's assets in South Africa. Spike's movies usually encompass a whole lot, and *School Daze* is no exception. It's a musical comedy as well as a satire and social commentary. The stars are Larry Fishburne, Art Evans, Ellen Holly, Tisha Cambell, Kyme Hersi, and Branford Marsalis. Ossie Davis does a

Spike Lee directing Larry Fishburne (left) and his co-stars in *School Daze.*
Photo by David Lee.

cameo. But we're also working with a lot of unknown actors—people who can sing, dance, and act.

It can be a hassle at times, because some of the less experienced actors aren't really familiar with SAG rules, and they want to blame us for certain problems that we don't have much control over, whereas if they would read the SAG book they'd know what was going on. On the other hand, some of the more established stars can be lazy, or they're prima donnas and you have to cater to them. But despite these problems, I enjoy working with the talent because they're still hungry, just like we're still hungry.

DOING YOUR HOMEWORK

The advice I would give to anybody who wants to be an independent filmmaker is to understand that it's a business and every business is a risk, and even though your product is a movie instead of maybe a ball bearing, you still have to treat what you're doing *as* a business. You have to learn how the "big boys" put their films together. Start a personal library—spend every extra $20 on film books instead of going out and blowing the money. You don't necessarily have to attend film school to become a good filmmaker. But you have to be serious about it, you have to join organizations that promote films, and so on.

There are so many avenues of getting into the business that people fail to

A huge location setup for the closing scene of *School Daze.* *Photo by David Lee.*

explore. They all talk about going to Hollywood. But the main point is that if you're really interested in making it, the information is out there. People are out here doing it every day, and it's just a matter of whether you're willing to study and sacrifice to become the filmmaker that you want to become.

PART II

THE BASICS

"You've gotta get your hands on the hardware and make sure you have a basic mastery of a lot of the different skills. Know as much as you can about all the different areas of production, because you can get knocked off by your own crew guys if you don't know what they're doing. It's sort of like building a house. If you don't know anything about plumbing, the plumber can tell you the sink is good, and the first time you turn it on it pops out of the wall."

GEORGE A. ROMERO

5

Movie Equipment—
The Nuts and Bolts

TO MAXIMIZE your chances for success in the movie business you have got to learn the technical stuff—the "nuts and bolts" of filmmaking. I'm not going to get into a mundane recitation and comparison of the "specs" (specifications) of the various cameras, magazines, lenses, light meters, editing, lighting, and sound gear, etc. The specs are available from equipment manuals, the bible of these being the *American Cinematographer Manual.* But I will give you an overview of your choices, on both a professional and an amateur level.

Once you choose the type of equipment that you want to learn on, it will be up to you to read and observe and practice, practice, practice until you become fluent in the *language* of filmmaking: in other words, the technology behind the creativity. Trying to make a film without understanding technically what the filmmaking process is all about is like trying to write a story without thoroughly understanding grammar and syntax.

Maybe you think you can merely direct the actors in their performances and rely on a good, knowledgeable crew to back you up so you won't get egg on your face and wind up with a mess of good takes that can't be edited. It's been done that way before. Some directors have even been successful at it. But those kinds of directors are working with one arm tied behind their backs and most of the crew snickering behind their backs, too, because seasoned film crews take deep pride in their professionalism and have a cynical contempt for anyone on the set who appears less than professional.

However, you can take your first steps toward becoming a professional without immediately rushing out to buy or rent professional equipment. By using inexpensive amateur equipment, you actually can learn to make films professionally—in terms of correct camera, lighting, and editing technique.

You can learn how to work with actors and how to tell a story effectively. You'll be able to see where your action flows smoothly and where it's clumsy or boring. In fact, you should be able to achieve a high level of craftsmanship as far as basic filmmaking ingredients are concerned, except your finished product won't be in a professional format. But once you've mastered the basics and you get your hands on professional equipment, you won't find it difficult to learn how to make it work for you. You may rest assured that professional gear works on the same principles as the amateur stuff. It's just bigger and heavier with different kinds of buttons to push, different compartments to load, and so on.

AMATEUR EQUIPMENT YOU CAN LEARN ON

There are four categories of equipment you need to make a movie:

- Camera gear
- Sound gear
- Lighting gear
- Editing gear

Camera gear consists of the camera itself, with its lenses and filters, film compartment and/or magazines, and power supply. It also includes camera support equipment: tripods, shoulder pods, and dollies.

Sound gear consists of the sound recorder, microphones, microphone baffles and filters, microphone booms and fishpoles, sync cables, sync generators, and power supply.

Lighting gear consists of movie lights and filters, light stands, cables, generators, and batteries.

Editing gear consists of sound readers, film and/or videotape viewers, synchronizers, splicers, dubbers, and mixers.

You may elect to add numerous accessories and refinements to your basic equipment package as you become proficient in the use of your equipment. You will become acquainted with these options by observing and talking to other filmmakers, reading technical magazines and books, and visiting camera stores to find out about the latest products to hit the market.

Professional gear stays pretty much the same for years and years. It is the amateur equipment that changes and improves so quickly that whatever is new this year is obsolete the next. That's why I'm going to discuss the amateur equipment in general terms, rather than making specific brand and product recommendations that might be out of date by the time you read this book.

Your first important decision is the format that you will work in. Your choice is basically between film and videotape. On an amateur level there is

8-millimeter (now pretty much phased out) and Super 8-millimeter film; and there is 8-millimeter, Super 8-millimeter and half-inch videotape. It is cheaper to make movies in the smaller formats, but the image quality is not very good. And if you start with a poor image, it is only going to get worse by the time it is printed or dubbed to a finished product, which will be a generation or two away from the camera original. So I recommend that you choose either Super-8 film or half-inch videotape to begin learning how to make movies.

Super-8 Film Gear

CHOOSING A CAMERA

The camera is always the most important part of any equipment package. Select one that operates smoothly and quietly so that the noise of the camera motor will not intrude on your sound track. Make sure the lenses are of top quality and that the camera can accommodate a variety of lenses, including a zoom lens and a range of fixed-focus lenses, from wide-angle to telescopic. The more lens flexibility you have, the more freedom you will have in framing and composing images.

Make sure the camera can record sound. Super-8 film has a magnetic sound stripe on it that runs the length of the film on the side of the film opposite the sprocket holes. Therefore, you will be recording synchronous (sync) sound while you are shooting your pictures. A microphone should be built into the camera. Before you buy your camera, test the mike to determine that it is sensitive enough to record with sharp fidelity even when you are filming a person talking at a distance of ten to twenty feet from the camera. Also, make sure that an auxiliary mike can be jacked into the camera; that way, the camera can be filming from a distance, yet the mike can be placed close enough to the subject to record good sound.

If the camera has automatic focus and exposure features, make sure that you have the option of *not* using these features so that you can focus your lenses and set your apertures manually whenever you need to. You will get more precise lens settings by doing it manually, the way professionals do. But you will need to buy a light meter and learn how to use it properly to set your exposures by hand; if you don't have a light meter, it is better to use the automatic settings than to risk getting images that are so dark or light that you can barely see them.

Try to buy a camera that enables you to vary the film speed. Many motion picture special effects depend on slowing the film down or speeding it up. And some effects depend on being able to run the film backward through the camera. For instance, if you want to see an actor's hat fly from the ground up onto his head, you reverse the film and shoot the hat falling off; then, when you project the film forward, it looks as if the hat is leaping up by itself.

It is also helpful to have a single-frame capability on the camera. This enables you to shoot stop-motion or animation effects.

Another important feature to look for in your Super-8 camera is the ability to build in fades and dissolves while you are shooting. This allows you to make time-lapse transitions from one scene to another in your movies.

Choose a camera tripod that is solid enough to support the camera without vibrating while the camera motor is running, because tripod vibrations will show up as "flutter" on your film. Check the tripod to make sure it functions smoothly without sticking, whether tilting, panning, or craning up and down.

SUPER-8 EDITING EQUIPMENT

When you edit Super-8 film, you will be physically handling the film itself. Usually this means that you'll be handling the very film that went through your camera, not a print of it (which would cost more money and not look as good as the camera original). Professionals don't handle the original film; they edit a second-generation print, sometimes called a *slop print* or a *work print*. Then, when they're satisfied with the way the edited movie plays, they conform (match) the camera original to the spliced work print so that finished prints can be made from the camera original and will be of top quality. Making a print, editing it, then conforming it to the original is generally too time-consuming and expensive for beginning filmmakers.

In any case, you will need Super-8 editing equipment to make a finished movie from the film you've shot. The equipment includes

- A projector that can project Super-8 film and play back magnetic-stripe sound
- A movie viewer with a set of rewinds
- A film splicer
- A sound reader
- A tape recorder
- A tape splicer

The projector is used not only to screen your movies, but also to dub new and/or improved sound onto the tracks. To do this, you need a projector with an input sound jack that will allow you to record directly onto the magnetic (mag) stripe of your film as it passes through the projector. With this type of projector, you can add musical passages to your movies by dubbing the music from a tape recorder onto the actual film. And there are many other sound effects you can add, depending on your ingenuity and the amount of effort that you are willing to put forth.

The movie viewer and the sound reader (two separate pieces of equipment, with separate rewinds) enable you to see and hear your film footage over and over, at reduced speed, so you can determine the best places to make edits.

Then you make the edits by using your film splicer to splice selected scenes together at the precise frame lines you have chosen, in the order that you want the scenes to appear in your finished movie.

The tape recorder is for recording music, voices, and sound effects that you wish to add to your movies and for dubbing these sounds onto the mag-stripe track. If you have more than one tape recorder, you can do overdubbing and segueing. A *segue* occurs when one sound fades out as another sound fades in; this technique is often employed in making a smooth audio transition from one piece of theme music to another. With your tape splicer and sound reader, you can make precise edits in quarter-inch sound tape. By dubbing back and forth from one machine to another, you can build up multiple audio effects, then dub the whole works onto your film's mag-stripe track for a viewing of the finished product.

With hard, painstaking work, wondrous results can be achieved in Super-8. As your picture and sound edits become more and more complicated, approaching a professional level, you may elect to take your finished picture and track elements to a sophisticated motion picture laboratory to have composite prints made, with built-in effects that will outclass what you can do in bits and pieces on your own equipment.

SUPER-8 LIGHTING EQUIPMENT

For shooting interior scenes, you will need movie lights, which have tungsten filaments designed to emit the range of lightwaves that register natural colors truly and accurately on motion picture film. At least three lights are generally required to properly illuminate one or two people in a relatively close shot that does not reveal much of their surroundings. It takes about six lights to properly illuminate a moderate-size movie set or location such as a bedroom or an office when the shot is going to be so wide that most of the room will be seen along with the people in it.

Some very important accessories come with the lights, including diffusion filters, reflectors, and "barn doors" (for aiming and focusing the light). Red, green, blue, and orange filters can be used to alter the colors that will register on film. There is even special daylight filter material that can be stretched across windows in a room where sunlight is intruding so that the sunlight can be used to augment the artificial movie light without imparting a bluish look —which sunlight, unfiltered, will do—to the subject that is being photographed.

Warning: These powerful movie lights can be very dangerous. The standard filaments are usually rated at 600 to 1,000 watts, so hot that if you touch one with a handkerchief the cloth immediately catches fire. Some years ago, when we were making a TV spot for Arsenal sausage, we actually fried eggs and sausages out in the woods on one of these lights powered by a portable generator. You need heavy-duty three-pronged electrical cables for the lights, because flimsier cables can melt or burn. The connections should always be grounded properly to avoid the danger of electrocution.

Used with common sense and proper safety precautions, these lights will do their job without burning anybody. I haven't seen anyone get burned by them in my twenty-two years as a filmmaker, but I have seen some close calls.

Half-inch Videotape Gear

I've stated that half-inch videotape will give better image quality than 8-millimeter or Super-8 videotape; this is particularly true when it comes to dubbing, which is an essential step in editing videotape. Film can be physically edited, spliced, and then screened—you can actually project the edited camera original—but videotape can be edited only electronically. The videotape itself is not cut and spliced; instead, selected shots from the videotape that went through the camera are dubbed onto a brand-new videotape to produce a finished movie. I make this explanation as a way of leading up to a discussion of the major *dis*advantage of working with half-inch videotape instead of 8-millimeter videotape:

Currently, 8-millimeter home video editing gear is more sophisticated than similar gear in the half-inch format. In 8-millimeter you can make edits that are very clean and professional—in other words, glitch-free—without ugly color smears or image breakup.

But the sophisticated editing gear now only available in the 8-millimeter format will soon be available in the half-inch format too. So I'd still opt for half-inch because of the better overall image quality and because most aspiring filmmakers already own a half-inch VCR. If you do already own a half-inch VCR, you need to buy only a half-inch camera to start editing your movies, because the camera itself can be used to select and dub shots onto the VCR in an edited sequence.

CHOOSING A CAMERA

Most of the things I've already said about choosing a camera for shooting Super-8 film apply to choosing a video camera. Tape runs more smoothly than film, so gear noise is not usually a problem. Look at some tape shot with the camera so you can see whether or not the lens is sharp. Most video cameras are equipped with a zoom lens, but wide-angle lenses and close-up lenses are desirable extras.

Buy a solid-state camera, not one that uses tubes instead of microchips. The solid-state cameras do not cause the image to strobe (streak) when you pan, while strobing is a big problem in cameras with tube circuitry. Solid-state cameras are more efficient and dependable and do not require a warm-up before they will perform their various electronic functions.

All video cameras record sound with a built-in microphone. This kind of mike will probably be okay when you are shooting someone talking up close, but you will need to buy an auxiliary mike for more complex situations, so make sure the camera has a jack for the auxiliary mike.

Make sure also that you are not limited to automatic focus and automatic exposure and can perform these functions manually whenever you need to. You won't need a light meter with your video camera since you can see the image you are getting on tape in video feedback through the eyepiece and can adjust the aperture or the focus until the image looks the way you want it to.

You won't be able to change the speed of the tape going through the camera (for special effects such as slow motion) because all video cameras record at one very fast speed for optimum image quality. You won't have single-frame capability either. And you won't be able to run the tape backward. If you really want to create the kinds of effects that these devices facilitate, do them on film, then transfer to tape. Or you can do them when you edit your tape—if you buy one of the newer VCRs that can produce slow motion and still frames, play in reverse, and copy all these effects onto another VCR.

You will be able to build fades and dissolves into your footage while shooting, because all video cameras have this capability. The problem is that doing them while shooting is the hard way, because it takes too much advance planning and because you'll probably end up discarding most of them and going with straight cuts. It is better to be able to select the exact place where a shot should fade or dissolve when you are editing, but you won't have this luxury unless you buy some very expensive video editing gear. So fades and dissolves probably won't make up a large part of your beginning video repertoire.

I recently bought a half-inch video camera that has given me excellent results, even on occasions when I've transferred my half-inch tape to three-quarter- or one-inch tape for professional purposes. Here is a list of the accessories I acquired to make sure I could do a near-professional job with my camera:

- Wide-angle lens
- Two-hour battery to supplement the one-hour battery and the AC power supply/battery charger that came with the camera.
- Separate microphone with jacks and extension cable to be used instead of the built-in mike
- Lens and camera cleaning kit
- Tripod

In choosing a tripod for a half-inch video camera, you won't need to go overboard on sturdiness since modern camcorders weigh only about four pounds. But make sure that the camera mount is secure and won't twist or wobble when you pan, tilt, or crane. I had to buy a different attachment screw from the one that came with my tripod, and I had to drill a bigger hole in the camera mount to make the new screw fit. But I ended up with a very secure mount.

I also bought a supply of videocassettes made especially for use in camcorders. The brand was Scotch EXG (Extra High Grade) Camera T 120, for VHS systems. The manufacturer claims that this videotape "was developed to deliver optimal results in video camera recording" and that it has static-fighting elements that help ensure that all video programs will be drop-out-free and in bold, brilliant color. I have found this to be true. The EXG Camera T 120 is vastly superior to ordinary half-inch videotape.

HALF-INCH EDITING EQUIPMENT

The simplest and easiest way to edit half-inch tape is to have two VCRs and dub your selected takes from one VCR to the other. As I mentioned before, you can actually use your camera as a VCR, but don't do it that way if you can afford not to. Your camera will last longer and will take sharper pictures if you can avoid running miles of tape through it during the editing process.

In videotape editing, two VCRs and a television monitor take the place of the projector and movie viewer with rewinds that are needed for Super-8 film editing. But you will still need a sound reader, a tape recorder, and a tape splicer so that you can build sound tracks with music and/or multiple effects, then dub the finished sound onto your edited video movie. You can use one or both of your VCRs for this purpose instead of buying an audio tape recorder, but the videotape will be far more expensive than using quarter-inch audio-tape, and it will subject your video equipment to unnecessary wear and tear, so I would advise against it.

When dubbing and making edits, always use the VCRs at their fastest running speed as this will produce the best quality. Connect the two machines with separate cables for audio and video dubbing rather than using a single coaxial cable, which will not give as clear a signal. If you can afford it, use two monitors, one for each VCR, which will allow you to see what you are dubbing and review edits without disconnecting and reconnecting your cables over and over. Ideally the dubbing VCR should be one that will play back your shots even when you're going at fast forward or reverse so you won't have to rely solely on your footage counters to find particular shots and select precise segments for editing.

REFINEMENTS FOR GLITCH-FREE EDITS

As I mentioned earlier, manufacturers currently build devices for glitch-free professional-looking edits into 8-millimeter videotape gear, but these refinements are now only beginning to show up in half-inch VCRs and camcorders. The cleanest cuts are made with machines that have flying-erase heads. This kind of head erases the tape in the same diagonal pattern in which it was recorded, so there is no image overlap and blurring when two shots are edited together by dubbing the head of one onto the tail of the other.

Another desirable device to look for when you buy your half-inch VCR is the jog-shuttle dial. It is used to control tape movement during stops and starts so that edits can be made more precisely, thus further reducing the chance of smeary images.

A feature called *video insert* or *video dub* is available on some VCRs. It is designed to eliminate glitch between edits when recording video on top of video by applying a higher current to the recording heads and thereby suppressing evidence of the signal that is being overdubbed.

Some VCRs have an edit switch that will minimize the loss of sharpness during dubbing. But even with such a switch, image quality will begin to suffer noticeably if dubs are made more than one generation away from the camera original.

There's no way to copy a videotape without some image loss. The best way to minimize the loss is to use a high-quality original, shot at fast speed, on the best videotape available for your camcorder and then dub it onto a high-quality VCR.

When editing, you are not limited to one format. You can copy 8-millimeter tapes onto half-inch VHS or Beta systems and vice versa. You may want to exercise these options to gain access to editing refinements not available on your present VCR. You may even want to "bump" (dub) half-inch videotape to three-quarter or one-inch for editing in a professional video studio.

Some two-machine half-inch editing systems made for amateur purposes actually approach the professional level in terms of the flexibility and precision that they will deliver. For instance, some of these systems will mark and store a tentative edit so it can be previewed, each machine automatically playing its tape on cue. The location of the edit points can be fine-tuned, and when you're satisfied that you have a smooth action flow you push a button telling the VCRs to carry out the edit.

Desktop video—the use of computerized equipment to edit, title, and add special effects to home video productions—is making tremendous strides. There are now software edit controllers that are essentially video computers that enable video footage to be timed and marked to precise frames, as in editing film. Scenes can be experimentally cut and rearranged; then the computer will automatically create a final cut with all the scenes in the selected order and with titles and special effects built in.

If you choose to work in a video format, you'll have the advantage of all the new technology that is rapidly being developed for so-called amateurs. But the technology is becoming so advanced and refined that the gap is narrowing between the amateur and the professional. Already movies shot on half-inch home video equipment have been sold to major videocassette distributors. This trend will probably continue in the future, and more and more new filmmakers will take advantage of it to make a name for themselves.

VIDEO LIGHTING EQUIPMENT

The same type of lighting gear that is used with Super-8 film is used when you're shooting on videotape. Fewer lights may be needed since videotape is much more sensitive than film and will record at lower light levels, but I would recommend that you purchase the same lighting package that I described earlier (page 35). Having extra lights will give you the capacity to shoot bigger setups, and it is wise to have backup lights in case one or two of them fizzle.

Note: The same kinds of lights are also used with semiprofessional and professional videotape and movie gear. Therefore, to avoid being repetitious, I will dispense with any further discussion of movie lights in this chapter.

SEMIPROFESSIONAL EQUIPMENT

The next step up from Super-8 film is 16-millimeter film, which actually can be considered a professional format since most commercial films are shot in 16. Many theatrical films have also been shot in 16 and blown to 35-millimeter for international release. However, there are 16-millimeter cameras that are semiprofessional rather than professional. Some of these cameras cannot shoot sync sound. Some don't have reflex lenses; in other words, you don't see what you are shooting through the lens, but through a separate optical system. You can't use a nonreflex lens for focusing, but must rely on the secondary apparatus, which is not always accurate. Furthermore, some semiprofessional cameras have lenses that are not of optimum quality, so they don't always produce sharp images.

Similarly, semiprofessional double-system synchronous sound recorders are available for purchase or rental. But often they have a tendency to lose sync, or they don't record with high fidelity.

Personally, I would not fool around with these types of cameras and recorders unless I had no choice. You can rent legitimate professional gear for just a few dollars more per day. It is desirable to begin to *shoot* in 16-millimeter with synchronous sound, so you can begin to learn how to *edit* in 16, which is the smallest format with which you can acquire professional movie editing techniques.

It is even harder to draw the line between semiprofessional and professional videotape equipment. For instance, a high-speed Betacam was used by Christopher and Linda Lewis to make their first home video hit, *Blood Cult.* This type of camera is considered professional for news-gathering purposes, but it would probably have to be considered semiprofessional when it comes to making feature movies. However, in order to edit, Chris and Linda dubbed their half-inch Betacam tape up to one-inch, which is a professional format.

As soon as you step up from half-inch to three-quarter-inch videotape, you will be obliged to do your editing in a professional studio (or else buy a professional setup for yourself). With a professional setup, you will have all the technological refinements anyone could desire. You will very easily acclimate yourself to this luxury, for you will have already learned the basic principles by working on your own half-inch gear at home. At a professional studio, you won't be running the editing console on your own; you wouldn't be left with all that expensive computerized electronic equipment unless you forked out enough money to buy the place. But it won't take long, with a good studio technician at the controls following your directions, for you to become as proficient as you'll ever need to be at editing your movies on videotape.

Of course in 16-millimeter film you can choose to hire a professional editor instead of digging in and learning how to do it yourself; someone else can operate the machinery while you still make the editorial decisions. But don't succumb to this temptation. First off, you probably can't afford to pay for the technician as well as the equipment. Even if you can, don't do it. Don't deny yourself the opportunity of learning firsthand what the total filmmaking process is all about.

PROFESSIONAL EQUIPMENT

There is no way of learning how to use professional camera, recording, and editing gear except to get your hands on it. It is like driving a car; no amount of reading about it can replicate the actual experience. Fortunately, learning how to operate professional gear is just as easy as learning the amateur stuff. When you jump from Super-8 film to 16-millimeter film, in many ways filmmaking becomes easier instead of more complicated because the equipment does more things for you, and does them better. The jump from 16-millimeter to 35-millimeter is even smoother; the operation of the equipment doesn't change much, and the improved quality of the finished product is exhilarating. The same is true when you jump from amateur to professional videotape formats.

Professional Videotape Gear

If you want to make movies on videotape and bypass theatrical distribution, the best way to do it is to shoot on film and edit on videotape. That way you get the "film look" that most people find aesthetically pleasing, but you still end up in the medium that you will use for distribution of your product. I have already given you an overview of the professional video editing process (which doesn't involve teaching yourself how to use the equipment, because you will edit in a professional studio, using the technicians that the studio provides).

If you elect to shoot your movies on videotape instead of film, you will probably use either a half-inch high-speed Betacam, which even though it uses half-inch tape is a professional-level camera costing about $35,000, or a three-quarter-inch camera, perhaps a Panasonic. These cameras aren't difficult to use, and they yield excellent quality. I'm not going to go into detail about them, because at this stage in your development as a filmmaker it is likely that you will be working in film instead of videotape.

Videotape can substitute for film in some applications. I've already shown that it can be an excellent learning medium. Videotape, in its 8-millimeter and half-inch "amateur" formats, can look more professional than Super-8 film because of the computerized editing software available in those formats. But most "real" movies are still being made on film for screening on 35-millimeter projectors in theaters. Therefore, for theatrical as opposed to television programming, the step up from amateur to professional involves leaving videotape behind.

Professional Film Gear

To make a professional movie, you need the same categories of equipment you required to make a movie on the amateur level: camera, sound, lighting, and editing gear. Once you have a finished edit, your film and sound track elements go to a motion picture laboratory/mixing facility for final dubbing and composite printing. You will supervise the lab and studio technicians in this work, but you needn't know how to work the equipment yourself.

CAMERA GEAR

Professional cameras, whether 16-millimeter or 35-millimeter, can be divided into three basic categories determined by their ability or inability to shoot sync sound and the way they are built or modified to achieve this ability:

1. *Wild cameras* are called "wild" because the speed of the camera motor cannot be synchronized with a sound recorder; therefore, wild cameras cannot shoot sync sound.

2. *Blimped cameras* can shoot sync sound, but a special soundproof housing—a "blimp"—must be fitted around the camera so that the noise of its motor and gears will not interfere with sound recording.

3. *Self-blimped cameras* can shoot sync sound and require no external blimp because excellent soundproofing is built into the camera itself and the motor and gears are designed to run very quietly.

Obviously, the noise of a wild camera's operation is of little consequence since you won't be recording sound while you are shooting film. Wild cameras rent for much less than sync cameras and deliver excellent picture quality. Therefore, on a low-budget shooting schedule it may be wise to do all the sync shooting in as few days as possible, then use a wild camera for the rest of the production.

Blimped cameras are very heavy and awkward. In the "olden days" all lip-sync movies had to be shot with blimped cameras. The blimp itself weighs about eighty pounds, so huge and heavy that it denies camera maneuverability; that's why movies used to be shot mostly on sound stages and rarely on actual locations. We shot *Night of the Living Dead* with an old-fashioned blimped 35-millimeter Arriflex. It delivered excellent picture and sound quality, but the camera setups were such a slow, grueling chore that I'd never want to work that way again.

The best modern cameras are self-blimped. They weigh little more than wild cameras do and are just as easy to operate. They can fit into tight places. They are very maneuverable and provide tremendous flexibility in framing and composing shots. They make it possible to do numerous camera setups in a day's work, many more setups than used to be possible on the old studio soundstages.

The most commonly used professional cameras are:

- Arriflex
- Eclair
- Mitchell
- Auricon
- Panavision

Professionals most often use Arriflex when a wild camera is called for, in either 16-millimeter or 35-millimeter. When it comes to shooting sync sound, the old blimped Arriflexes are rarely used anymore, although they can be bought or rented very cheaply compared to the more sophisticated cameras.

The self-blimped Arriflex and the self-blimped Eclair, both available in either 16-millimeter or 35-millimeter, are generally the cameras of choice for professionals when they must shoot sync on modest budgets. Mitchell and Auricon are excellent alternatives but are a bit more cumbersome and harder to load.

Panavision is unquestionably the best camera to use if you can afford it. Most Hollywood pictures are shot on Panavision cameras, which give crystal-clear, rock-steady images. But if your production budget precludes this luxury, the other types of camera will still do an acceptable job.

You can learn to load and shoot with an Arri or an Eclair after some very brief instruction from someone who already knows how to use the cameras.

George Romero plugging in the blimped Arri, on location for
Night of the Living Dead.

You can even teach yourself by reading the operating manuals. The beauty of modern professional gear is that it has been engineered and refined to be as uncomplicated as possible while still delivering top quality. Anyone who can operate a home video camera can learn how to operate professional movie cameras with comparable ease and efficiency.

There is a wide choice of lenses, tripods, dollies, and other accessories accompanying each camera. When you start to rent this gear, you will get valuable initial advice from equipment suppliers, who will encourage you to take specific kinds of camera equipment packages. These packages have been put together because they will handle most professional jobs properly, so you can't go too far wrong in opting for a complete equipment package built around your camera of choice. You will learn how to modify the package according to your own preferences as you gain experience and learn from your initial mistakes.

Cameraman Paul McCollough with the self-blimped Arri that we used to film *The Majorettes. Photo by John Russo.*

SOUND GEAR

When you make films in Super-8, you are using *single-system* sound, whereas professionals use *double-system* sound. *Single-system* means that both picture and sound are being recorded on the same piece of film ("on film"). Your takes are therefore always in sync, and you don't have to worry about sync while you are shooting. But when sound is on film, obviously if you want to make a sound splice, you *have to* make a picture splice too—there is no way around it. Professionals often need more editorial flexibility; they want to be able to edit picture while letting sound run or vice versa.

For this reason, professional camera and sound gear is always *double-system*— the recorder is entirely separate from the camera, and the two machines are kept in sync by a sync signal and a sync generator. This is the reason behind the proverbial clapstick, which is clapped before each sync take so that the takes can be "synced up" in the editing room. The editor marks the first frame of picture where he can see the black and white bars of the clapstick coming together, and then he marks the first frame of sound where he can hear the clap. When these elements are "laid up" side by side in a synchronizer, they can be kept in sync for viewing and making editorial decisions.

The separate sound recorder for professional sync recording is the Nagra. Other types of sync recorders exist, but the Nagra is unsurpassed and is almost universally used on all types of movies, from the lowliest TV spot to the biggest Hollywood extravaganza.

Older Nagras require cables that tie into the camera, but the newer models operate independently. The camera is governed by its internal electronics to run at precisely twenty-four frames per second, and the Nagra also runs at precisely twenty-four frames per second, so they are always in perfect sync.

Professionals record sound with extremely sensitive directional microphones. A directional mike is one that will record with high fidelity any sound that it is aimed at directly, while not picking up unwanted fringe sounds. The most accurate directional mikes are the long-barreled "shotgun" mikes. A shotgun mike makes it possible to record a person talking in an area where there is heavy auto traffic, and the person's voice will be picked up relatively "clean," without being overpowered by the traffic noise.

Professionals sometimes use special microphones for special jobs. For instance, Lavelier mikes and wireless mikes are generally part of a sound equipment package. A Lavelier is very small and can easily be clipped behind a collar or a necktie. A wireless mike can be hidden beneath a shirt or a blouse; it is used for shooting especially wide shots where a mike hooked to a cable cannot be used because the cable would be seen in the shot. But wireless mikes often pick up interference and static, so they should be used only in special circumstances.

Professionals usually "boom" their mikes whenever possible; in other words, they use an apparatus that can dangle the mike near the actors and aim it at their mouths from a position just outside the framing of a shot. The boom can be a huge apparatus that looks almost like a small crane, or it can be a "fishpole"—an extendable bamboo rod that truly does resemble its namesake.

Scenes are often shot with the aid of sound baffles, which block out extraneous noise by cutting off portions of the set or location, or with the help of windscreens that fit around the heads of the microphones so that they won't pick up the whispering or whistling of the wind.

Like professional cameras, professional sound recorders can be powered by house current or by portable battery packs—one more reason today's movies can be made virtually anywhere.

EDITING GEAR

The simplest kind of professional editing setup, in either 16-millimeter or 35-millimeter, includes the following:

- A projector for viewing raw footage
- An editing table with lightbox
- A synchronizer
- A movie viewer with rewinds
- A sound reader
- A film splicer
- A tape splicer

All these pieces of equipment can be bought separately; in other words, they are not tied into each other mechanically or electronically. While this is not the most efficient way to set yourself up for professional editing, it is, at a cost of roughly $2,000 to $3,000, the cheapest. Every film I worked on during my five years with George Romero at The Latent Image was edited on this kind of equipment, including *Night of the Living Dead*. The work print and the sound track had to be cranked manually through the synchronizer, through the viewer, and over the head of the sound reader so that spots could be marked for edits and the edits could be seen and heard at an approximation of natural speed—twenty-four frames per second. How closely the natural look and sound could be approximated depended on the skill and practice of the editor. George had an uncanny ability to get it right—sometimes he'd be cranking those rewinds by hand, and the footage would play almost as if it were running through a sync projector. For me it was more difficult; when I was doing the cranking, the picture and sound tended to slow down or speed up at rhythmic intervals instead of staying pretty close to twenty-four frames per second.

To overcome these difficulties highly sophisticated editing tables have been developed. The main brands in use today are Steenbeck, Moviola, and KEM. These machines enable you to thread up picture and sound on separate decks and play them together in sync. Usually one roll of picture is viewed in sync with two rolls of edited sound, but it is possible to buy or rent editing machines with more decks, more viewers, and more sound readers so that more rolls of picture and sound can be played in sync simultaneously.

Once you have this kind of equipment at your disposal, you can edit picture and sound according to the same principles that apply when you're working in Super-8, but of course the end result is much more polished and sophisticated.

Your final mix will be done at a professional studio, where your camera original will be conformed to your edited work print. Then the sound mix and the conformed original will be printed onto a single roll of film to give you the very first print—the composite "answer print"—of your finished movie. If you've chosen your equipment well and used it well, screening your answer print will be an exhilarating experience that will fill you with pride.

6
Making Your Movies Look Professional

LET'S ASSUME that you have a camera and know how to zoom and focus and push the buttons to record sights and sounds on celluloid. Now that you've been introduced to the "nuts and bolts" aspects of filmmaking, we can cover the basic techniques of cinematic art and craftsmanship that will enable you to get the most out of your equipment.

For some of you this will be a refresher course. But stick with me. You might learn more than you expect, even if you don't learn as much as those who are getting into these things for the first time. If you put the tips I'm going to give you into practice, your work will shed the stigma of "home movie" and begin to look truly professional. In this chapter I will discuss fundamentally important techniques such as using camera angles optimally, making smooth camera moves, and achieving good composition and continuity. I'm also including tips on using lighting to best advantage and on avoiding pitfalls in recording sound.

Reading this chapter once won't be enough to make the fireworks go off in your head in a brilliant blaze of total comprehension. But if you read, then go out and practice, then reread and analyze your mistakes, the correct principles and techniques will gradually sink in, and you'll earn the professional status you desire.

COMPOSITION: CAMERA ANGLES AND FRAMING

The camera is the eye of the audience. It is also the eye of the filmmaker—the director/cinematographer—who must use the camera's capability and versatility not merely to present subject matter but to *portray* it with dramatic slant, flair, and vitality. Choosing effective camera angles is of prime importance in getting any scene across in the best way possible. The right angles and framing will let the actors work to their best advantage, capturing people's attention, holding their interest, and having a powerful effect on their intellects and emotions. Basic camera angles and types of shots are the cinematographer's stock in trade:

MASTER SHOT. A broad overall view of everything and everybody in a scene or sequence, the camera continuing to roll until all the action plays from beginning to end without a cut.

WIDE SHOT. A broad view of all or part of the action in a scene. The framing could be equivalent to that of a master shot, or it could be a little less encompassing.

What distinguishes a wide shot from a master shot in the strictly literal definition is that in a *true* master shot the whole scene is allowed to play clear through. It is quite expensive always to film master shots, even though it is desirable to have them for safety. Sometimes only *partial* master shots are filmed to save time and money. For instance, the director will figure out in advance what portions of the master shot he will cut to during editing and will actually film only those sections of the scene in the widest setup. These wide shots then substitute for a complete, uninterrupted master shot.

MEDIUM SHOT. What somebody calls a wide shot somebody else might call a medium shot. The definitions are loose, and how the terms are used depends on the eye and the temperament of the particular filmmaker. So a medium shot is basically something less than a wide but not as tight as a medium close-up:

MEDIUM CLOSE-UP (MCU). A fairly close shot, but not generally so close as to show a subject filling the frame, for instance, an actress shown from her waist to the top of her head.

CLOSE-UP (CU). The subject shown full-frame, for instance, an actor's head shown from forehead to chin.

EXTREME CLOSE-UP (ECU). Usually framed so tightly on the subject that its full dimensions are cropped. For instance, this shot is so tight that you see someone's blinking eyes with the upper and lower part of the face cut off, or you see the label on a beer bottle looming at you to emphasize the brand. Close-up rings can even be put on the camera lens so that tiny objects like insects or marbles can fill the entire frame in excruciating detail.

TIGHT SHOT. Another term for the various kinds of close-up. This term, again, is used loosely.

TWO-SHOT. When the camera is framed on two actors within a scene. There are also three-shots, four-shots, and so on, all the way up to crowd shots.

OVER-THE-SHOULDER SHOT. Usually used in filming conversation be-

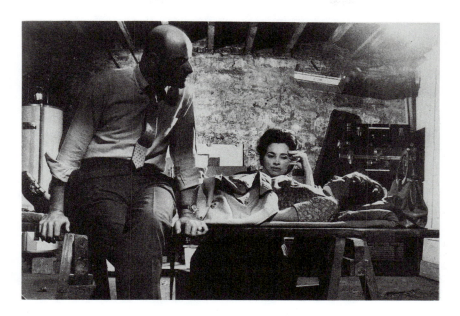

A medium-wide shot in the basement set for *Night of the Living Dead.*

tween two people. The camera is framed on one of them, while an aspect of the other is seen in the foreground so that we see the person he is relating to from his point of view (POV).

Since some of the above terminology is rather ambiguous, to specify more precisely what he wants, the director may call for a head shot or a head-and-shoulders shot of a particular actor. He may also ask for a "beauty shot"—an extremely flattering close-up—of anything from an actress's face to the cheeseburger she is helping to sell.

Of course the camera can frame these types of shots from a variety of positions, or *camera placements.* There are *down-angle* shots and *up-angle* shots, depending upon which way the camera is pointing. *Tripod* shots and *hand-held* shots refer to the way the camera is supported. Don't forget that the camera is capable of making slick moves while the film is rolling; compositions needn't be *static* (perfectly still)—that's one of the big advantages of moving pictures; we're not doing still lifes. The cinematographer can make his scenes play to their best advantage by making the camera *dolly, pan, tilt, crane,* and *zoom.* He can even shoot from a helicopter or *SteadiCam;* from the top of a building, a bridge, a speeding car, a roller coaster, or a hot-air balloon. Or lying on his back on the floor.

A *dolly shot* is any shot where the camera is rolling on wheels, whether on an actual camera dolly made for that purpose or from a moving car.

A close-up (CU) of Judith Ridley in *Night of the Living Dead*.

A *pan* is a rotation of the camera from side to side, made by swiveling the tripod mount or by moving one's body while hand-holding the camera.

A *tilt* is a swiveling of the camera up or down.

A *craning shot* is one where the camera is moved perpendicularly up or down.

A *zoom* is a shot where the lens itself does the work of making the subject larger or smaller in the frame, and the camera does not move nearer or farther from the subject.

A *Steadicam* is a recently invented, patented device that enables the camera to make rock-solid shots even when it is mounted on something that is moving—like a car, a plane, a roller coaster, or even the shoulder of a person who is walking.

Despite the obvious advantages of all this camera maneuverability, it is wise to remember that certain scenes can be hurt by too many bizarre angles or too much camera movement. Sometimes a static camera is best. A traveling shot might distract from what the actors are doing or saying. It might be jarring, unnecessary, or simply too expensive and time-consuming for your shooting schedule and budget.

Using Angle Changes to Avoid Bad Edits

In order to make your movies look professional when they are finished (not just when you are screening raw footage), you must carefully plan your shots in advance, always looking ahead to the ultimate editing process. Otherwise, the raw footage that looks so beautiful when you first lay eyes on it will turn ugly and awkward when you try to put it together to tell a good, logical story. All the action ("business") within a scene must be completely covered (explicitly filmed), and it must be shot from angles that ensure the scene can be edited smoothly.

To this end, you *must* change angles and framing *every* time you intend to cut from one shot or *section* of a shot to another. When you start putting your scene together in the editing room, you cannot splice action *out* of a shot just because you want the beginning and ending of the take but not the middle; you must splice another shot in between. If you don't, the audience will see the action or the film itself jump (see "jump cut" defined below) at the point of the edit, even after the two pieces of film are printed together (instead of just physically spliced). To avoid this kind of visual disturbance, the audience's eye must be diverted by an intervening shot. This intervening shot can be a new angle on the same subject, or it can be a *cutaway*—a shot of somebody or something else that is going on within the scene, apart from the main action. And the cutaway must be pertinent and logical; not, for instance, a meaningless shot of a subject's folded hands, as is sometimes done in a TV newscast so that there won't be *jump cuts* in somebody's on-camera interview.

A *jump cut* occurs when two pieces of film are edited together and the action clearly does not match—an actor is in a different position or is doing something different in the first shot from in the follow-up shot. The action therefore does not flow continuously and logically. A jump cut can be fixed only by going to a different angle with matching action and/or dialogue or by inserting a proper cutaway shot between the two shots that don't flow the way they should. A jump cut is always startling because it is *wrong*. It is an error of filmmaking craftsmanship, except in those rare instances when it is used intentionally and expressly for the purpose of startling the audience, as in a bizarre dream sequence or flashback.

When you intend to cut from a wide to a tighter shot in depicting a piece of business, if you change the camera angle as well as the framing it will help "cover" slight variations in placement of props or actors' head and hand positions, making discrepancies unnoticeable. However, *within* a particular piece of business, shots shouldn't jump back and forth from wide to tight so many times that the editing becomes jarring and blows the audience's concentration. If you are directing, this will be your judgment call based on your experience and aesthetic sensibilities. But try to film your dialogue and action in long enough segments without blown lines, etc., so you can cut where you planned to, not where you are forced to. Otherwise, your edit will look choppy instead of smooth and clean.

Composition: Balance and Perspective

Bear in mind that clever composition can be used to enhance the audience's impression of a character. Shooting *up* at someone makes him appear imposing or powerful. Conversely, shooting *down* can make a person seem meek, cowed, or oppressed by whoever seems to be looking down at him.

If you are featuring two people in an intimate setting, for instance sitting across from each other in a quiet restaurant or cocktail lounge, you will want to film close-ups from their eye level to preserve the intimacy of the scene by enabling the audience to relate to them the way they are relating to each other.

If you have two equals in a scene, the framing on their close-ups (how much of them you see in the frame) should be balanced, about equal. Otherwise, as you cut back and forth you will diminish one character and enhance the other in the audience's eyes, even if this is not your intention. Besides, you can actually slight an actor by inadvertently making his presence, his delivery, seem less powerful or impressive than that of the actor he is working with.

As a corollary, you may use the camera to *build up* a performer who is not as impressive as you would like. His close-ups can be framed more tightly, and thus made stronger than those of other actors in the same scene. He can be flattered by dramatic camera angles that show off his best physical characteristics. His voice can be made louder, fuller, and more resonant electronically when his sound takes are transferred for editing.

George Romero squeezes the hand-held camera between a wall and a mike boom to steal an action-packed close-up for *Night of the Living Dead.*

Always be on the lookout for the most attractive features of actors and models who were cast for their attractiveness in the first place. Unflattering camera work can make a beautiful woman actually look ugly. Don't be too lazy to move the camera around and find the exact placement that results in a stunning close-up. The actors and actresses will be grateful to you and will perform at their best once they realize you have their best interests at heart and are going to make them come across well. And your movie will turn out well, too!

Avoiding Illogical Composition

The importance of logical composition really hit home when I was making a political documentary in Alabama. I had to film one of the judges on the state supreme court who was going to give an impromptu testimonial for our candidate, Governor Albert Brewer (who was running against George Wallace). The ad agency rep who had hired me came up with the idea of establishing the judge in his black robe, standing at the top of a spiral staircase, with me shooting up at him from down in the stairwell. It was a helluva dramatic shot. *But* it was the wrong thing to do. Why? Because the judge was going to be talking *to* the camera, which as I said before is the *eye* of the audience. Were they going to be looking up at him from deep in the stairwell for the whole ten minutes he was to be on-screen? Furthermore, we had to go from our establishing shot to a close-up so we could *see* the judge's face; if I zoomed in on him from the bottom of the stairwell, such a drastic angle would make his face look weirdly foreshortened and distorted. So the camera had to come up higher for the close-up, and the only place to set the tripod for this purpose was at the *top* of the stairwell.

What's wrong with that?

Well, I would have to cut back and forth from the establishing shot to the judge's close-ups in order to edit his impromptu speech—which was going to come from his being interviewed by the ad agency guy off camera. So, when all this stuff was edited together, the audience's eye contact with the judge was going to jump up and jump down in a bizarre, disturbing manner.

The ad agency guy didn't believe me and insisted on shooting the scene his way. So, in the finished film the sequence stands out like a sore thumb. The shots spring back and forth from the stairwell to the landing, two flights up, making the viewer feel like he's on a visual pogo stick.

This illustrates why, in your choice of camera angles and framing, you must strive for good, *logical* composition, balance, and perspective. Don't be so beguiled by a dramatic or unusual type of shot that you throw common sense out the window. Always remember the motive and purpose of a scene. Let the camera help you convey your ideas instead of interfering with them. In the case of the judge, we should have sacrificed the more dramatic shot for a series of shots from his eye level.

Making Smooth Camera Moves

Strive for smooth pans, tilts, zooms, and other moves. Don't let the audience become too aware of the camera. You want them to *experience* your movie almost as if it's real life. But they won't suspend disbelief if you keep bugging them with faulty, obtrusive camera technique.

A dramatic up-angle shot from my movie *Midnight. Photo by Paul McCollough.*

That is not to say that you shouldn't always be on the lookout for interesting or even unique shots that do suit your purpose. It can become boring always to shoot your actors from straight on, the way some people shoot home movies. Artful shots can be composed by shooting through a wrought-iron railing or with leafy foliage in the foreground, to name just two examples. In certain horror films—like *Halloween* and *Friday the 13th*—the camera contributes to the ominous mood by constantly filming the prospective victims from behind trees, around corners of buildings, or through window blinds, as if they are being spied on by somebody with sinister intentions. This is excellent use of an unusual camera technique that helps set the audience on edge, filling each viewer with suspense and dread over what must be about to happen.

Whatever shot you're using, don't try to hand-hold the camera when you should be using a tripod. On the big screen what you thought was "rock-steady" will be full of jiggles and bounces. If you have to hand-hold, use a shoulder pod and a wide-angle, preferably fixed-focus lens (not a zoom lens). The "longer" the lens and the farther away it is from your subject, the more pronounced the camera jiggles will be. A "long lens" is one that has a long focal length (in millimeters) and a narrow *depth of field*—objects not exactly on the focal plane will appear blurrier than they would on a wider-angle lens. Therefore, if you try to hand-hold a camera with a 50-millimeter or 75-millimeter lens, you are putting yourself in double jeopardy: the lens will "bounce" more, and the subject probably won't remain sharply within focal range, especially if the subject is an actor on the move.

BLOCKING

Before you shoot a scene you must figure out *how* you are going to shoot it: what the shots are going to be and how you are going to put them together when you edit. This is called *blocking a scene.* To help you do it, your screenwriter should have provided you with a *shooting script,* maybe even a *storyboard,* or at least a *shot list.*

A *shooting script* is a complete screenplay, containing not only dialogue and action descriptions, but also all the shots numbered and described exactly the way they are intended to appear in the finished film.

A *storyboard* is a representation of a film in illustrated panels, almost like a comic book. The panels are shaped like a movie screen, and key shots are depicted in each panel, in sequence, often with dialogue underneath, so that the director and others connected with the production can visualize how the shots should be framed and how they should flow.

A *shot list* is a list of the shots that must be executed based on the blocking of the scene in the director's mind.

Sometimes the screenplay will be pretty sketchy in its shot descriptions and as director you will have to work all the shots out for yourself, without any help. Some directors won't work without shooting scripts and storyboards. In producing big-budget TV commercials for major advertising agencies, storyboards are almost *de rigueur,* composed in lavish artist's renderings or sometimes in magazine-quality still photographs illustrating frame by frame exactly how the creative director envisions each segment of the spot. But I believe that a good shooting script and/or shot list is sufficient in most cases, and storyboards are often redundant, except to help impress a client and make him think he's getting everything some agency is charging him big bucks for.

Now, in certain very complicated productions, like the *Star Wars* movies, where shots are state-of-the-art combinations of matte work, computer animation, elaborate sets, props and backdrops, and live action, and all these elements having to come together harmoniously and realistically—then storyboards are essential. George Lucas and Steven Spielberg swear by them. But I don't think most lower-budget productions need or can afford an array of storyboards.

Everybody has his own particular style of working, and what one director might think indispensable another thinks is superfluous. Fellini sometimes wrote scenes on a napkin in a restaurant in the morning and shot them in the afternoon. He mustn't have been bothered by the lack of a storyboard. But I know people who go bananas if they don't have all the tools and crutches.

As long as I have a good dialogue script with guidepost shot indications, I'm satisfied. I like to block a scene only after I've rehearsed the actors on the actual location or set, with the actual props that they are going to use. Then my mind is open to on-the-spot changes and improvisations. Invariably something on location—something favorable or something adverse—will upset the best-laid plans of a shooting script and force the director to resort to his own ingenuity. Sometimes some special feature of the place—a statue, a nice fountain, whatever—inspires the blocking of the scene. And sometimes something unexpected happens that prevents the scene from being filmed the way it was written, and an alternative but just as effective way to block must be devised.

When the director does block a scene, he usually does it according to a basic formula:

You take a master shot of the entire scene. Then you do your wides, your mediums, your reverse angles and your close-ups, until all the action is covered all the ways you want to choose from when editing. One reason Hollywood films cost so much is that *every* conceivable angle is shot so that the editor is given an enormous wealth of material to work with, much of which will ultimately be scrapped. Low-budget pictures can't afford this luxury, so the director must often rely on his ability to "preedit" the picture in his mind, then make it come together and *work* the way he envisioned it.

Hollywood pictures usually are shot on a footage ratio of about twenty-five to one, which means that twenty-five times as much film is shot as is going to end up in the finished movie. Low-budget independent pictures usually have a footage ratio of around six or eight to one. This barely allows for properly capturing all the action since you are always going to have blown takes, and also it is desirable to have, at minimum, two good takes of each piece of business, for safety. Safety takes can truly be saviors if something terrible happens to your best take—like getting scratched in the lab.

Here is a section of the script from my low-budget movie *Midnight.*

In making *Midnight,* I was working on a very low film footage budget, four to one, so I had to shoot only the angles I envisioned working best in the final edit. This gave me very few takes to "play with" in case I made a judgment error on location. I've added the numbers on the left of the script as a key so I can tell you how I ended up blocking the scene when we actually shot it.

(1) Camera ZOOMS past Tom and Hank to reveal Nancy hiding behind some bushes some distance away. Afraid, she stays in hiding. From her point of view, we see Tom and Hank being handcuffed.

(2) A close-up shows Hank trembling, reaching a point of panic. Suddenly he starts to run, trying to get away.

(3) Deputy #1 crouches and fires twice. Hank crumples and falls down, sliding on his chest and face, then lying very still, obviously dead.

(4)   TOM (yells)
You killed him, you stupid redneck!
You didn't need to do that! We're
innocent! Innocent, goddamn you!

(5) Standing over Hank's body, Deputy #2 takes careful aim at Hank's head and squeezes the trigger. There is a loud report, then silence.

(1) The distributor who was supplying the equipment package neglected to send me a zoom lens, so the zoom had to be eliminated. Instead, I blocked out a wide shot from Nancy's POV, shooting through the foliage; this gave a nice visual effect and served to remind the audience that she was observing this spooky scene from a hiding place.

(2) I shot this exactly as written.

(3) This had to be broken into more than one shot, as Hank ran quite a distance away from the bad guys. I filmed a wide shot showing Hank running desperately away from camera, with the two deputies in the foreground, both firing their weapons like crazy. I inserted a new shot, not indicated in the script, of Tom yelling, in close-up: "Run, Hank, run!" Then back to the wide, to see Hank fall and roll over onto his back.

I repositioned (4) and (5), reversing their order. I showed the deputy striding up to the helpless Hank and taking slow, careful aim at Hank's head. Then, since we had special effects expert Tom Savini on this job, I shot a close-up of a "gore" effect of the trooper's bullet blasting into Hank's forehead. Only after that did I cut back to Tom yelling, in close-up; but I eliminated "You didn't need to do that" and "goddamn you" because we were getting lots of interference from airplanes passing overhead, and it became wise and expedient to strip away unnecessary dialogue.

In rehearsing and blocking, you must evaluate the action flow of the scene as well as dialogue deliveries. *Pace* is all-important. Business might have to be invented or changed to fill "holes," places where the scene seems to be flagging or dying because it is not clicking along interestingly or excitingly enough. Pay attention to your actors; they often have good ideas. But don't let them get carried away; sometimes they want to do stuff that won't work editorially, won't jibe with your concept, or might blow too much time and money.

Rehearsing thoroughly when filmstock isn't grinding through the camera will save dollars in takes that won't be blown. And it is *fun*. It gets everybody "into" the scene, working as a team, and feeling important.

When you finalize your blocking, make sure you stick to it and actually accomplish it before you say, "It's a wrap!" Don't leave the location until you're absolutely sure you've filmed everything you need; otherwise you might be stuck with dumb camera moves or jump cuts. Taking actors, crew, and equipment back to a location to pick up a shot you missed is *very expen-*

sive. And sometimes going back is out of the question because the season has changed, the location has been altered or no longer exists, or some of your props were destroyed in the "action" and can no longer be duplicated.

After you've reached a certain level of expertise in shooting and directing, you should let your instincts take over to a substantial degree. During the filming of *Midnight*, ignoring my instincts caused me to waste a long, cold night shooting lots of takes that I never used.

We were shooting a campfire scene involving Nancy, Tom, and Hank. I worked according to the usual formula, knocking off a master shot—which played beautifully; the actors were really on. My instincts told me I could go with the master alone because the framing and lighting looked great and the actors had done a beautiful job with their timing and deliveries. But I plunged ahead, getting all my mediums, two-shots, and close-ups. It was a rough, complicated gig; we were lucky to get it all in the can before the sun came up. Weeks later, editor Paul McCollough and I tried to cut the scene the way I had blocked it, with a pattern of wides, close-ups, etc. We wasted almost a full day at the editing table, then ended up going with that terrific master shot and *no* cuts, which is what I should have done from the moment we shot it.

Continuity

In blocking you also have to remember to preserve *continuity* in your movie. *Continuity* is the logical order and consistency of what is seen on-screen. Props mustn't jump in and out of scenes. If we see a cigarette lighter on the table in the establishing shot, it must still be there, in its correct position, if we see the same table top again. An actor can't be smoking a fresh cigarette in his wide shot and be down to a one-inch butt a second later when you cut in tight.

Hairdos, costumes, sashes, scarves, buttons, and the like must be consistent within a scene. Mike shadows have to be kept out. Makeup, including special appliances like fake wounds, scratches, black eyes, and what have you mustn't vary from one take to another illogically.

It is important to guard against unintentional anachronisms. For instance, one day I was shooting a scene that was supposed to be taking place in a drive-in in the 1950s, and I almost didn't notice that the inspection sticker on our vintage 1958 Buick said "1987." We scurried around and found a good way to cover up the modern sticker, then finished shooting our scene.

Continuity "blivets" (cinematic errors) ruin many movies that are excellent in most other respects. Sometimes they're merely unsettling; other times they can be hilarious. I once saw a Mickey Rooney western where stagecoach passengers were being robbed by a gang of outlaws, and a Greyhound bus went by in the background. And the picture wasn't *supposed* to be a comedy.

SCREEN DIRECTION

A key element of continuity to which you must pay strict attention is *screen direction,* which is the direction from which the camera perceives its subject and the direction that the subject moves through the frame with respect to camera point of view. The concept of screen direction is often not fully appreciated, even by filmmakers who are otherwise quite professional, so that shocking screen direction blivets mar their movies.

Screen direction is a complicated business, and whole chapters are devoted to it in books on cinematography. You should study the subject thoroughly to make sure you understand it fully. But in the meantime, here are some basic principles of correct screen direction:

1. When an actor exits an established location, moving from screen left to screen right, subsequent shots must also show him going left to right (except for "neutral" front-angle or rear-angle shots) until he gets to the new location. This device keeps the audience mentally *oriented.* It's a cinematic convention that has been established and adhered to ever since the pioneering days of filmmaking. When the good guys chased the bad guys from the ranch to the town, they always galloped in one single direction regardless of the number of shots in the montage. What if we inserted a medium close-up of one of the good guys galloping the other way? It would look like he chickened out and was suddenly running from the bad guys. Furthermore, when the good guys returned to the ranch, they always galloped in the opposite screen direction, so the audience never got upset trying to figure out where the actors *were* in relation to the two basic locations. If you keep changing screen direction, it will seem like your characters are confused, running in circles.

2. If an actress (Jane) is talking to an actor (Jim) across a table in a restaurant, and the establishing shot shows that Jane's dominant view is of the left side of Jim's face, don't go in for a close-up of Jim from Jane's supposed POV that is shot over Jane's *left* shoulder instead of her right, for if you do, the shot will feature the *right* side of Jim's face instead of the left, and it will seem to the viewer that Jane popped into a new position without even moving her chair.

3. Be *consistent* with your audience's point of view; think about it carefully before placing the camera. In a "Romans versus Christians" flick, I saw a major screen direction blivet when a Roman tossed a spear from screen right to screen left, and in the next shot the spear traveled from screen left to screen right and struck a Christian—it was very hard to believe it was the same spear.

Screen direction is vitally important. Just remember, if you want to take people on a cinematic adventure, they won't enjoy the trip if spotty craftsmanship keeps derailing them. They want to have the feeling that they're in the firm hands of somebody who can navigate with logic, cleverness, and consistency.

LIGHTING TIPS

Much of the time, good camera work is really good lighting. Assuming that the composition of a shot is satisfactory, then the quality of the lighting can transform a mediocre shot into a great one. On the other hand, good composition can be blown if the subject isn't lit properly. I've seen attractive people made unattractive by flat, pallid lighting, light "kicks" (undesirable reflections), "hot spots" (overbright patches of light), or unnecessarily harsh shadows.

It is not within the scope of this book to give a full course in cinematic lighting. But, if you intend to do the lighting yourself, you will need to study and practice lighting many, many scenes; if not, you will have to work with someone who specializes in it. You cannot have a good movie without good lighting.

Luckily, with the extremely sensitive color film that is available today, lighting a scene is not nearly so difficult and time-consuming as it used to be. It takes fewer lights to achieve a strong light level. With today's high-ASA (fine-grain, light-sensitive) filmstock, you will obtain excellent picture resolution and depth of field with lower wattage than was needed a decade ago.

The higher-ASA filmstocks used to be too grainy and too high-contrast to be used by professionals. But fortunately for you, that is not the case nowadays. Being able to use fewer lights means less discomfort for cast and crew— they don't need to sweat to death anymore.

I'm assuming here that you will find a way to learn and practice basic lighting techniques. My goal here is to give you some pointers that you can't easily learn on your own and that you won't find in lighting manuals. For example, a filter can be used to impart a natural look to a lit background setting or to prevent the background from standing out more than the person who is the primary focus of the scene. When muted lighting cannot be achieved by filtering, you may want to use indirect lighting. For instance, the light can be "bounced" (deflected) from a wall or ceiling or from a paper or metal reflector.

Careful use of natural or artificial light will enhance your subject matter. You can create sparkles and highlights in your actors' hair and eyes. You can bounce, filter, and/or diffuse sunlight or movie lights to soften an actress's countenance or eliminate unwelcome shadows and blemishes.

As a general principle, by using your own discerning eye and good taste, you can light an interior scene by augmenting, with your movie lights, the natural and artificial light that is already in the room, if that is the look you wish to preserve. But the artificial light may have to be filtered or overpow-

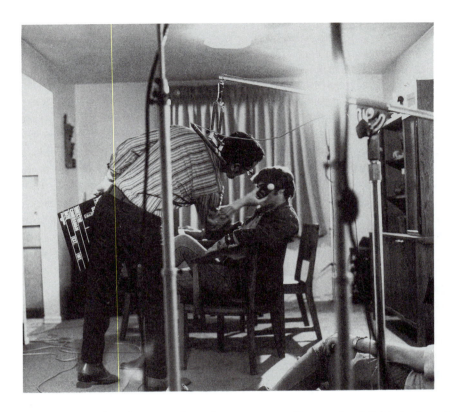

Shooting *The Affair* in my overheated apartment, amid a tangle of light stands and cables. That's me with the clapstick and light meter.

ered by your movie lights according to the ability of your film stock to register true color when used with indoor and outdoor lighting combinations.

When you are going to cut from shot to shot within a scene, the lighting of those shots must be *balanced* so the cuts won't be jarringly dissimilar in resolution, hue, shadow density, and so forth. Sometimes various filters must be used to help balance the lighting so the shots will edit into a visually pleasing sequence.

Lighting and makeup go hand in hand because ordinary makeup materials often won't register true color on film. Movie makeup salves, powders, and rouges are color-balanced so that actors' flesh tones will register with a natural look.

If you intend to blow up your finished print, from 8 millimeter to 16 millimeter, or from 16 millimeter to 35 millimeter for theatrical release, you should take special care that all your scenes are lit brightly enough to be shot at higher lens settings (because this will produce the best blowup with the least graininess). This also applies to scenes that will eventually be dubbed to videotape. Shots that are too dark and shadowy often look unclear, even smudgy, by the time they get onto videocassettes.

SOUND RECORDING TIPS

The quality of a movie's soundtrack can make or break the entire production. I don't have the space to give you a comprehensive course in sound recording, but I can give you hints that usually come only from experience.

As discussed previously, some amateur-level cameras have built-in microphones, but using that kind of microphone certainly doesn't give you freedom of mike placement for greater fidelity and elimination of extraneous noise. You will get better sound quality with a separate mike, and most cameras with built-in mikes have a jack where you can plug in the auxiliary mike and bypass the circuitry of the built-in mike.

Professionals usually rely on booming their mikes into a scene because it is too much trouble and too inhibiting to always have to look for or contrive a place to hide a mike *within* a scene. Of course, professionals have the advantage of extremely sensitive and directional microphones that can pick up high-fidelity sound even when boomed from outside the frame lines of wide shots, far from the actors. Trying to boom a cheap nonprofessional mike will not work in many cases because you won't be able to get it close enough to the action without its creeping into the shot, and yet if you back it off it won't be sensitive enough to do a good job. So it will have to be hidden within the scene (behind a cereal box or some other prop, ideally one that logically belongs in the scene).

Mikes hidden under actors' clothing are very problematic since you will hear the slightest rustle of clothing when the actors move, even if they try not to move very much (which can inhibit their performance). So this method is a last resort, both for the amateur and the professional.

Whatever the method, the goal is always to place the mike so that it will record strong, sharp sound with a minimum—hopefully an elimination—of extraneous background sound. Voice takes must be as "clean" as possible. Otherwise, when they are edited together, background noise will "jump" from splice to splice and will be utterly obtrusive and disturbing. If you keep your voice takes clean, you can always add any *desirable* ambient sound later by dubbing and mixing.

Postdubbing or *looping* of voice takes is more hassle than you will normally want to get into, although it can be a last resort for short takes or when sync is not critical. In this procedure, actors listen to and watch their sync takes in a studio and practice repeating the lines exactly as they said them on location, then record new voice takes that hopefully will look as in sync as the unusable ones that were recorded during actual filming. Some actors are excellent at this, and others are terrible—I have been through it many times, and I assure you it can be a real nightmare. But sometimes it is the only viable alternative when you run into an insurmountable problem on location that makes it impossible to record usable sound.

If you realize during shooting that you are going to have to postdub a take, it will behoove you to record *reference sound*—actual location sound to be used as a guide for *slugging* (cutting in) the replacement sound later. For that matter, even nondialogue takes should usually be shot sync instead of wild so you will have reference sound for footsteps, incidental sound effects (SFX), etc. Remember, any essential SFX that you fail to obtain during shooting will only have to be recorded later and painstakingly edited into your movie. Therefore, recording these SFX clearly enough on location means you will save enormous time, energy, and money in the editing room because you won't have to build effects tracks from scratch.

MASTERING CINEMATIC CRAFTSMANSHIP

I cannot overemphasize how important it is, in today's tough competition, for aspiring filmmakers to thoroughly learn their craft and become accomplished in most aspects of it. This comes only from practice. You can't get it all out of books, although good books and courses can certainly help.

In the next chapter, you're going to meet a self-taught filmmaker whose story will amaze and inspire you. I'm talking about Lizzie Borden, director of *Working Girls* and *Born in Flames.* She was in her mid-twenties when she fell in love with filmmaking and decided to teach herself how to do it. She succeeded phenomenally. Read what she has to say and you'll believe even more strongly than you do right now that the obstacles can be conquered and that you too can succeed!

Lizzie Borden, director of *Working Girls. Photo courtesy of Lizzie Borden.*

Lizzie Borden studied painting at Wellesley, graduated Phi Beta Kappa, and moved to New York, where she became "politicized by feminism." She also became enthralled by filmmaking, although at first she didn't know a thing about the technical end of it. Working on grants and her own rent money, she made *Working Girls,* a clinical, comical look at one day in the life of a middle-class brothel that has earned critical praise worldwide and so far has grossed over $5 million.

7

Lizzie Borden
Grass-Roots Filmmaking

★ My name, Lizzie Borden, is sort of a self-fulfilling prophecy, because what I like best about filmmaking is the editing—the cutting and chopping. The magic of splicing two pieces of film and waiting to see what it looks like as it flows through the viewer!

The immigration officials on Ellis Island couldn't spell my family's original name, so they gave us the name Borden—very Waspish for a Polish Jewish family. My real first name is Linda, and as I grew up in Michigan there were two main nicknames that were appropriate for the last name Borden—Elsie, after Elsie the cow, for Borden's milk, which I hated, as any girl would; and then Lizzie, for Lizzie the ax murderer, which of course I loved because my parents hated it so much. They cringed every time someone called for Lizzie.

My whole life on a certain level was rebellious, not in the way that meant I was rebellious at school, but I did find my own way of going through it. My heroes and heroines were the art teachers. When I went to college at Wellesley, I really didn't like it very much because it was such a closed-off women's school with girls like Muffy and Buffy, all these wealthy women, at a time right before women's colleges were given a new life by feminism. My major was art history, but I took over the basement in one of the dorms and just painted like crazy. I think ultimately I wasn't a very good painter; I mean, in high school and junior high I was much freer about painting because I didn't know that much, but later I knew every painting that anyone ever made, so I was becoming very self-conscious about my own work.

MAJOR INFLUENCES: FEMINISM AND GODARD

After I graduated and came to New York, I went to Queens College because they offered free studio space. At the same time I started writing for *Artforum* magazine, which put me in conflict with some of the professors because they were all for figurative art, and there I was at twenty-one writing for a magazine that was on the opposite pole.

I became very politicized by feminism. This was during the early 1970s, when feminism in New York was in its heyday. It was politicizing me in a way that the Vietnam war hadn't, because the antiwar protests seemed so concerned about the draft and therefore alien to me as a woman, although of course I was against the war.

Then I started to look at films, just kind of by accident. When I was growing up in Michigan, an "art film" was Ingmar Bergman, and I've never been drawn to that kind of cinema. But I saw a retrospective of Godard films at the Carnegie Hall cinema, and they just *grabbed* me! He threw away all the rules. He was able to deal with graphic elements, paintinglike elements, yet I felt that his ability to make films as essays rather than just stories was incredible. His whole body of work, his approach to film, proved that it could be a personal voyage.

This was around 1974, and I had been writing for a few years and meeting a lot of artists and being drawn to different kinds of art from painting. I was really jealous because these filmmakers were doing something that I wanted to do, and it just struck me like a lightning bolt going off in my head: Well then, fool, just do it! But how? I knew I didn't want to go to school, because I had just gone through six years of it, Phi Beta Kappa and the whole bit, and what did I come out with? Just an overeducation about art that made me nervous that I was doing what someone else had done before me. I decided not to let that happen with filmmaking once I got into it.

LEARNING FILMMAKING FROM GROUND ZERO

I wasn't one of those kids who grew up with Super-8, making my own little Spielberglike epics at age seventeen. I didn't even know that I could make films or that I could personalize them in any way. But I figured that somehow I could teach myself filmmaking. It had to be something that was understandable technically, by just trial and error. For me, it meant starting out with Bolex cameras and old, junky Nagra recorders. I just wanted to get over my fear of the technology. And a lot of the stuff I shot at first came out black or with no sound on it, but by doing it like that you learn the thrill of finally getting an image.

My first film took two years to make, from 1974 to 1976, and I taught myself everything on it. It's called *Regrouping,* and it's a really bizarre little film. It's not a documentary, it's got fictional parts in it, but it's really about voyeurism; it's about being on the outside of a women's consciousness-raising group and *feeling* like an outsider. I would follow these women around the streets, and I'd shoot them when they didn't know—they knew I was going to do it; they just never knew when. And a lot of the film came out—well, I didn't load it in the camera right, so it would bounce through the frame line. When I had the first stuff I could edit, I rented a Steenbeck editing table, but I didn't have a clue what to do with the thing, so I called up a friend of mine and said, "How do you load it?" She came over and showed me. My editing room looked like spaghetti hit by a fan, but somehow I knew where every piece of film was. Editing I just loved, right from the beginning. *Regrouping* was created through the editing. It cost about $10,000 all told, and I financed it myself, in bits and pieces.

I ended up with a black-and-white ninety-minute movie, and it hardly was shown anywhere but the Edinburgh Film Festival and the Whitney Museum. The women who were in it hated it. They felt so exposed that I finally decided I couldn't show the film. They knew my methods ahead of time, but the point was that they didn't really expect me to do the things I was going to do. I became a maniacal person, and I would trail them around with the camera. I like discovering secrets about groups that are closed to me, whether it's groups of black women or prostitutes or whatever. It makes me feel a little like an anthropologist.

MAKING *BORN IN FLAMES* IN SPARE TIME ON SPARE CASH

My second film, *Born in Flames,* takes place in the future after a Social-Democrat cultural revolution. It was about women in the vanguard of trying to make the culture go back toward the left, and it showed how black women had no dialogue with white middle-class feminists. Their language was different, and yet their aims were so parallel. The black women wouldn't call themselves feminists at all, because that wasn't the political framework they were in, yet they were fighting for the same kinds of things as the white women. The women in the film are not actresses. I would grab people off the street, women out of bars, and I would hire camera people for $25 a day and rent cameras very inexpensively. I would shoot stuff involving real people inside a fictional framework. I knew that I had to dispense with a lot of the rules that other films are governed by. I had to say good-bye to continuity because I could only shoot once a month.

I was supporting myself by working as a film editor in my own house. That way I could use the Steenbeck at night for my own purposes. Four hundred dollars a week is what I charged, which is nothing, and that's why I got jobs —I was certainly cheaper than any kind of union editor. And I'd sometimes

Lizzie Borden directing "real people" (nonactresses) enlisted off the streets to star in *Born in Flames*. Photo courtesy of Lizzie Borden.

get short ends to shoot with. There was a guy in New York who sold short ends—leftover remnants of 400-foot rolls of film that somebody else hadn't completely shot. Sometimes the film is fogged, and even when it isn't you have to load these little sections of film, maybe only three or four minutes long, instead of a full ten-minute roll, so you have to constantly reload the camera. But I decided I had to work within those obstacles, and I didn't care how long it took me. I knew I had to make my own films from the bottom up.

Born in Flames took four years to make, from the late seventies to the early eighties, shooting once a month. As soon as I had enough money to do another shot, I'd pull everyone back together and go out in the streets and do it. I'll never work that way again, because you lose people all the time, and you have to change your story when you lose people. Or people gain thirty pounds, or lose thirty pounds, or change their hair. Strange! But for me it was an important method because I approached the making of the film with a desire to have it teach me what I didn't already know. I couldn't write a script that put words into the mouths of black women, because I didn't know any. I thought, my God, this is a world I don't know, I've gotta find a way to understand it. And I knew I had to shoot the movie in bits and pieces because I would never have enough money to shoot it all at once, so I tried to turn that liability into a virtue. I was constantly gathering material and structuring it, seeing what worked and what didn't, on the editing table. I was learning how two cuts kind of vibrate together, that some jump cuts are thrilling and other jump cuts are clunky. There was often just a tiny difference between clunkiness and beauty.

THE MAKING OF *WORKING GIRLS*

It's taken me a very long time—from 1974 to 1987—to make my three movies. *Working Girls* took about two years, starting at the end of *Born in Flames.* It was around 1982 when I met the head of a prostitutes' organization called COYOTE (Call Off Your Old Tired Ethics). I found her fascinating, even though I didn't have a notion that I wanted to do a film about prostitution—it just seemed very alien to me. When I thought "prostitute," I got the image of a street hooker. Then, when a couple of acquaintances of mine from the art world admitted to me that they worked in brothels, I went to visit a brothel, and I realized that there was this world of middle-class prostitution that I'd never seen on film before. I'd seen street hookers, and I'd seen high-class call girls, but I'd never seen this very middle-class kind of prostitution. I really wanted to make a film about it.

It was a world that would've completely closed to me had I wanted to go in there with a camera. So what I attempted with *Working Girls* was to have a lot of control—over the script and so on—from the first moment.

I needed people on the crew who were mature and compassionate and had a sense of real responsibility. In *Working Girls* some of them were doing jobs they had never worked before, because they had done jobs maybe one union level beneath that. For example, the woman I had doing sound recording is in the union for continuity, and she'd operated the mike boom before, but she'd never done sound recording on a feature, so she needed a feature credit. My A.D. (assistant director) had been my intern from NYU, and people said you can't have a twenty-one-year-old doing the A.D.ing, yet she was the one who helped me with the casting from the beginning, and she had such a wonderfully mature personality that I knew she'd be great. And she was.

I found the sweetest guy in the world, Kurt Ossenfort, who agreed to build the set for cost because he wanted to be production designer; he had done some music videos but no features before. And Larry Banks was in the union as a gaffer and couldn't work for me as a gaffer, so he was my lighting designer. He created a lighting scheme where the lighting changed from flat lighting in the day to very shadowy lighting at night. He had worked on TV spots for well-known commercial directors, and he had a much more subtle sense of lighting than I've seen in a lot of independent films. To me that was really important.

Judy Irola was my camerawoman. I needed a woman to shoot *Working Girls* because if I failed, if I made a film that ended up being pornography, I didn't want people to say it was because there was a camera*man*. There's an article by Laura Mulvey, a British theoretician who claims that the gaze of the camera is inherently male; it's called "The Gaze of the Camera," and it was sort of a classic among film students. I wanted to prove that the apparatus itself is neither male nor female. So in the bedroom scenes I was trying to do all the shots from a woman's point of view, and because of that somehow I was aware that even though I was showing sex, there would be a balance between people getting some kind of voyeuristic impulse fulfilled and having their voyeuristic impulses squashed. Somehow the door would close in their faces, and they wouldn't get any kind of sexual feelings from those images. It was a constant balancing act.

Difficulty of Filming Bedroom Scenes

The bedroom scenes were the ones that were closest to me, and I was responsible for determining them frame by frame. For the downstairs stuff I worked with Judy Irola a lot, especially when there were dolly shots. The European term is *plans séquences*— you know, where an entire scene is done through one dolly and you have to orchestrate the actions of all the characters into one long shot. I had never used a dolly before, and I had never worked with actors, so I rehearsed a lot with the women beforehand so I would feel very comfortable. I knew all their strengths, I knew their weaknesses, and I realized I could shade their performances just by knowing what felt real and what didn't.

I was very uncomfortable with the idea of the camera at first. Where do you place the camera? How do you decide where you want to shoot from? I really didn't have a storyboard except in the bedroom scenes. The first week of shooting on *Working Girls*— and I shot mostly in sequence—I feel was quite awkward because I was getting to understand all of the crew elements. If I had the kind of budget that would have allowed me to reshoot the first week, I would have.

In the second week I did all the bedroom scenes, one right after the other. I wanted to get them out of the way because everyone was very tense about them. And I wanted Louise, who played Molly, to really feel like a "working girl." Even though all of the sex is simulated, there's still a lot of physical contact, and it was unpleasant in some ways for her. She was really glad when those scenes were over. I was also afraid to do the downstairs scenes with the men first, because I was afraid they'd later chicken out of their bedroom scenes.

Sex is really hard to shoot, and the actors and even some of the crew people were quite nervous about it, so we did a video rehearsal, and everybody got to wear underwear and giggle about it and be really silly. Then what I did to make the actors trust me was guarantee them the framing I would use, so they knew that if they took all their clothes off I wasn't going to shoot them from weird angles. Consequently, at that point I was forced to make a storyboard. And I was so happy I did, because it gave me confidence that it would be my vision and somehow it would work. Because the bedrooms were all about fantasy, I didn't have to film scenes that would cut together in a conventional way. So I could just play with the editing of them, and it gave me the confidence to go back downstairs after we finished the bedroom scenes and be able to have a surer hand in directing.

Since I was working in a restricted space, I had to make that space as vivid as I could, with as much color and movement and camera activity as possible, so the eye would not get bored. What I tried to do was go back and forth between the *plans séquences* and shooting with master shots and close-ups.

Lizzie Borden checking the framing of a scene. The burnt piece of cloth hanging behind her arm is a quilted mat used as a sound baffle.
Photo courtesy of Lizzie Borden.

With *Working Girls* I was trying to work within the economic framework of three grants totaling $75,000, plus $25,000 in rent money that I had put in escrow for several years while I had been fighting—and I'm still fighting—to keep my loft. I got the grants as a result of having done *Born in Flames:* $25,000 from the National Endowment for the Arts, $25,000 from the New York State Council on the Arts, and $25,000 from the Jerome Foundation. I figured, Hey, if I'm kicked out of my space because I can't pay my rent, at least I'll have done a movie. And I built the set in my loft, figuring I'd use the loft one last time. Luckily, *Working Girls* has done well enough that paying the rent hasn't been a problem lately.

I was also fortunate that I got to use SAG actors because the Screen Actors Guild read my script and decided it was pornography. I kept trying to convince them it was a feminist film, but they kept reading the script back to me and ignoring my attempts to explain that even if it sounded like pornography it wasn't going to be shot that way. I told them I wanted to pay into their Pension and Welfare Fund, and they said they were sorry. I thought they were telling me I couldn't use SAG actors, but then they said, "Your film is outside our jurisdiction, and if our actors want to be in this kind of movie, it's up to them." So I said, "Are you telling me that if I say my film is pornography then I can work with SAG actors and pay them whatever I want to and it's okay?" They said, "Yeah." So I said, "Can you please put that in writing?" To my amazement, they did, and that's how I got around SAG.

I was planning to do my film on as little as possible, and had I really cut corners after it was shot I probably could have turned it in for about $180,000. But there were a lot of deferrals. I could have saved maybe $75,000 by not paying people who never even expected to get paid. There were people in the film who got paid a token, and then later we gave them more money because we were able to. And the postproduction costs were high. The film was shot in Super-16, so I had to pay for a blowup.

I didn't want a cheap sound track, because that's a killer. I had two sound effects editors and two dialogue editors. At one point I just tore the brothel set down and brought four Steenbecks into my loft, and it became in effect a postproduction studio.

A lot of the other costs were legal fees, because it started out as a $100,000 movie financed by grants and my rent money and it went to a $300,000 movie financed partially by a limited partnership. Andi Gladstone decided she wanted to be my co-producer, and she had never done a feature before. She had really liked *Born in Flames*, so she wanted to work on *Working Girls*. She put together a limited partnership through a lawyer and started to try to get people to finance the finishing costs, so while I was editing my film there was a constant stream of people coming in to look at it, and a lot of them would say, "Well, where's the killer? Where's the hot sex?" So we never got money from big-time investors. Things kept dragging on and on, and finally Andi just got people to put in $1,000 here, $800 there. And thank God we were invited to attend the Directors' Fortnight (a section of the Cannes Film Festival that's really great for directors who are unknown because it brings a lot of attention to their work), because we owed the lab $90,000 since I shot a very high ratio of film. We managed to sell some European territories, so we got money to pay the lab. Then the mix cost $20,000, and the blowup was $15,000, and the internegative was another $15,000. But Du Art gave us a

Super-16 camera for free for having our lab work done there, and Spike Lee later used the same camera for *She's Gotta Have It.* My lighting designer lit for blowup; certain scenes were overlit so they'd blow up with less grain. The good thing about Super-16 is that you have a frame that's more similar to 35-millimeter. It really helped, because all the costs were 16-millimeter costs up to the end. Still, I'd love to work in 35. It's so gorgeous.

SUCCESS AND ITS CHALLENGES

I think everybody finds his or her own method of directing, and mine is more collaborative. But if an idea doesn't fit my vision, I don't use it. My greatest challenge next time is going to be figuring out how I can follow my own vision even though I know it's somebody else's money. I've sensed that pressure when I've talked to certain filmmakers who've worked for the major studios, and they say that the studios often question everything, even their choice of actors, camera angles, locations—they put them through the wringer.

Right now a lot of studios and a lot of distribution companies that have production arms are willing to finance movies for between $1 million and $5 million and not feel that there's a tremendous risk, because video and foreign sales make that money back. It really seems to have opened the way for filmmakers who might have been considered marginal before.

I'm interested in people and relationships, not special effects. I see some directors move to Hollywood and really screw themselves up. There are some women I have in mind who started out doing documentaries, then did their time in Hollywood and made multimillion-dollar movies that ended up being box office disasters, and then they were unable to make another movie. Out there there's so much censorship of ideas before they happen.

I don't want to censor my ideas before even thinking them through. *Working Girls* would have gotten an X, and that's why we put it out unrated. I thought it had no graphic images in it, and yet a lot of the shots, including the diaphragm shots, are really taboo, an instant X. This upsets me; it's quite unfair. We unofficially submitted the film to the MPAA, and they said to us, "There are at least forty violations; you won't have a film left by the time you get done cutting it." And their objections had to do with every one of the sex scenes, the diaphragm scenes. It's ridiculous.

There are things about women's hygiene that are so taboo. After I finished *Working Girls* I was reading about Martha Coolidge trying to get a diaphragm scene in *Joy of Sex,* and the studio refused. As it turns out, Susan Seidelman had a diaphragm scene in *Making Mr. Right,* but you just can't show someone trying to insert it, as I did in *Working Girls.* Do underage kids who see the object think it's a flying saucer? Maybe these days, with AIDS, birth control elements in films will be looked at more positively.

I've always thought that I want to do a porn film, but I would probably finance that myself on a really low budget. I wouldn't want anybody to meddle in it. The purpose would be to make a really positive statement about eroticism. We women have to make a statement about what's erotic for us, because all this controversy about pornography and whether it's good or bad denies our right to produce the kinds of erotic images we like. So it's actually about claiming a whole set of images for ourselves. The conservative right would call any erotic film I would do "pornography."

A MILLION OFFERS

It's amazing that if a film does well at the box office for its cost, all of a sudden you have a million offers. I have every agent in the book calling me, and I have to approach a lot of this with a grain of salt, because I'm the same person I was before the film started to register at the box office. My big question right now is, do I want to be considered for films I haven't had anything to do with conceptually? Do I want to be hired as just a director? So far I've seen a lot of scripts that other people have written, and I just don't feel close enough to them to devote that much time of my life to working on somebody else's movie.

At this point, if the financing is there, my films don't have to take as long as they have taken so far, where I've had to do everything, every step of the way, even after the films were released. I was the one, not the actors, who had to travel and promote *Working Girls,* because I was the one who knew the issues. Some people in certain cities didn't even want to talk about the movie; they wanted to talk about the issue of prostitution.

One of the difficulties of being an independent and a "control freak" is that every element of the film is determined by oneself, from the conception to the execution. Then all of a sudden it's in other people's hands, and they do what they want with it. Basically that's their job as distributors, to make people want to see this movie. Although I had many objections at first, I realize now that the campaign for *Working Girls* did work, because it brought people to the movie who normally might not have been interested. Because I'm a woman, I would have attracted the feminist audience anyhow. But some of the raincoat crowd that came for the matinees were walking out quite sober, and I know my film put a little dent in their preconceptions about prostitutes.

Some filmmakers go wrong when they try to control the advertising for their films. The filmmaker doesn't always know best. What I'm aware of now that I wasn't aware of before *Born in Flames* is this whole megaworld of distributors and trade journals and all of that, and it's a world I don't feel all that comfortable in. Let them play with it—that's *their* art form. Mine is just to develop ideas for the movies I want to make. I hope I'll be able to start another movie soon, because there was a point in traveling with *Working Girls* where I just began to feel like a PR person. I need to write and direct in order to feel like a creative person.

8

Earning and Learning on Commercial Gigs

IF YOU CAN'T support yourself and still make your own movies and pay for them—the way Lizzie Borden did—in your spare time, then perhaps you can earn while you learn, by breaking into the commercial film business. Working on TV spots, sales films, documentaries, political films, etc., is wonderful on-the-job training, and the pay ranges from moderate to marvelous. It's a fine way of supporting yourself, making contacts, and filling in gaps in your expertise while you wait for the chance to make your first feature movie. It can even give you easy access to the equipment and facilities you'll need to make that movie.

Every single thing you learn by doing commercial work makes you better in your profession and more insightful as a person. What you're absorbing now, sometimes subconsciously, might someday find its way into one of your movies or screenplays. You learn how to make inherently dry subjects as cinematically interesting as possible. You see how to keep from boring your audience when you must present scenes that are fundamentally informational instead of wildly dramatic.

Cinematically, the best TV spots are state-of-the-art. Because people are constantly being bombarded by attempts to sell them stuff, they become jaded, immune to any attempt to capture their attention with a sales pitch. Therefore, any brand-new cinematic innovation is bound to be snatched up and employed by Madison Avenue if it will make people pay a little more attention for a while.

All these new techniques become part of your education and experience if you happen to be working for a commercial production company that lands work for a big, rich client. It takes considerable filmmaking technology and expertise to put a tiger in people's tanks, race them through mountain curves in the Grand Prix, land them on the moon, make a ten-foot-tall giant hand them a roll of paper towels, or cause a miniature Conestoga wagon to pull a load of dogfood through their kitchen. By working on this stuff, you learn how to *do* it while someone else is paying. Then you can apply the same kinds of concepts to some far-out premise you may want to try in your own movie someday.

Even if you never get to work on big-budget jobs, the day-to-day production of a commercial company is an invaluable training ground. In the lowliest TV spot, sets have to be convincing, props have to look real and function correctly, actors and models have to be astutely cast and costumed, and every aspect of the cinematography, editing, scoring, etc., has to hit professional standards.

Making spots teaches you a lot about *pace*. You discover how to tell a story, get a point across, and influence people's drives and emotions in the space of sixty seconds, thirty seconds, even ten seconds. You can learn how to work with everyone from "name" talent to absolute amateurs. You face the challenge of keeping costs down while still delivering a slick piece of work.

Longer films like industrials, training films, and sales films add to your wealth of insight into all sorts of production problems. You'll find out how to budget for location filming that includes crew and cast travel. Working in factories, mines, maybe even nuclear installations, you'll sometimes encounter delicate or dangerous situations.

BREAKING INTO COMMERCIAL WORK

Unfortunately, it can be darn near impossible to get hired onto a production crew if you've never worked on one before. Producers want experienced crew people. Yet, they won't hire you so that you can gain the experience they require.

The reason for this "catch-22" is that the slightest mistake by the lowliest crew member can blow a small fortune. Only crew members of proven astuteness and reliability are trusted with as elemental and mechanical a task as loading and unloading magazines. It's not a hard thing to learn. But if you make a mistake, causing a scratch to appear on a roll of film, or inadvertently exposing it to a light leak, you can blow a one-time shot that might have cost a couple hundred thousand dollars. There are many horror stories about that kind of error, and they make producers extremely reluctant to take a chance on a shining new face.

Still, you say you're determined. You know you can make it. You just need that single chance. And you can't get it. Hold on. Don't lose hope.

Don't be so impatient to make the big leap into producing and directing that you fail to recognize an opportunity when it's right under your feet. Get your foot on the ladder even if it's on the bottom rung—or close to the rung but not quite touching it—or on the wrong ladder but right next to the one you'd rather climb. *Start* almost anywhere you can. Keep striving. And don't take your eyes off your true goal. Here are some tips that might help you crack the stalemate:

1. Don't rely on a mere résumé; it can't really tell anyone what kind of work you can do. You want to be a filmmaker, so use film to sell yourself, not paper. Put together the best sample reel you can make—*clips,* not complete prints, of your finest work. Strive for variety and professionalism and work in 16 millimeter if possible; then make videotape dubs of your film and send the cassettes to prospective employers along with your résumé. Make sure your work is truly professional-looking and exciting; today's filmmakers expect someone they'd want to hire to have samples in keeping with the kind of knowledge and information that's out there today. They may not be after perfection, but there is a new level that you've got to hit. If one of the filmmakers likes what he sees, he might remember you next time a grip gets sick and he's desperate to fill up a crew.

2. Don't try to reach only the higher-ups (producers, directors, cameramen). Try to meet some people who are already working on film crews as grips, gofers, or gaffers. One of them might gain points with a producer if he recommends a good fill-in someday, so he might be willing to do you the favor.

3. *Volunteer* if you spy a chance, but perform as if you're the highest-paid person on the production staff—be reliable, punctual, flexible, hardworking, uncomplaining, and self-sacrificing—then maybe someday you will be. These professionals won't let you into the club if you don't show that you deserve to belong.

4. Don't wait too long for somebody else to hire you. Instead, strike out on your own. You can free-lance a few gigs in your spare time even if you have to hold down some kind of steady job to keep food on your table. Some businesses need tapes and films made so cheaply that any sort of production house is way out of their league, but they may hire a one-man crew to make them a nice little ten-minute videotape that they can use to show off their services or sell their "widgets." This kind of work not only helps you gain filmmaking experience; it's also grist for your sample reel and gives you great references for getting more work. It can even lead to a job offer from one of the established production companies that ignored you before.

5. Think about *related* areas of employment that might get you closer to where you really want to make your career. For instance, all the major advertising agencies, and most of the smaller ones, have broadcast production departments, where you might be able to get hired as a production assistant, a secretary, a storyboard artist, a copywriter, or an agency producer or assistant producer. All of these jobs will add to your experience, help you make contacts, and possibly serve as a springboard to your ultimate goal. Besides ad agencies, many other types of companies have departments that produce corporate films. USX is one; Westinghouse Corporation is another. There you'll meet people in the types of companies where you want to be, and your contacts within the corporate world will be an incentive for some film production company to hire you once it realizes you now have an "in" with some of the people the production company must sell to if it is to continue to land film contracts. Working at a TV station can also be a good way to begin your career. Lots of production takes place even at small independent stations— the news, the weather, locally originated panel shows, specials, and so on.

6. Making political films can be extremely enlightening since it gives you a lot of insight into people. Over the years at The Latent Image, we made commercials for many famous politicians, including Senator Ted Kennedy, Governor George Romney of Michigan, Governor Hernandez Colon of Puerto Rico, and presidential candidate George McGovern. We also filmed celebrities like Jimmy Stewart, Ann-Margret, Buddy Greco, Tony Martin, and Johnny Cash. Scientists Willy Ley and Wernher von Braun. Sports stars Willie Stargell, Maury Wills, Bobby Layne, and Franco Harris. And many, many others.

The filmmaker brings his talents to bear in the making of TV spots and/or "documentaries" that are often a slick package of artfully contrived hype in the guise of a factual presentation. Let's face it, it's propaganda—you have to always photograph, record, and edit the candidate so he shows to his best advantage. Therefore, the ethical and moral considerations of such propaganda may force you to make difficult personal choices—is the gig worth a crisis in conscience? It's up to you. However, working on political films adds to the comprehensive training you get from commercial work, which can be invaluable when it comes to making your first feature movie. It gives you not just skill in filmmaking, but in budgeting and managing diverse productions. Handling complicated, tangled-up logistics. Dealing with actors, crews, and unions. Publicity. Marketing. Once you have a feel for all these things, your chances of making a good picture and getting it sold are greatly improved.

7. Making documentaries is another possible stepping-stone. Tobe Hooper, for example, traveled around the country a lot doing films about experimental educational programs right after the Kennedy administration, when exciting things were happening in documentary films. He made more than sixty documentaries and probably that many special education TV spots. In so doing, he's been tear-gassed in Memphis on the anniversary of Martin Luther King's assassination and been in a crowd with Ted Kennedy in a riot. More education and experience.

KEY STEPS IN MAKING A COMMERCIAL FILM

Every film, whether it's a feature or the lowliest TV spot, has to be taken through these key steps on its way from initial concept to finished print:

1. Scripting
2. Budgeting
3. Preproduction planning and preparation
4. Shooting
5. Postproduction (editing and finishing)

This book is not designed to be a treatise on commercial filmmaking. If you want to make commercial films, you will find out how to do so either by freelancing or by working your way up through the ranks of an established production company or agency. You will learn all you need to know about steps 1, 3, 4, and 5 by practicing filmmaking on your own and by digging in and doing whatever work comes your way.

But if you want to go out and try to *land* commercial jobs after you feel you've attained sufficient skill to execute those jobs, then you'll first have to know how to draw up budgets and make bids. This is a skill you don't usually get unless you're at management level within a company. So I'm going to teach you the basics, which will give you a head start on pulling in commercial work and producing it without losing your shirt. Knowing how to budget commercial films will also make it easier for you to accurately budget your first feature.

Basics of Commercial Film Budgeting

Drawing up an accurate budget is a matter of figuring out with certainty how many days it's going to take to produce a particular job, what personnel you are going to need at what rates of pay and on how many days, what equipment will be required, how much you will need to spend for props, sets, costumes, and special effects, what outside suppliers (such as animation or art houses) will be required and what they will charge you, and how much time and money will be spent in postproduction (editing, mixing, lab services, and the like).

As a beginner, you could come close to figuring out the cost of just about all the above through a bit of research, but the thing that will throw you is the *time* factor. I can give you a few tips, but this is one of those lessons only experience can teach. You'll have to learn how long you take to shoot, to score, to edit, and so forth. How can you lose your shirt trying to produce a "little" thirty-second spot? Consider: It costs roughly $9,000 to put a relatively small film crew on location for a day. If you have three actors in a scene at SAG minimum that's another $1,000. So if you estimate three days of shooting and it takes five, you just lost $20,000. If you were making a feature movie . . . at this rate you would end up millions of dollars in the red.

So watch out for those few extra camera setups. Or special effects that are exceedingly painstaking and time-consuming. Or a location near an airport with planes flying over you every ten minutes so that you can roll clean sound only in the gaps, when there's nothing taking off or landing.

The best I can do to help you understand the basics of budgeting is to show you the steps I took and how I arrived at a bidding figure on a fairly simple TV commercial. I wrote and produced the following for the Contemporary Institute of Broadcasting (CIB); George Romero then directed it as part of a series of spots and a documentary filmed at the school's headquarters in Philadelphia:

| The Latent Image, Inc. | CIB Script #2: "Students" |
VIDEO	AUDIO
Open with 10- 15- second montage: ECUs of students talking about CIB—their triumphs, the new confidence they've attained through CIB. Get a brief success story, if possible.	Sample comments (lip sync): "I have a good voice, but I didn't know if I could learn to project it." "It's not easy. You have to practice and work hard."
Montage starts with quick cuts then eases into a more relaxed but still up-tempo pace.	"But you're learning from experts. It gives you a real confidence." "Not everyone in television is good-looking."
Students' montage will be improvised, so we hope to work with selected students who can pull it off.	"I have twenty hours on camera already. I can't believe it!"
Students' comments go voice-over as we DISSOLVE to shots of the learning process in the school. Narrator takes over as sounds of talking students segue out.	"You learn by doing . . . that's the only way to make it stick." NARRATION:

VIDEO	AUDIO
Continue to end of spot with dramatic, interesting shots of school activity. Make sure to feature broadcast personalities who act as instructors. Show good-looking females if possible. Cuts are quick, pace is up-tempo, lighting is dramatic.	That's right! You learn by doing at the Contemporary Institute of Broadcasting. CIB is a no-nonsense school that can prepare you for an exciting, stimulating career as a broadcast personality. CIB has top-notch, well-known instructors who have proven their own audience appeal and are anxious to help *you* make the grade. If you have the basic raw talent, and if you're willing to work hard, you already own the ingredients for a successful career in radio or television.
Montage continues.	CIB can show you how to use your talent effectively by teaching you exciting new skills that can propel you into a glamorous, high-paying professional career.
Montage FREEZES on shot of instructor adjusting headphones on student at control panel or some other interesting setup.	
SUPER CIB address and phone number.	If you have what it takes, CIB has a place in your future. Call or write today for free information.

Because CIB was hurting for enrollment, we knew it didn't have a lot of money to spend. (Incidentally, this is a good example of a case where the client came to the film production house directly, without an ad agency in the middle, so we were in effect acting as agency *and* producer, doing what our brochures bragged we could do—furnish "full service from script to screen.")

Key factors are:

1. Our on-camera "talent" consisted of students of unknown ability. Although they didn't have to be paid anything (they would sign releases), they could drive the production costs up by blowing takes.

2. We would be filming in a location that we had never scouted. Although we'd been assured of certain basic requirements—that it looked good, that there was enough electrical power, etc.—we wouldn't know for sure until we got there.

3. If anything went wrong, the crew might have had to stay in Philadelphia longer than the bid allowed. So we decided it would be best to take a small crew, as long as they could handle the job under circumstances that might be loaded with unpleasant surprises.

Most of the production considerations were fairly ordinary. No props for us to furnish—they'd be on the premises. No big special effects. No "period" sets or costumes, as would have been required if I had written some "gadgety" concept—like Patrick Henry telling the Virginia Assembly how he learned his oratorical skills at CIB. We were using the school's own assets to help it sell itself; this is a plain, direct, practical approach. In the way of special lab costs, I had only one freeze frame and one super at the end of the spot.

Okay. I decided to allow two days to film this spot: one day to get the lip-sync comments from the students and the second day to knock off as many camera setups as we could, all around the school—in their classrooms, studios, broadcast booths, etc. The lip-sync shots are all ECUs, so we could film them all in one room, varying backgrounds only slightly. Also, we wouldn't have to go outdoors, so the shooting couldn't get hung up by bad weather. Hopefully we could even knock off all the lip-sync stuff in one morning, gaining more time to film the wild setups.

Since The Latent Image was not a union shop, the crew would work as late each day as necessary to avoid using a third day on location. So I had a hedge against going over budget in this department.

Because we were going to work with relative amateurs as on-camera talent, and because we were going to shoot a lot of wild setups, I allowed for a high footage ratio. (Usually commercial film ratios are much higher than feature film ratios because most commercial films are made up of many, many very short shots—lots of setups covered by constant narration.) With luck, it would be possible to shoot our spot on one 400-foot roll of 16-millimeter filmstock (ten minutes per roll), but I knew from experience that we'd probably use three or even *four* rolls. George guns off more than most cameramen. So, to be safe, I budgeted for four rolls.

If we ran into problems on location, we might wish we had a six-man crew. But I decided to go with just four, counting myself. I could act as producer and still help lug equipment, string cables, set lights, and so on. This would help keep the bid as low as I sensed it had to be for us to land the job. And, because I knew the capabilities of our staff, I was confident that four of us could handle this thing, barring extraordinary complications; if we did need help, we could probably pick up a stringer in Philadelphia.

So, let's write down what it would cost us to pay four guys for two days in Philadelphia. Right?

Wrong. We had to pay them for *four* days: two days of shooting *and* two days of travel, one on each end of the shooting schedule.

Anything not *in* the script? Something I might have forgotten?

How about music? This spot would require music to help carry the narration along. But it could be library music, not an original score, and we could get it for a flat fee of about $125.

Bearing all these considerations in mind, let's list the factors and costs that would go into our bid:

On-camera talent (no cost; students and instructors sign releases)	xxxx
Narrator (record in our own studio)	300
Filmstock, processing and work printing	800
Quarter-inch and 16mm sound tape and transfers	300
Editing and interlocking (equip. and personnel)	800
Super and freeze frame	250
Music	125
Mix	.90
Lab finishing costs to one A/print	250
Script	250
Producer (4 days x 350)	1,400
Director/cameraman (4 days x 350)	1,400
Asst. cameraman/gaffer (4 days x 250)	1,000
Recording engineer/gaffer (4 days x 250)	1,000
Meals, airfares, lodging	1,000
Equipment (Eclair camera, Nagra, accessories)	2,000
	$10,965

What did I forget? Overhead costs were built into the charges for personnel, time, and equipment in this particular bid. But how about *profit?* The Latent Image needed to make something on this deal, so let's "plus it" by 10 percent, or $1,096.50. That brings us up to $12,061.50. However, I may have wanted to add another 10 percent as a "contingency"—in case any of the things that had me worried actually did go wrong—and if I did this, the total bid would come in at $13,158.

A bid is a product of *your* costs and your *desired* profit versus how much the client *should* pay or *will* pay. If the client can't be charged what you would like, you must decide whether the job is still worth it to you at a reduced price. Conversely, if you know you can get away with charging the client more, you have to figure the point where you will be pushing beyond a fair, realistic price for your talents into an area where you will be just plain milking the client.

You won't stay in business very long if people find out you're overpriced. Other filmmakers, just as talented but less greedy, will take the business away from you.

Perhaps right now you're the one who's talented and hungry. So you may be able to cut into other people's territory—people who have become fat and complacent, like our competitors were when we started The Latent Image, Inc. Pittsburgh isn't the only big city that has lots of commercial film production. Your city or town might be full of untapped opportunities. Look around. Ask questions. Gain a foothold and start making a living as a professional filmmaker.

A SHORT LESSON IN STEALING

Suppose you're a freelance filmmaker in Philadelphia, and you get wind that Contemporary Institute of Broadcasting is thinking about some TV spots and maybe a recruitment film to bolster student enrollment. You hear about this from a young lady you're dating whose friend is the daughter of one of the instructors. You'd dearly love to have a chance to pitch yourself for the job, but your girlfriend's friend really doesn't know you or your work well enough to recommend you, and it seems it would be too big an imposition to try to show your sample reel to her father and then try to get him to give you an intro to the school officials.

If you're going to bomb out, you might as well bomb out at the top. So, you get your hands on one of CIB's brochures, which lists its address and phone number and the name of the president. You write him a letter on your snazzy, businesslike stationery:

Dear Mr. CIB:

My name is Bob Filmmaker, and I understand that CIB is contemplating production of some TV spots and possibly an enrollment film. I can do this work for you, smoothly and professionally, at an affordable price. If you've already gotten bids, I believe mine will undercut them, with no loss of quality in the finished product. May I please phone you for an appointment?

Sincerely,
Bob Filmmaker

Now, if your letter has sufficient impact on the CIB president, he won't wait for your follow-up call; he'll phone you. In case he doesn't, at least you've primed him instead of blundering in cold.

So, three days later you make your call, and his secretary won't put you through to him; instead she takes a message, and another day goes by, and he still doesn't get back to you. But you persist—after all, the world isn't going to blow up if this guy gets mad at you for bothering him. He takes your call the next morning.

You are very polite but enthusiastic. "Hello, Mr. CIB. Thank you for taking the time to talk with me. My name is Bob Filmmaker, and I'd like to come in and show you why I'd be the right person to produce films for your broadcast school."

"What have you done before?" asks CIB skeptically.

"I have some nice stuff on my sample reel. Some TV spots and some clips from two films I made for XYZ Travel to help sell their cut-rate tours. Mr. Jones at XYZ was very pleased with my work—I handled all the production, including writing the scripts—and they're now having a lot less trouble booking the tours."

"Well," says CIB, "it's probably too late for me to talk to you at this point. I just came back from Pittsburgh, where I met with a fairly big, established commercial film company. You say you're a one-man show? How can you give me as good a job as *they* can?"

"Because I'm an excellent cameraman and a director, and I work with the best backup crew in Philadelphia. I don't have to pay them when they're not working for me . . . I shell out on a per-job basis. So my overhead is *very* low. That's where I can save you a lot of money."

Now, you know CIB can't be a flush operation because it needs these films to bolster sagging enrollment. So your pitch is right on target—aimed at CIB's pocketbook. But, like most people, CIB is not going to buy a piece of crap, even if it's *cheap* crap. So, when you get your appointment, you've got to convince the president that you can deliver the genuine goods *and* save CIB money.

To help convince him, you say, "Mr. CIB, you've already spent money flying to Pittsburgh when there are good filmmakers like me right here in Philadelphia. That out-of-town company has to charge you for airfares, hotel bills, meals, the whole works. That money doesn't put better pictures up on the screen. Neither does the big overhead. I don't have a huge studio, and I don't need one for your films, because they're going to be shot on location, right *here,* where I can be at your service all through the production, every single day."

Your initial meeting is a success, and CIB gives you a chance to write some sample scripts and work up a bid. You end up writing a script similar in concept and content to the one written by The Latent Image (although you do not know this at the time, since you are not given a peek at that script). In bidding your script, there are some costs that are inherently the same for you and your competitors; no way you can knock them down. But you will save money in overhead, crew travel, lodging and meals, and the amount of money *you* will have to make on this job, because you are interested in making decent cash without pricing yourself out of the market. So your bid ends up looking like this:

On-camera talent and narrator	xxxx
Filmstock, processing, and work printing	800
Quarter-inch and 16mm tape and transfers	200
Editing room rental (2 days x 200)	400
Super and freeze frame	250
Music	125
Mix	45
Lab finishing costs to one A/print	250
Asst. cameraman (2 days x 200)	400
Recording engineer (2 days x 200)	400
Lighting supervisor (2 days x 200)	400
Three gaffers and grips (2 days x 350)	700
Meals for crew (2 days)	200
Eclair camera, Nagra, other shooting equip.	800
	$4,970

Since you are *in* Philadelphia, you prefer to take advantage of the availability of one of the CIB broadcast personalities to be your narrator. You can record him right in one of the CIB studios, on a separate day from your shooting days, when you are not paying a big crew to hang around. You can afford a *bigger* crew, since you are paying them only for the two shooting days, not for any travel days. And, only their direct cost to you, not production company overhead, is built into your bid.

There are no syncing, editing, or conforming charges, because you intend to do all this work yourself. And there are no overhead charges built into the transferring and mixing costs; you have listed only what you will be charged by the postproduction house.

So far, it looks like you have cut the competition's bid in half. But you haven't paid *yourself.* How much do you want to make for writing the script, producing, directing, editing, conforming, supervising the mix, the interlock, the lab finishing, etc.? Here's how long it will probably take you to do it all:

	No. of Days
Preproduction meetings	2
Writing script	1
Hiring and coordinating crew and equip.	1
Shooting	1
Postproduction	5
	10

How much is ten days of your time worth? Two hundred dollars per day? That would be $2,000. But you feel pretty sure you're going to undercut the Pittsburgh outfit by a wide margin. Besides, you have some overhead of your own—light, heat, rent, phone bills, stationery, etc.—that ought to be covered; plus, there ought to be some contingency money in case something goes wrong. So, let's plus the bid by $3,000. That brings it in at a final figure of $7,970—about $5,000 less than the out-of-town outfit.

Remember, although $3,000 is not an unusual amount of money for a freelancer to clear on a job like this—and although it looks like a *lot* of money for ten days' work—one of the main hazards of freelancing is that you do not land enough gigs to keep you working every single day. So your per-diem rate has to be high enough to compensate for the rest of the time, when you will be hard at work without pay, spending your own money in fact, pitching prospective clients and trying to sell them your services.

This time, however, you come out on top. CIB ends up liking your sample reel *and* your price, and you succeed in landing the gig, stealing it away from your supposedly bigger, stronger competitors.

Congratulations, Bob Filmmaker!

MAKING SURE YOU GET PAID

At The Latent Image we had a bidding policy that was designed to ensure that even if a client never paid the full bill, at the very least we wouldn't get stuck for any cash out of our own pockets. Our bids were always at least three times the total of our estimated out-of-pocket costs—and we always asked for an advance that was one third of our bidding price. So, if the job went bust, we'd be out our *time* (in other words, our overhead), but at least we wouldn't owe our suppliers any money. Most of our clients graciously paid the advance, since the same payment policy is followed by almost all commercial production companies. The standard payment schedule is one third in advance, one third when filming is completed, and one third when the first print is delivered.

For political films we always asked for an advance that was one half instead of only one third of the total bid, and we wanted the other half before we would deliver a print. That was because losing political campaigns are so notorious for not paying their debts—far worse in this regard than ordinary commercial clients.

Makeup artist Dick Smith takes this precaution one step further. "On certain lowball productions," he advises, "you have to be concerned about checks bouncing. Never deliver anything that you've made without getting a certified check or cash, because once you've delivered, you have no way to make them pay. Never take a deal for postponed payment of any sort, even if the producer says he'll pay you much more if you wait until after the film is released, or if he wants you to work for less on this particular production, claiming he'll hire you for bigger money to make up for it on his next project. These kinds of promises almost always turn out to be lies. Don't be afraid of arguing and standing up for yourself. If the producer acts amazed that you would question his so-called integrity, just tell him it's business and nothing personal."

RUSS STREINER ON USING THE AD WORLD AS A SPRINGBOARD

After we made *Night of the Living Dead,* Russ Streiner and I co-produced and George Romero directed a "youth picture" entitled *The Affair,* which wasn't nearly as successful as our horror movie, so we had to keep doing commercials for a few more years. During that time, Russ and I teamed with Rudy Ricci (author of *The Affair)* to form our own company, New American Films, while George Romero stayed at The Latent Image. When financial difficulties caused New American Films to fold, Russ landed a high-paying job with a major advertising agency, and I kept on writing books and making low-budget feature movies, while doing a few commercial jobs on the side. One of the last commercial films I produced, for United Way, won a Golden Reel award in 1980, and the job came through Russ because his agency was handling the United Way account.

Russ got his advertising job because he knew virtually every aspect of film production, due to his experience at The Latent Image and at New American. He rose quickly to vice president—largely because his expertise contributed importantly to the growth of the agency from billing of $12 million a year to over $200 million annually. Russ is now once more into feature production, working with George Romero and me on a remake of *Night of the Living Dead* and on several other projects. But he doesn't feel that his career was sidetracked; instead he says its potential was enhanced by the ten years he spent as an ad exec:

"One of the great things it did for me was give me a firsthand glimpse at how the corporate world works. When you get that in perspective, it also applies to the movie business. The business aspects of production don't change whether it's a thirty-second spot for a bottle of ketchup or a feature-length film. It's *all* a business, and there is bottom-line accountability regarding budgets and deadlines. My exposure to the business world all these years has given me the ability to look at making movies as an art without losing sight of it as a business. I took a great deal of pride not just in working with the major national clients but with some of the smaller ones that drastically needed help, where I could feel that I had a direct, hands-on effect on their becoming successful. I feel that I've already proven myself in the advertising arena, and now I want to get back to producing legitimate entertainment."

Russell W. Streiner as he looks today and as Johnny in *Night of the Living Dead.*
Photos courtesy of Russell W. Streiner.

It's possible that you might become so successful as a commercial film-maker that you'll build a career in the ad world and forget about making feature movies. The financial rewards can be enormous—and enormously seductive.

Some highly successful commercial filmmakers charge directing fees of thousands of dollars per *day,* with a three-day minimum guarantee before they'll agree to work for a prospective client. They're making much more money than most feature directors earn, so it's pretty hard for them to justify taking time out to make a feature, no matter how strongly they want to. What if the feature bombs? Maybe those big commercial clients won't come back to a reputation that has been "tarnished" by failure.

If Madison Avenue opens its arms to you, it will be up to you to decide how tightly you want to be hugged. Tom Bernard, Vice President of Market-ing and Distribution for Orion Classics, put it this way: "Most people are not willing to make the financial sacrifice it takes to go back and start from ground zero. They are making too much money shooting industrials and commercials to take a gamble and a year out of their lives to make a feature—so they talk about the film, but they never make it."

Joe Pytka. *Photo by Jane McCann.*

Joe Pytka and I met when we were both starting out as Pittsburgh filmmakers in the early sixties. Now Joe is one of the top commercial directors in the world. The week I interviewed him, *Newsweek* had done a full page on him. He's the only director to win the Grand Prix at Cannes two years in a row. He's won dozens of CLIOs. Currently he's working on a Pepsi commercial and a music video with Michael Jackson. And he's about to direct his first feature movie, *Let it Ride,* for Paramount, starring Richard Dreyfuss.

9

Joe Pytka
Commercial Gold

★ I always had a passion for movies—I can remember knowing directors' names and so on before I was even in grade school. I grew up in the fifties, so the filmmakers that I loved in those days were John Ford, George Stevens, Alfred Hitchcock—especially John Ford. The cavalry trilogy, *Fort Apache,* and so on—those are great movies; they have a wonderful sense of people and place and tradition. Every time I see a John Ford movie, I get more satisfied by it. I loved George Stevens' *Shane.* And *Gunga Din,* a wonderful action-adventure film. As I grew older I started looking at Antonioni, Fellini, Godard, and Truffaut—and I'm studying Godard now, because I'm trying to get an "antitechnique" thing going in my work. But his films don't tend to satisfy me, because they're too intellectual, and I think filmmaking is more of a media process.

MAKING MAGIC MOMENTS

Back in Pittsburgh, the first films I got involved with were documentaries for public television. When you're doing documentaries, you have the sense of looking at something and photographing it, much like a photojournalist. That carried over into most of my filmmaking. I love movies, but I don't really look at them for style—I try to set up a realistic scene and photograph it. I kind of like to see something happen at the point of impact. I'm talking about a certain kind of magic. When we shoot the Michelob commercials, we try to set up a situation where sparks will fly. It may take a day to get two shots. We try to get a moment we can capture, a moment of interest, a moment of tension. In many cases the people are ad-libbing. I play tricks on them to get something I can use. I may put them in a situation they're uncomfortable with, just to get spontaneous looks. Sometimes I shout at them, then shoot them in slow motion. It's kind of cruel, maybe, but it can result in a piece of magic that people vividly remember.

Every project has a different solution. You have to be sort of quick on your feet to understand what you have to do. If you have a terrific actor, you just want to set a great tone for what he has to do and make everything as quiet and peaceful as possible so he can operate. In the case of Bartles & Jaymes, it's a matter of setting the stage and being very efficient from a production standpoint.

To tell you the truth, Bartles & Jaymes ads are fairly cut and dried. We do up to ten of them a day. They're simple to produce. The ones on the porch, we can knock off three or four before lunch and five or six after lunch. They're little witty one-liners. We do them on TelePrompTers. It was funny when we went to New York with those guys, seeing them on Madison Avenue being deluged by all the Yuppies. One guy is a farmer from northern Oregon, and the other is a contractor from Santa Rosa, California. So they're non-professionals; they're both "real people." The writer did the casting. I can't take too much credit for the commercials. They're basically simple for a director. It's a matter of being careful and efficient, knowing what your setups are, getting the shots, keeping a good attitude on the set, and so on.

WORKING WITH MICHAEL JACKSON

The Michael Jackson stuff I did was aired in early 1988. I shot a music video for him, and I shot the Pepsi commercials, which are very complicated technologically. They contain virtually every kind of special effect that you can do. They're kind of James-Bond-like; there's a surrealistic conflict. It has to do with being chased.

Jackson is a certified genius, probably the only genius I've ever worked with in my life. He's a phenomenal performer, incredibly quick to understand complicated concepts, and his movements, his control of his body, are unbelievable. I've done a lot of commercials with fabulous athletes like Michael Jordan, Moses Malone, Edwin Moses, and a lot of football players, baseball players—but I've never seen a human being with Michael Jackson's physical ability. Before I did the music video with Michael, I studied all the great old dance movies, and Astaire had an incredible elegance in his style, Gene Kelly had a tremendous physical presence and athletic ability, but nobody combines the qualities that Michael has—the singing, the dancing, the eroticism, the sensuality—he's very contemporary. I'm sure there were restrictions on Kelly and Astaire at the time, and I'm sure that people are gonna be pulling their hair out when they hear me saying these things. But being close to this guy and seeing him perform in person, there's been nothing like him on the face of the earth in my lifetime. He hasn't even scratched the surface of his abilities.

He's absolutely stunning. He's a perfectionist. And he puts his talent on the line. We flew him in wires for the Pepsi commercial. He asked me flat to my face, "How's the stuntman look?" I said, "He's okay, but he's a stuntman. People will say he's a stuntman." He asked, "What should we do?" I said, "The only thing is for you to fly." He's in wires and a harness, way off the ground, at the mercy of grips—and here's a guy worth millions of dollars to the marketplace, and for a Pepsi commercial he's up there jeopardizing himself. Anything could happen. But he did a great job. And he was in the middle of recording an album; he could have broken his leg or separated a shoulder. He'd be recording all night, and then he'd come to our studio— totally dedicated and an electrifying performer.

A FEATURE IN THE WORKS

There are a lot of successful directors who have gone from commercials into features. Guys like Howard Zieff, who was probably the best commercial director. He did *Slither, Private Benjamin, Hearts of the West.* Adrian Lyne, who did *Flashdance* and *Fatal Attraction.* Tony Scott, who did *Top Gun.* And Michael Cimino, who won the Academy Award for *The Deer Hunter,* was a great commercial director in the sixties and seventies. The success of commercial directors is due mainly to the look of their films. A lot of feature guys can do a film, but they don't have a "look." Nowadays a look is very important to the way a film is received. In a curious way, the industry is much more interested in filmmakers today than it used to be in the past. And part of the success of films like *Flashdance* and *Blade Runner* is their look, the filmmaking look—the lights, composition, editing. These are things we admired in directors of the forties and fifties.

Nowadays, not only are commercial directors making a successful entry into features, but feature directors are doing commercials. Federico Fellini, Roman Polanski and Franco Zeffirelli all do commercials in Europe. John Badham, who directed *Saturday Night Fever* and *WarGames,* has done commercials. Michael Chapman, who directed *All the Right Moves* and *Clan of the Cave Bear* is directing commercials, too.

For my own first feature, I would have preferred to make one from a script of my own, but I was offered a beautiful script called *Let It Ride,* a comedy that takes place during one day at a racetrack. Richard Dreyfuss was already committed to star in it and the writer was Nancy Dowd, who wrote *Slapshot* and *Coming Home,* so it was just too good to pass up. Paramount needed a director in a hurry and were considering several, but when I showed up they liked me and, bang, I got the project. The producer is David Giler, who wrote *The Parallax View* and produced *Alien* and its sequel, *Aliens.* I met him on a Friday and we had a deal on the following Tuesday. Four days! It was a miracle that happened mostly because the film had to go into production immediately in order to retain Richard Dreyfuss. For me, it was almost like landing an industrial film that falls in your lap late one afternoon and you only have a week or so to get it in the can.

One thing that helps me handle the pressure is that as a commercial director I actually have a lot of experience working under hectic conditions. Most feature directors do maybe one film a year or even every two years, so that means they're shooting 60 or 70 days over a two-year period. But I've been working on set at least 150 to 200 days a year. I'm in active production virtually constantly. I like the idea of working in commercials for the simple reason that it keeps you sharp in terms of your technique. If the only time you shoot a film is when you're doing a feature, then I'm not sure how you can keep your skills intact. It's almost like being an athlete. If you're off for that length of time, some of your skills may erode.

The things I'm addressing in doing a feature—the handling of subject matter, hiring crews, lining up locations—are things I've done many times for commercial productions. So the logistics of the movie aren't so tough, but the dovetailing of all the characters is very difficult. We have eighty important roles to cast—a slew of colorful characters at the racetrack and in the saloons. But there are so many good actors available for features as opposed to commercials; virtually everyone coming in to read has a strong capability. Many times in commercials you're dealing with actors who are really models, and their theatrical skills aren't highly polished. I'm overwhelmed by the quality of the actors we're casting in *Let It Ride*. Richard Dreyfuss is a brilliant performer, and his ability to inspire other actors is incredible.

I'm concerned that I do a good job, as always. Even when I do a commercial, I have the same concern. You're always concerned when you're facing the unknown. When I used to race motorcycles I'd get worried about races all the time beforehand. But there's nothing you can do about it. All you can do is face the problems one at a time, do your best, and hope that it works out. I'm comforted by the fact that I have a good script and good people to work with. I think *Let It Ride* at the very least will be entertaining, and if all goes well maybe I can make it into something that's a little bit transcendental. That's my hope, and I'll certainly give it my best shot.

PART III

CAST, CREW, AND CO-CONSPIRATORS

"It may well be pointless to try and isolate the great powers of the movie industry. Stars, studio executives, directors, and producers all circle in the same orbit . . . all joined at the hip, locked in an uneasy alliance, groping sometimes—but by no means always—toward the same mist-shrouded goal: a hit."

WILLIAM GOLDMAN
Adventures in the Screen Trade

10

On-Camera People

MOVIES ARE MAINLY about people. Even in movies that rely heavily on special effects, such as *Star Wars* and *E.T.,* all that wonderful gimmickry wouldn't add up to a hill of beans if the audience didn't care deeply about the people (even the non-Earth people) on the screen. It is therefore one of the filmmaker's prime responsibilities to make sure that the characters in his movies are engrossingly realistic and believable. To achieve this goal, he has to fill the roles with good actors and then get them to perform to their full potential.

The easiest way to do this is to cast highly experienced professional actors. But sometimes a movie's budget is too low to afford them. And sometimes it may be desirable to go with an inexperienced or untrained actor in a specific role because of a certain kind of charm and/or "screen presence" that the director perceives in that actor.

For instance, we wrote the part of Judy into the *Night of the Living Dead* script because we had been so impressed with Judith Ridley when she read for the part of Barbara (the female lead). Judith had no acting experience at all; she had done a bit of modeling in industrial films and that was about it. We didn't want to take a chance on giving her the lead role, where her inexperience might have caused us to shoot lots of retakes, blowing our meager footage budget. So we wrote in a part for her, enabling us to enhance our movie with her ingenuous beauty while not allowing the entire production to hinge on her performance. As it turned out, she performed very well indeed, and the on-camera experience that she acquired helped her land the lead in our next picture, *The Affair.*

Casting nonactors in important parts doesn't always pan out, so every filmmaker should understand the pluses and minuses of working with people of varying acting ability. They can be broken down into the following main groups, even though there is much overlap among the various categories:

- Professional actors
- Semiprofessional and avocational actors
- Untrained actors and models
- Nonactors
- Stars

WORKING WITH PROFESSIONAL ACTORS

You get more from professionals than just their acting ability. Since acting *is* their profession, their sole means of making a living, they are immediately available and "on call" to a production once they are signed on to it. They don't have some other job to distract them or absent them from the shooting schedule. They are punctual and dependable, in rehearsal and on the set. They prepare themselves thoroughly and learn their lines well. They are ready to deliver on time and on cue.

Because they understand costumes and props, they can furnish or find exactly the right stuff when you ask them to. They know how to do their own makeup and often prefer to, saving you the trouble and expense of a special makeup person—or freeing the makeup person that you have hired to concentrate on the less accomplished actors.

Professionals have location savvy, which means that they always know where the camera is and what it is doing (whether panning, tilting, dollying, or zooming). They can "play to the camera" accordingly, making the job of the director much easier.

They not only can give excellent line deliveries, but they do it with remarkable consistency. A vibrant laugh that sounds wonderfully natural and spontaneous in rehearsal will sound just as fresh take after take. And they'll "hit their spots" consistently, too—always doing a piece of business the same way on the same cue so the takes can be filmed and edited smoothly and expeditiously, without time lost covering continuity blivets.

Professionals usually have worked their way up from high school plays to acting school to community and "straw hat" theater and so on. They've worked in TV spots, industrial films, documentaries, soap operas, TV movies, and theatrical movies. They know what plays and what sells. Therefore, their ideas are often cinematically sound as well as dramatically sound. They can give a good performance cold if need be, after rehearsing by themselves off in a corner, and then shade it to the director's taste as soon as he has time to give a listen. And they can help him experiment and innovate to come up with something better and more on target than either the director or the actor may have thought of before the camera was rolling.

Furthermore, they give a production *class*. When you hire professional actors, it tells everyone that you are doing an important piece of work. The other actors—and the camera crew—respond by working enthusiastically on your movie. The same psychology works favorably on people outside the production that you need to impress—agents, distributors, theater owners, movie critics, and the general public—setting them up to believe that your movie must be one that is worth waiting for and watching.

WORKING WITH SEMIPROFESSIONAL AND AVOCATIONAL ACTORS

There are many excellent semiprofessional and avocational actors, often capable of doing such a fine job that the only thing that separates them from true professionals is that they do not make their living by acting alone.

If these kinds of actors can be cast in roles that cater to their possible limitations, sometimes they can do just as well as full-time professionals. Their range may be a bit narrow, so the parts may have to be tailored so as not to demand quite as much from them, or they might not have quite the "leading man" or "leading lady" looks that you desire, obliging you to settle for a close compromise, but the biggest problem in casting semiprofessionals is their lack of availability. The usual shooting schedule on a relatively low-budget picture is thirty days spread over six weeks, and anybody who gets a major role is usually needed on ten to fourteen of those days, scattered throughout the schedule. Some of the "days" will actually be nights—exteriors shot after dark—requiring everybody to lose sleep and possibly miss work on the following day. Nonprofessionals have real-life jobs. It's tough for them to take enough time off to fulfill a heavy commitment to a feature movie. So the shooting schedule ends up being tied to *their* schedules—and when you have a cast made up largely of nonprofessionals, their availabilities conflict, making scheduling a real nightmare, dragging out the number of days in the shooting schedule and driving up production costs.

WORKING WITH UNTRAINED ACTORS AND MODELS

Untrained actors are those who have not taken any acting courses and whose experience in films, TV, and/or live theater is very limited. Models can fit into this category, too, when their commercial production experience is limited to looking right and striking suitable poses without delivering many lines.

The advantage of using models over rank amateurs is that they have an affinity for the camera and for the entertainment business in general. They *look* like they should be on-camera. What they do when they get there may be another story.

Sometimes when models come in to read for parts in my movies, it makes me think of the days when talking pictures were ending the careers of the old silent-screen stars. Some of them couldn't make it when they had to use their voices: swashbuckling heroes would squeak or lisp; gorgeous, sophisticated-looking damsels would be unable to stifle a nasal twang or a harsh Brooklyn accent. People who look good on-camera don't always sound good. And the ability to pose—to radiate charm, believability, or sex appeal in short, undemanding bursts—does not necessarily translate into an ability to deliver the goods over the long haul of a full-length dramatic presentation.

On the other hand, every once in a while you can find a "diamond in the rough," as we did with Judith Ridley in *Night of the Living Dead* and *The Affair.* You may find a model or an untrained actress who has much stronger screen presence and is much more appealing to the audience, in a natural way, than any of the professionals or semiprofessionals that are available for your movie. Screen presence—the ability to dominate the audience with the force of one's image—is an intangible quality that seems to have little to do with talent or training. Some have it, and some don't. The ones who have it—like John Wayne, Greta Garbo, Kirk Douglas, Lauren Bacall—can enhance a movie and can even become stars, without ever taking an acting course.

If you choose to give one of these diamonds in the rough his or her first break, please bear in mind that you will have to make compromises and adjustments. Sometimes you will have to take an exceptionally long time in rehearsal. Other times, too much rehearsal will kill the natural charm and spontaneity of a delivery—it will die after the first or second take, to be recaptured nevermore.

Don't overburden an unskilled actor with matters of blocking and continuity, because the performance that you hope to get out of him is too fragile. Give him too much to think about, over and above the acting itself, and he'll start to lose it. You'll have to block your scenes so you can shoot your way around potential blivets. Come in tight enough, for example, on close-ups so that you won't see the actor's hands—that way it won't matter if they're in a different position on each take. Devise angle changes and cutaways to cover errors and inconsistencies of playing to camera and hitting the mark.

It will be up to you to decide if your production can afford the time delays and additional costs that are usually caused by working with untrained actors. Don't be so beguiled by someone's personal charm that you are lured into a fatal casting error. On the other hand, don't be so closed-minded that you fail to discover a legitimate talent or screen presence who will help your movie become a big winner.

WORKING WITH NONACTORS

There is a fad right now of casting nonactors in TV commercials. The most famous of these is probably the late Clara Peller of the Wendy's "Where's the beef?" campaign. Sometimes nonactors bring a certain raw, unpolished flair to a role simply because they *are* raw and unpolished—a shade outside the audience's normal expectations. This causes us to pay fresh attention in a way that we might not have done if we were looking at a trained actor.

The ad agencies that are using these nonactors spend a fortune looking for them. They can afford to scour the country. They can foot the bill for these people to take off from their regular jobs for an extended period. Also, the people that they find that are so "right" for certain roles only need to *be* right for a few seconds on-screen. A zillion takes might have to be shot to obtain those precious few seconds, and the ad agency can afford to squander the money.

Most feature movies cannot afford to operate that way. Therefore, don't use nonactors except in very small parts; even then I assure you it will usually be quite noticeable that they *are* nonactors. After all, if nonactors did not have certain rough edges that subtly distinguish them from real actors even when they're cast painstakingly to fill a precise role, the commercial fad I talked about would not work at all. But it does work. It works marvelously well.

Sometimes it can even work in a feature movie, if you get lucky. Many people have a great deal of untapped natural acting ability. But if they lack professional training, you have to be careful of how you channel their raw talent. Usually you have to typecast—select a nonactor whose presence and personality seem exactly right for one narrow role. A gruff, boisterous person may be the perfect guy to play a tough rural sheriff, but he may fail dismally in any other part. George Kosana, the sheriff in *Night of the Living Dead,* was a memorable character, a great asset to the picture, and he had never acted before—most people seem to think we typecast him perfectly. A sexy, brazen young woman may make a great go-go dancer in your movie, as long as you don't ask her to get too subtle with her facial expressions or her line deliveries.

Sometimes casting nonactors is a total bust. Even the ones who give great readings in casting sessions tend to freeze up on-camera. On occasion, they can't handle the pressure—the hot lights, the bustle of the crew, the unglamorous jumble of props, backdrops, and tangled-up electrical cables. When they find out it's not all fun and games, their interest wanes and their self-doubts take over, making them wish they were somewhere else.

George Romero rehearses a scene featuring George Kosana as the sheriff in *Night of the Living Dead.*

WORKING WITH STARS

When he was chairman of Columbia Pictures, David Puttnam said, "Stars aren't stars by accident. By and large, they're really quite good actors. You find yourself with a star because actually that is the most talented actor you can get. A star is a good actor whom the public, over the years, has gotten to like."

Well, we filmmakers are part of the public, and we like stars, too. We like working with them and finding out what they're really like. It's part of the fun—the glamour and excitement of the movie business.

With a star you get the talent and professionalism described earlier, with a bonus: a guaranteed box office draw. So you have to pay more and treat the star like someone special, because he *is* special, and he knows it. Even if he doesn't feel so special—even if he's inwardly shy and modest and insecure—he can't afford to show it, or his market value will drop and he might lose his "star" status.

Many projects are conceived and written with specific stars in mind for the lead roles. These are projects conceived by big-time producers, writers, and directors who have the kind of reputation and track record that gives them reason to believe that they can actually cast the stars they have in mind. To land a star, it is imperative that the lead roles be big and impressive (except in the case of cameos). And of course the story must be a powerful one that has a real chance of becoming a major hit. At least that is how it is *supposed* to work—sometimes the strategy fails miserably. Here is one common scenario for this type of failure:

A dynamite script is written for which Star A and Star B would be absolutely perfect as the leading man and leading lady. All goes well at first, and Stars A and B actually commit to the project, signing letters of intent to appear in the picture. With this terrific package in hand, the producer begins approaching the major studios for financing. A big studio loves the project at first but then starts second-guessing story details and production costs. Because of the delay and a commitment on another picture, the director has to pull out. Star A stays with the project, but Star B doesn't want to work with any other director, so she pulls out, too. Now another star must be found with just as much box office clout, and the new director, the studio, and Star A must all agree that the new star is a fine replacement. But a suitable new director can't be found in time, and now Star A has to bow out. By the time the project is finally salvaged with umpteen directorial and casting changes, the stars who ultimately appear in the picture do not have the same kind of screen chemistry that the creators originally envisioned, and the picture bombs. The only solace is that it might not have been a hit even if the original stars had stuck with it: witness *Ishtar*, a $40 million flop created to star and sure enough starring Warren Beatty and Dustin Hoffman.

A well-conceived casting strategy can bring triumph. In *Premiere* magazine, James L. Brooks talked about how important it was to him to land William Hurt for his hit movie *Broadcast News:* "I went through days when I felt on the brink of madness. . . . I needed somebody who when he went into a room caused a stir. You don't *act* that, you *do* that . . . then he said yes . . . in an Italian restaurant. . . . I felt such electricity going through me, because it meant I was going to do my movie."

If you become famous and successful enough to work with stars, you'll already be in a sense a star yourself, on their level or close to it. Once they've signed their contracts, with all the star-treatment perks written in and satisfied, you'll be able to work with them pretty much as you would with any other professional. But you'll still probably be nervous about doing it. As blasé and cynical and worldly-wise as most of us try to be, we are still not completely immune to the special charisma that seems to surround a true movie star.

OLIVER STONE ON CASTING

Choosing the actors that are right for the roles in your movies is one of the most exciting aspects of filmmaking—and getting them can be exasperating. But the creative possibilities are endless today, as Oliver Stone attests:

"I've worked a lot with non-SAG people because I like to try to use real people in movies, and sometimes it works and sometimes it doesn't. There's no formula on it. I'd say it has a fifty-fifty chance of success. I've always done the same thing on every film. I hire my casting agent either out of New York or Los Angeles or the Philippines or Mexico if need be. And it all depends on the agent's feelings about you as a filmmaker. For example, on *Salvador* very few people knew my work, and I didn't get too much in terms of offers from talent. The agents weren't too hot on the idea. But I made the movie anyway. I got Jimmy Woods. I got John Savage and Jim Belushi. I cast it. It was done independently. The old days of casting through the studios are really gone. There is no such thing. So it's a question of your individual inclinations."

11

People Behind the Camera

THIS CHAPTER will acquaint you with the various job categories to be found in motion picture production. This does not mean that every production will employ someone in each category. In general, the lower the budget, the smaller the staff. Independents working with few dollars must either wear many hats or design their projects so that certain production services are not required. But every filmmaker should know the types of services that are *available,* should the need arise.

PRODUCERS

There are many types of producer, with varying degrees of involvement in the various stages of motion picture production, which accounts for the confusion in lay people's minds as to what, precisely, a producer is supposed to do. Some producers do little more than provide the money to make the movie. Other producers are prime movers during every phase of a movie from start to finish. This kind of producer may:

1. Decide what film is going to be produced, including devising the concept or helping to write the script
2. Come up with the money, either out of his own pocket or from various banking and investment sources
3. Hire the entire production staff, including the writer(s) and the director and all the acting talent
4. Supervise every aspect of production from start to finish
5. Negotiate and sign distribution deals

6. Manage and allocate income from distribution during the entire income-producing life of the movie

Nowadays it is fashionable for the director to be singled out as the *auteur* of a movie and to be thought of as the person most responsible for it creatively. But it was the producer who used to hold this lofty position in most people's eyes. It is a mystique that probably neither the producer nor the director fully deserves, since making a movie is a vast, cooperative enterprise with many people intimately sharing in the creative process. However, the fully *involved* type of producer certainly can lay claim to a hefty portion of the praise or the blame for the success or failure of a film.

Producers who are knowledgeable enough to understand exactly what is going on and effectively supervise all phases of production have come to be known as *line producers.* This is the most valuable kind of producer to have. At the other extreme are *executive producers,* who either do not know production or choose to be absent from the nitty-gritty of it—they simply put up a share of the money.

A producer may work with a co-producer or may delegate responsibilities to various people who are given subsidiary titles like *assistant producer, associate producer, production manager,* and *production assistant.* There is much overlap in the duties that may be performed by anybody and everybody holding these titles.

As a practical example of how all this works, let's take a look at my movie *Midnight.* My friend Don Redinger raised half the production money, so he got the title of producer even though he ended up not working on the picture at all; I became in effect the line producer as well as the director and screenwriter. I did not have a production manager to help me do script breakdowns and fine-tuned budgeting, so I did these things myself. I did have three production assistants during filming, one of whom, my wife, Mary Lou, was an unpaid volunteer; they helped gather props, drive actors to and from the set, provide meals for cast and crew, etc., etc.

Independent-International Pictures Corporation (IIP) put up the other half of the production money in return for the right to distribute the picture, so Samuel M. Sherman and Daniel Q. Kennis, officers of IIP, became the executive producers. They never showed up on location, nor did I expect them to; but they read the script and gave me suggestions for changes and advice as to casting. They helped me cast Lawrence Tierney, a "name" actor, in an important role. They screened rough edits at various stages of production in order to help guide things along. In other words, they performed in a removed, but quite involved, supervisory capacity from start to finish.

Another thing they did at the outset was assign an employee of IIP, Steve Jacobsen, to be the official liaison with me and my location crew. Steve ordered equipment and filmstock for us and made sure we got it on time. He also picked up and screened raw footage from Technicolor Laboratory so we would know as soon as possible whether the footage was looking good or if we would have to schedule any emergency reshoots. Steve could do this more easily than we could since he was close to the lab, in New York, while our filming was taking place in Pittsburgh. Since he was doing this work at a distance, we referred to him as an associate producer.

WRITERS

Writers usually are not present on the set, especially on major studio productions. Once filming is to begin, the director takes over as the creative head and does not want anybody else interfering with his "vision." During preproduction the director and producer may have worked very closely with a writer or a whole string of writers, but after that the writers' job is considered over. The exception to this is when the writer is also the producer, the director, or perhaps a *technical advisor*—in cases where his knowledge of certain details and how they should be portrayed accurately on-screen is considered extremely valuable to the production. In low-budget independent productions, it is highly likely that the writer will also be the director and maybe the producer, too!

Some writers are better at writing action, and others are better at writing dialogue. Some are excellent novelists but poor screenwriters. Some write more cinematically than others, especially if they've studied filmmaking or have been involved in making films themselves. Major productions often employ many writers instead of just one because some movie executives believe that they can have the best of all possible worlds by milking the different talents and abilities out of a slew of different writers. Sometimes this works, and sometimes it fails miserably, resulting in a script that doesn't have a clear idea of what it is doing and where it is going.

Many times a producer or director prefers to write his own scripts or to work closely with one particular writer whom he especially trusts. In fact, many a director has demanded a clause in his contract granting him the prerogative to bring in his own writer to rework the existing script.

Sometimes writers become upset over this state of affairs, where they do not have control over rewrites of their scripts and their creative input is not welcome once they have put words on paper. Sometimes they get so disgusted that they decide to stop being just writers and instead also become:

DIRECTORS

The director is responsible for translating the script into sights and sounds on film so that they tell the best, most involving story possible. To accomplish this, he works closely with the producer(s) and writer(s) during preproduction, and then he becomes the creative leader and decision maker all through production and postproduction.

He is intimately involved in designing the "look" of the movie in all its aspects: props, costumes, sets, locations, casting, special effects, et al. He doesn't usually do everything personally, but he delegates authority as wisely as he can and then oversees the work of the people to whom this authority has been delegated. He may have one or several *assistant directors* to help him liaise with crew members or key production personnel and to handle much of the paperwork and legwork involved in any motion picture production.

Sometimes one of the assistant directors may work as a *dialogue director.* The function of a dialogue director is to rehearse line deliveries with the actors, bringing them to a state of preparation that can then be molded and fine-tuned by the director prior to and during actual filming. The dialogue director may also work with actors who need to affect foreign accents or special "character" accents to make sure these accents are believable and consistent through take after take.

One of the most important types of assistant director that the main director hires is the *director of photography.* The director of photography is greatly responsible, along with the director, for making sure that the images being registered on film are impressive and effective; in other words, that they enhance the performances of the actors and help give the movie the proper slant and power. To accomplish this, he works closely with the camera operator and the camera operator's assistants and with all the other members of the motion picture crew.

CREW MEMBERS AND THEIR FUNCTIONS

The *camera operator* is responsible for operating the camera so as to obtain the images that the director desires in terms of composition and movement. These desires are usually communicated to him by the director of photography, although on low-budget productions the camera operator and the director of photography will probably be the same person.

The *first assistant cameraman* helps move and place the camera for each shot. He changes lenses and sets them for sharp focus and accurate light readings. He also is responsible for maintenance—making sure that the camera and all its lenses and accessories are clean and functioning properly at all times.

The *second assistant cameraman* aids the first assistant cameraman and the camera operator in all their duties and also loads and unloads film, slates takes with the clapstick, keeps camera logs, ships exposed footage, and receives it after it has been processed.

The *gaffer* is the chief electrician, responsible for the safe and efficient setup of movie lights, cables, and accessories. Under him are his main assistant, called the gaffer's *best boy,* as well as various electricians and riggers of cables and electrical equipment and generator operators for situations where power must be supplied to remote locations.

The *sound mixer* is the recording engineer, called a *mixer* because he must often record and balance sound levels when more than one microphone is used in a camera setup. He is responsible for recording clean, high-fidelity sound, whether sync or wild, slating the takes, and keeping sound logs on every take. To assist him, he has a *boom operator,* who makes sure that the mikes are placed or boomed correctly without intruding into shots or casting shadows into shots. He also may employ a *cableman* to string all cables relating to the sound equipment, moving them and placing them so they won't be seen on-camera.

Grips are the people who assist the camera and sound crews by helping to move equipment, props, and costumes. The *key grip* is in charge of the grip crew. Included in the grip crew is usually a *dolly/crane grip,* who specializes in operating and maintaining dollies and cranes but may also assist with all the other grip functions.

The *production designer* is responsible for the artistic look of a movie. This includes overseeing the design of props, sets, and costumes and the choice of locations in order to give the movie an overall design that is consistent with the aesthetic sensibility of the director. The production designer may work with specialists such as art directors, prop makers, costumers and costume designers, set decorators, architects and draftsmen, and even model makers for situations where aspects of a set or location must be built in miniature.

The *wardrobe master* and his staff stock the costumes needed for the movie and keep them in the required condition, whether sparkling clean or ripped, bloody, and dirty.

The *still photographer* takes stills of the movie's action, on camera and behind the scenes, for publicity and promotion. He works closely with the *unit publicist,* who is responsible for all publicity regarding the production.

The *construction foreman* is responsible for building sets, scaffolding—any and all heavy construction connected with a movie. Working under him will be various painters, plasterers, carpenters, carpet layers, drapery hangers, welders, and whatever specialty is needed for a given job.

Craft Services are the people who supply meals and snacks for actors and crew. Just as many prison riots are caused by bad food, much ill will and lack of cooperation on the set (and Union grievances) can be traced to this same cause.

Miscellaneous production personnel may include the drivers and mechanics who drive and maintain production vehicles, chauffeurs for actors and executives, first-aid specialists, and various people who perform such necessary tasks as cleaning and polishing, baby-sitting, and guarding sets and locations.

12

Special Effects People

SOME OF THE most important behind-the-scenes people in the movie business are the tricksters—the illusionists and the special effects people who make us suspend disbelief and truly experience movie magic. The main tricksters are wranglers, animal specialists, firearms and explosives specialists, stunt coordinators and stuntmen, makeup artists, animators, and special effects construction experts.

> "Tremendous numbers of young people are aware of the glamour and excitement of what is popularly known as *special makeup effects.* They think that's a category in itself, but in fact *special makeup effects* is simply the name given to the higher forms of makeup that regular makeup artists do; I mean artists like me who have gained a certain reputation. You can't just go in and be a special makeup effects artist. Generally speaking, you have to work your way up from the bottom."
>
> Dick Smith
> Makeup artist

I'm going to describe what these people do, which may be somewhat boring for readers who already know. But, for those who don't, the descriptions will serve as a valuable guide to production services and personnel whose expertise can make or break a project.

Wranglers handle and direct livestock such as horses, sheep, and cattle, making them do pretty much what the director wants, as close to on cue as is possible. Sometimes the wranglers only have to take care of the animals. Other times they have to engineer a realistic stampede, get horses to jump a gorge or plummet over a cliff, or make animals fall down and fake death from arrows, bullets, and the like.

Animal specialists train and supervise wildlife such as monkeys, lions, and tigers, making them perform with genuine-seeming but harmless ferocity. Usually when we think of movie animals we have in mind some of the more exotic beasts of the jungle, but the animal specialists also have to contend with smaller, creepier animals, like the hordes of rats in *Willard* or the thousands of giant tropical cockroaches in *Creepshow*.

Firearms and explosives specialists supply weapons and blanks and make sure they are used safely and effectively; they also create horrendous fires, bomb blasts, and other types of demolitions effects.

Stunt coordinators and stuntmen design and execute the stunts in a movie. Often the stunt coordinator acts as a second-unit director, actually directing actors and camera crew in the filming of the stunts he has designed for the production. He may also direct all the action built around and leading up to the stunts (for instance, an entire car chase sequence) so that the sequence will flow smoothly and believably within the overall movie.

Makeup artists not only do regular makeup that makes the actors and actresses look handsome and beautiful, but also do special makeup effects that can be weird, awesome, comic, or gruesome.

Animators bring strange and unusual creatures to life on the screen. To do this, they must animate characters that are drawn on paper or molded and sculpted out of various substances such as clay, plastic, or latex. They shoot the movements of the characters one frame at a time—twenty-four frames and twenty-four shots for every second that the animated sequence will appear on the screen. Naturally, that is a painstaking process; but in a sense it's the easy part. The tough part is being able to sculpt the characters and make them move so they don't look like fakes. *E.T.* works only because we believe in the extraterrestrial; he is so well executed that he makes us forget he's merely a sculpted puppet.

Special effects construction experts devise props or sets that can be used in combination with certain filmmaking techniques to make the unreal look real —like rooms that move or turn upside down, as does the little girl's bedroom in *The Exorcist.* Sometimes special props are made to be used in combination with actors' makeup to create realistic illusions that can be weird, scary, or thrillingly entertaining—an arrow piercing an eyeball, a head exploding (like the heads in *Scanners),* a man changing into a reptile (in the sci-fi TV movie *V),* a man cruising the clouds in a Volkswagen Beetle *(The Love Bug),* a boy and an extraterrestrial pedaling a bicycle through the wild blue yonder *(E.T.).*

Sometimes the most effective and believable cinematic illusions are

"The first thing is that you have to love it, no matter what. You eat, sleep, and drink everything you can find on special effects work. You can read books, but there's no substitute for learning by your own mistakes, whether it's in mold-making, armature building, or whatever. You have to devour everything you can and then just go out and start making all the mistakes you can make. And then some good things will start to happen."

Rick Catizone
Animated Effects Specialist

achieved through a collaboration of several types of special effects people whose specialties often overlap. For example, a makeup artist may have to transform a live actor into a demon; then an animator has to sculpt a matching demon in miniature to make it sprout wings and fly and start to transform back again into a human being. If at some point the demon has to take a stake through his heart, a special effects prop maker may have to design the stake and execute the portion of the effect that involves the live actor in makeup and costume.

If an actor has to flip a car over and wreck it, a stunt coordinator has to design and direct the stunt and a stuntman has to double for the actor. A special effects construction specialist has to make the dummy that substitutes for the actor (and the stuntman) when the script calls for us to see the movie character being tossed through the windshield. A makeup artist creates the lacerations on the actor's face after he goes through the windshield. And a demolitions man blows up the car after it crashes into a stone wall.

If Clark Kent falls off a high building, a stuntman has to take the dive. An animator has to show him falling and taking his street clothes off, which may involve making a miniature model of Clark Kent. Then back to the live actor, as Superman, flying to safety—an animated effect that relies on shooting the live actor flying in a harness, then superimposing (matting) those shots over shots of the city so that the flying effect is achieved by cinematically combining two pieces of film.

The best of the tricksters rarely let a problem stump them, achieving the splendidly realistic effects in today's movies through inventiveness, daring, cooperation, and hard, intricate work.

FROM CREATING ILLUSIONS TO MAKING MOVIES

Just as commercial filmmaking or advertising agency work can be a stepping-stone toward making feature movies, doing special effects work can be a way of breaking into the business and eventually moving to other areas, including acting and directing.

Hal Needham, who directed *Smokey and the Bandit,* used to be a stuntman. But, remember, stuntmen and stunt coordinators often get first-hand experience directing the segments of the movies where the stunts appear. This puts their work in the limelight, where it can be noticed and appreciated by established directors and producers.

Like stuntmen, makeup men often stand in for actors or put their own makeup on themselves and play fill-in roles. They also help direct the sequences where their special effects are being used. Tom Savini, who built up a huge fan following by doing the special makeup effects in films like *Dawn of the Dead* and *Friday the 13th,* has recently signed a deal to direct two movies for New World Pictures. Tom's small acting parts led to bigger parts, most notably the Black Knight in *Knightriders.* His overall excellent work led to directing several episodes of the TV series *Tales from the Darkside.* And finally he got the offer from New World.

So once again the moral is: If you want to be a filmmaker, get on the set any way you can. Then make it happen for yourself.

If you already are a director, or if that's the only thing you *want* to be, you should learn about special effects because you might find yourself doing them some day, even if you don't want to. This holds particularly true for low-budget productions. When I was making *Midnight,* Tom Savini did all the special-effects during the principal shooting schedule, but after we had the picture finished, the distributor wanted me to write and film a new ending that contained lots of special-effects violence and gore. Unfortunately Tom was by then unavailable because he was working on *Knightriders.* Rather than hire someone else and shell out some big bucks, I got together with production manager Ray Laine and actor Greg Besnak, and we devised all the gun-effects for the last ten minutes of the film.

SPECIAL EFFECTS:
THE STARS OF TODAY'S MOVIES

Special effects are vital to many of today's movies because of the constant pressure to give people something that they can't see on television. Because TV movies are censored much more rigidly than theatrical releases, certain low-budget filmmakers have struck box office gold by loading their movies with special-effects gore and violence. Big-budget filmmakers like George Lucas and Steven Spielberg have given us special-effects extravaganzas like *E.T., Star Wars, Raiders of the Lost Ark,* and *Close Encounters of the Third Kind,* which don't rely on blatant gore and violence, partly because if you can afford to dazzle the audience with some of the more lavish special effects, you can entertain them and make plenty of money without giving yourself the headache of an R or an X rating. If you can make a good PG movie of this sort, your distribution worries are over. None of the theater chains will refuse to book your picture; newspapers and TV stations will readily accept its advertising; hordes of folks will come out of their houses to see it even though it doesn't contain sex or gore (the usual low-budget drawing cards); and it'll get huge television, foreign, and home video sales without having to be butchered in order to fulfill varying censorship requirements in the different markets.

Generally speaking, movies attract customers by offering:

1. Good stories
2. Good acting
3. Stars
4. Exotic props, costumes, sets, or locations
5. Sex
6. Violence
7. Special effects

If censorship robs or restricts you in areas (5) and (6), and a money shortage does you out of (3) and (4), then your high cards are (1), (2), and (7). And if you have any doubts about just how unbeatable (1) and (2) are, then you'd better make sure that (7) is your ace in the hole. That's why low-budget filmmakers often resort to bloody, realistic, but inexpensive special effects. Gore effects are relatively cheap. Battles in outer space are not. In any case, both low-budget independents and producers of Hollywood blockbusters have come to look upon special effects as an essential ingredient of their movies.

Economic factors aside, the tricksters and their bags of tricks are vitally important to the aesthetics of movie-making. We all love to be transported to another time and place, to indulge in vicarious experiences that look and feel momentarily real; to be shot at; to see things blow up; to confront the wondrous, the hideous, the frightening; to see creatures that breathe fire or fly through the air defying the logic of gravity, whether they be giant winged dragons or sweet ladies like Mary Poppins.

None of this can happen without the tricksters. They are our sorcerers, our co-conspirators. Knowing the kinds of things they can pull off can stimulate ideas and even form key concepts in the mind of a scriptwriter/director. *Not* knowing how to work with them effectively can cause a movie to fall flat on its face.

Every filmmaker should have an appreciation and an understanding of how these special effects people work and exactly what they can supply to a movie. They help us cast a spell over people, transport them to worlds of our own making, charm them, make them shudder and laugh and cry, awe them, tantalize them, and delight them. And sometimes these effects even help us open their eyes to reality by weaving our illusions so carefully that they can escape everyday life for a little while and come back with a fresher, truer perspective.

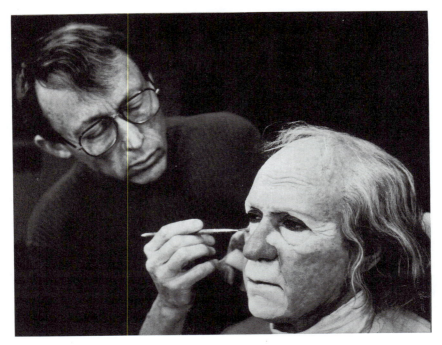

Dick Smith changing F. Murray Abraham into old Salieri—a four-hour makeup.

Known as Hollywood's premiere makeup artist, **Dick Smith** did the amazing makeup work in films like *Little Big Man, The Godfather, The Exorcist, Altered States,* and *Amadeus,* for which he won an Academy Award. For more than forty years he has spearheaded new advances and techniques that have captivated audiences and helped make box office magic.

13

Dick Smith
Makeup Wizardry

THE GOLDEN AGE OF TV MAKEUP

★ Back in the 1940s I was going to Yale University as a premed student and had gotten interested in makeup from watching films like *The Hunchback of Notre Dame,* so I started experimenting, making myself up as monsters and scaring my classmates—which was a great lark—and gradually I became more serious about it and decided this was what I wanted to do. I had never heard anyone in my circle expressing the slightest interest in makeup. There was no publicity about it in those days. All the behind-the-scenes trade secrets of Hollywood were *kept* secret.

I went through a brief stint in World War II, got out in early 1945, and tried to get a job in Hollywood based on photos of the makeup I had done. A lot of nice things were said, but no help came from anybody. After some months I tried to get into television and finally was fortunate enough to be offered the first staff makeup job in any TV studio, NBC in New York City. The person who hired me thought that television was going to grow and that my degree from Yale meant that I had the ability to eventually run a department. When I started, I knew almost nothing, but no one else did either, so I learned as I went along. And TV grew so fast that in five years I had a department of twenty makeup artists working full-time for me, all of whom I had to teach. In the good old days of TV we were doing several television dramas each week. We would do things like *Caesar and Cleopatra, The Three Musketeers, Cyrano de Bergerac,* as well as futuristic things, so the range of makeup problems that we had to deal with was enormous. I continued at NBC for fourteen years and developed all kinds of techniques for first black-

and-white live shows, then color television, for which I developed makeup bases that are still used today. They're called *CTV* for color television.

BREAKING IN NOWADAYS

But of course that kind of marvelous on-the-job training is not available today. Today there is very little drama in television, so working in television is not the stimulating educational experience it once was. Television is no longer a very creative field, excluding TV movies, which I consider film, not TV.

Makeup work in television and films is covered by two unions, one based in Hollywood and the other based in New York, and a professional makeup artist usually strives to become a union member. However, not all productions are covered by union contracts. Low-budget nonunion films are made all over the place. Also, people like me—or Rick Baker, Stan Winston, Tom Savini, and Rob Bottin—often find that a particular film calls for so much intricate work that it requires a crew, and the crew members are not really makeup artists but skilled artisans and technicians, so they generally are not covered by union contracts, and this is an area that is the most popular goal for young amateurs.

To get a job in this "shop work" or "lab work" as it's sometimes called, a person has to demonstrate that he is a skilled artisan or technician of some sort. The best way he can do this is to show the head of the shop good eight-by-ten photos of complete character makeups, fantasy makeups, puppets, or masks—any of the humanoid creations that are turned out today. The key talent that sells a person most quickly is realistic sculptural ability; I mean being able to sculpt a face that looks so realistic that you can't *tell* it's false. The artist has to make items such as false eyes, teeth; create the mechanisms to make eyeballs move in a false head or to make skin on a false head move in a realistic manner; make the jaw move, convey expression; make creatures move by means of radio-controlled devices. If a person wants to become known as a special makeup effects artist and work in such a shop, these are the things he must be able to demonstrate that he knows in whole or in part.

There are excellent books on makeup and special effects by people like Richard Corson, Lee Baygan, Tom Savini, and Vincent Keyhoe. There are also magazines like *Fangoria, Cinemagic, Cinefantastique,* and *Cinefex,* containing in-depth articles on all the technical aspects. Makeup videotapes are starting to come out now, too.

All the good makeup artists are basically self-taught. One has to stand on one's own. You're faced with unsolved problems constantly, and you have to be able to invent and solve and create; no one's standing there telling you what to do. A creative makeup artist is constantly facing new problems, and this is part of the challenge and excitement of the field.

This is not to say that a person who goes to a makeup school is going to be done any harm, but in my opinion he cannot rely on the school experience alone. As I state in my ads, my own course is not for beginners. I screen the applicants. I'm interested in dealing only with people who have already taught themselves the fundamentals and show enough artistic skill so that I think they have some hope of getting into this business. I require at least three good photographs of three-dimensional work that they have done. I don't want just painted makeups. I want to see appliances, I want to see sculptures, I want to see a complete and fairly competent creation.

I have a standard reply to anybody who says "I want to be a good makeup artist; I want to be just like you or Rick Baker or Tom Savini." I say "Okay, you really don't know what you can do, and I don't know what you can do. Maybe you *are* a genius. Spend the next six months studying and devoting all your spare time to working on yourself and all your friends; take photographs —start off with the simpler makeups and keep going. See at the end of six months whether or not you've accomplished anything. This test will determine whether you really *like* makeup. Do you want to get your hands and face dirty? Do you want to clean up all the mess afterward? Is it going to be a bore? Do you hate the feel of spirit gum on your skin? Or do you really and truly find it fascinating to transform yourself? Do you really want to work hard at it? Because that's absolutely essential. If enthusiasm flags after a couple of months of spending all your spare time, then you know right away it's not for you. On the other hand, if you complete this, then send me three pictures of what you thought was the best, and I will let you know if you have any talent, any prospects. If you don't have it, I'll tell you to forget it, you're never going to make it."

Even the ones who have more experience and are more talented have got to realize there are *hundreds* like them, all trying to get into this tiny little profession. All the people I hired in the early days of television were of mediocre talent. But when Rick Baker came along, I thought, "My God, this kid is a genius. He's gonna make it, no question." And so I backed him all the way. And during the last few years they've been coming out of the woodwork. I'm getting two or three "Rick Bakers" a year, kids that just knock you out with what they've already learned. They're doing work that's better than 90 percent of the existing makeup artists. It's great, but it's also scary because there're so *many* of them, and where in the hell are they all gonna fit?

TRAINING ON LOW-BUDGET PRODUCTIONS

There is, of course, a lot of nonunion film work, and it's an excellent area for beginners to get experience and a modicum of pay, as long as they're careful. There is more robbery and connivance and cheating than you can imagine. Not all the productions are that way, of course. But many are run by con artists.

Never lay out any of your own money for supplies. Get a cash advance; don't spend your own money. Make a deal in which you're going to get money up front or at least on a weekly basis. And if you don't receive your pay on time, stop work immediately. No matter what the pressure is, do not continue until you get paid. In many cases you will get terrible abuse. Producers will scream at you, "How dare you question my integrity? You're implying that I'm dishonest! No one else in the whole *crew* is doing what you're doing!"

My son David had exactly that experience with a man who was a Yale classmate of mine, but David stood his ground. On the last day he insisted he be given his pay before he would finish a critical makeup. He stopped work, took the check, and went to the bank and cashed it. Then he completed the makeup. And everyone on this particular production got screwed. Nobody got paid except David and one actor. The project was a total swindle.

HOW TO GIVE A DIRECTOR WHAT HE WANTS

At present I'm working as a consultant on *Poltergeist III*. But I don't plan on taking on too many big, heavy jobs in the future. I really prefer to do creative makeup jobs like Salieri in *Amadeus*. Those are the kinds of jobs I love.

If a director wants me to work with him, I never get involved until I've read the script. The director really has to know what he wants to see in terms of an effect and how much of it he wants to see all in one take without cutaways. He has to know what his optimum screen image is and what he'll settle for. Generally speaking, after reading the script I meet with the director, producer, and cinematographer, and we go through the whole thing and decide on each scene and each character. I suggest different ways of doing each effect at different cost levels. It may be that I have to go back and prepare sculptural sketches or photographs and pass them back to the director, or I may make a test on videotape and we screen it. We have to accept or reject various concepts, make adjustments, and home in on what will work best.

A makeup artist's work must be practical and lasting, but his obligations do not end there. He should be well prepared, both on and off the set. He has to be on time, he has to coordinate with the assistant director, he has to stay on schedule. He has to take care of the actors properly and maintain makeup through take after take. And he must be efficient and careful about removing the actors' makeup because the cleaning-up phase nowadays can be crucial. The adhesives are so strong that unless they are removed with great care the actors' skin can be so badly affected that shooting may be held up. This

F. Murray Abraham fully made up as old Salieri in *Amadeus.*

happened recently on a Hollywood film in which a makeup artist was careless. The next day the actor's face was swollen like a balloon, and he was out of action for about ten days.

A makeup artist doesn't necessarily have to obtain a college degree; he doesn't even have to have a high school diploma. But I feel that everybody should get the most education he possibly can. And he should pay particular attention to English, to communication arts of all kinds. I receive so many letters that are written on a piece of paper torn out of a loose-leaf pad, scribbled in pencil, barely legible, grammatically incredible, that I am tremendously relieved to get a properly typed letter that is in good English, perhaps even eloquent. Anyone who is going to go far in this field has to write not only good letters, but contracts, proposals, memorandums, and so on. It's amazing how many times in our daily lives and in our daily work these capabilities are necessary. The need for them can't be overemphasized.

Don't put all your eggs in one basket. Diversify as much as you can. The people who are weathering the entry into the makeup field are those who have some other skill, like model building, commercial art, or carpentry; or they're dental technicians, or they carve mannequins, etc. Those people are doing fine because they can fill in the blank spaces with this other work, and they don't have to wait on tables to pay the rent.

Rick Catizone beginning a triceratops sculpture. *Photo copyright 1988 by Rick Catizone and used with his permission.*

Rick Catizone did titles, credits, animation and matte work for *Night of the Living Dead, Creepshow, Creepshow 2,* and *Evil Dead II.* He is presently contributing to the special effects in George A. Romero's *Monkey Shines.*

14

Rick Catizone
Animated Thrills

THE POWER OF ANIMATION

★ When I started high school, I loved seeing films like *King Kong* and *Mighty Joe Young* and knowing that there was a creature moving that wasn't a drawn cartoon. These creatures had more weight and power than a marionette, yet you could never see strings. I was fascinated. Then I found a magazine somewhere that had a vague explanation of what I was looking at, and I found out it was called *stop-motion animation.* Finally I got hold of a couple of special effects books; they were fairly basic, but I ended up practically memorizing them. Then I took my own little 8-millimeter camera and built some fairly crude models out of wire and foam rubber and animated them. I kept doing my own stuff step by step, and about a year out of high school I got a job running an Oxberry animation stand for Bob Wolcott's company, The Animators, Inc., in Pittsburgh. I had a roll of 8-millimeter film that had some stop-motion work of some monsters and so on, and I had tried doing some split screens and rear projections, and I think one of the biggest things that amazed Bob Wolcott at the time was I was able to time my effects fairly closely even though I was working with the old 8-millimeter filmstock that ran both ways through the camera and was slit down the middle in processing. I would hit the right spot within a second or so, and my mattes were in the right place and so on, and Bob figured that if I was willing to go through such laborious, painstaking work to achieve my effects, then maybe I truly belonged in the animation business.

For the five years that I strictly did nothing but run the Oxberry, I used to wonder if I might burn it out, because it ran all eight hours of every day. Back in the sixties there was a great deal of film title work, filmstrip work, in addition to all the regular animated commercials and animated film segments, mostly cel animation because that's what people thought of when they wanted to do something that wasn't real—they thought of a drawn cartoon. But in my spare time I kept working on developing sculpted figures and armatures and so forth—as well as developing a crew of talented associates. Finally we got one or two jobs where I proved I could handle that stuff.

THE ANIMATED EFFECTS FOR *CREEPSHOW* AND *EVIL DEAD II*

In 1980 I started my own company, Anivision, and one of our first big jobs was creating the animation segments for *Creepshow*, which involved the tricky work of making a mock-up comic book. We had the pages printed up to size, cut them all out, registered them on acetates, and laid those over the comic book scenes that were done as artwork, so that you have a real book that turned and revealed the next page with all the actual artwork on it. We also helped Tom Savini with some of the sculptures because he was all tied up trying to do a million things at once. We did the hands, feet, and chest of the creature in the crate, and we did the basic hands with the bones protruding through the skin for the "Father's Day" segment, where the hands come out of the grave. We sculpted them out of clay. Tom had already made casts of the actor's hands and feet for the creature in the crate, and we did our sculptures over top of that. We also did a very quick thing for the segment called "Something to Tide You Over," where the girl comes back, and Savini wanted her to look sort of shriveled. He was pressed for time and asked us if there was any way to do it quickly, and I said that the fastest thing I could think of would be to take cotton, rubber, and so on and put it right over the face mold so you'd be able to build it up pretty quickly instead of doing a real fine piece of sculpture. We did that, and Tom took the idea a little further when he did the makeup for Ted Danson.

For *Creepshow 2* we contributed about nine minutes of screen time. We did the design and animation for all the characters. Originally our concept would have taken about twelve minutes overall, which would have been nice to do because it gave more time for character and mood development, but as we all know, budget doesn't always comply with script, so we had to pare twelve minutes down to nine. We executed it as tightly as we could without losing the thrust of what was happening in the three stories in the anthology. It was hectic.

On *Evil Dead II*, we were recommended by a couple of guys on the makeup effects crew, Mike Trcic and Mark Shostrum, because they had a scene involving a crawling hand that gets caught in a rat trap, and it had to crawl along and look real. Mike had seen the test footage I did for *Creepshow*, which involved a crawling hand that was later eliminated from the script even though it worked rather well. Mike and Mark liked it, so they recommended me to Sam Raimi. At first I was hired to do only that, but they had so *many* effects throughout the film that they had to farm more and more of them out. So I inherited the transforming of the Henrietta figure's face from the semi-possessed look to the full demon head, which also meant that her neck had to grow six or eight feet from her body.

For that shot we did a set of seven or eight wax heads that led up to our fully rubber head, which had a wire armature, allowing us to open the jaw, move the tongue, furl the eyebrows, and snarl the face. Live actors had to be simultaneously in some of these scenes, so all the scenes were shot against background plates. When the full-bodied puppet had to actually fight the lead character, background plates were shot of the actor miming the fact that he was fighting this creature. Then we had to take that footage and put our model in there and match eye lines and movement to get the feeling that the fight was actually taking place before the audience's eyes.

HOW TO WORK EFFECTIVELY WITH A GOOD ANIMATOR

If what I'm going to do is really going to count for something in a movie, I like to be called in as early as possible to hit on the basics. For instance, we've all worked on things where the budget has been set and no one has bothered to talk with the person who will be doing the animation. Somebody just plucks a figure out of the air and tells me that's how much money is available and what needs to be seen on-screen, and it's like he has $2 to spend and wants to see fourteen space aliens landing on the Earth and staging a battle. I'd rather have somebody come to me and have enough money to work with, and then I'll still try to cut costs while turning out an effective piece of work.

The other reason for me to get in early at the conceptual stage is that if I'm going to, say, design and animate creatures, I should ideally do the designs in time for everybody involved to get a feel for what the creatures will look like and how they'll behave. This should happen *before* the storyboards are created. You wouldn't want somebody to start doing storyboards with renderings of creatures that don't have enough power or snap, because when somebody sees these storyboards they become locked in, and I can't convince them to change the design into something that *looks* real and will actually work on film.

One *very* important point anytime animation is being combined with live action is that the filmmaker should always shoot his live action scenes with a camera that gives solid frame registration, like a Mitchell, so that when I rear-project the live action to build the animated figures into the scenes, the background plates won't float—they'll be rock-steady, and therefore the illusion of seeing the live actors and the animated creatures actually together on film will not be destroyed. When you're doing any kind of effects work, whether it's animation, animation–live action combinations or matte paintings, you need near-perfect frame registration to keep things from floating. Once your effects start floating, you have a hard time convincing the audience that something real is happening. When people shoot with cameras that don't have very good registration, they'll say they had the camera firmly locked down on a tripod, but when you super titles over the scenes, the words flutter up and down. The animator gets blamed for the screwup, when in reality the titles are rock-steady and the flutter was in the camera. Once a double-column Oxberry stand is braced, it weighs a couple of tons and isn't about to move anywhere.

One of my fondest wishes is to see filmmakers use animation effects more creatively. I'd like to see the techniques applied to lighter material. We know we can bring to life creatures that don't actually exist, but this doesn't mean that the creatures always have to be sinister. We generally tend to bring the dark, evil side to life, and I think that the successes of movies like *E.T.* and *Who Framed Roger Rabbit* prove moviegoers really want to see creatures that are more endearing and positive.

PART IV

LAUNCHING
YOUR FIRST FEATURE

"The right idea at the right time has always proved invincible."
INGO PREMINGER

"We are on the threshold of a technological and aesthetic revolution in movies which will inevitably restructure human consciousness and understanding. The independent filmmaker, whether he's working in Super-8 or 70mm Panavision, will be the nexus of the change to come."
JOSEPH GELMIS
Chairman, New York Film Critics

15

Ready to Take the Plunge

TO SUCCEED as a feature filmmaker, you have to be brave enough to take risks, skillful enough to make the risks calculated ones, tough enough not to become bitter over your losses, and wise enough not to let success go to your head.

Movie-making is not only an adventure; it's a crapshoot. One can never be entirely sure how any particular project will turn out. Public taste is fickle, largely unpredictable. Your movie will be going up against heavy odds, no matter how carefully you plan, no matter how good a job you do.

If your feature movie is to become a reality, it's going to have to go through: Scripting, budgeting, preproduction planning and preparation, shooting, and postproduction. I'm sure you'll remember that these are the same stages a commercial film must go through on its way from initial concept to finished print. But a feature movie must go through a few extra steps. Production money must be raised, a distributor must be found, and the movie must be marketed and promoted.

Those tough extra steps are the ones that make most commercial filmmakers chicken out and never make a feature movie. You don't have to go out and hunt for investors in a TV spot. You don't have to find a distributor for it. And you don't have to promote it, because it *is* promotion for some person or product. Whoever paid to have the spot made is also going to pay to put it on the air.

To make a feature movie, if you don't have a distributor lined up in advance, footing the bill, you have to go after investors. If you land investors and succeed in getting the picture made, you may not find a distributor who believes in the picture strongly enough to shell out money to put it before the public. And even if you get over that hurdle, the public may or may not buy tickets in sufficient quantity. In short, you may have a flop on your hands.

I *like* to make movies. But they are much too costly and time-consuming and energy-consuming to be made purely for fun. I have gotten paid, sometimes well and sometimes poorly, for every commercial film I ever made; and all five of my feature movies made money. More importantly, these films were seen by large numbers of people, which is what you ought to be after when you're working in the mass media. Don't blunder ahead and make a movie that will be appreciated only by you and your small circle of friends when you're sitting around drinking beer and eating pizza.

> "Don't exceed your limitations. Work within the framework of what you can afford. What was a warning to me was seeing a lot of people with half-finished films. For example, I know one filmmaker who decided to do a period piece—and if you don't have much money, to attempt a period piece is crazy. My God, renting two period automobiles can use up half your budget in some cases! Whatever your financial level, you have to try to do something that's within reach."
>
> Lizzie Borden

Before you set out on the grand and awesome adventure of making your first feature motion picture, be sure your filmmaking skills have developed to the point where you are not going to bite off more than you can chew. Do some soul-searching. Accurately evaluate your assets and abilities. Ask yourself some hard questions and think long and hard about the answers:

- What grounds do you have for believing that you will succeed in making a salable product and/or receiving critical acclaim when so many others have failed? What can you do to ensure that your expectations will be fulfilled?
- What are the resources you can draw on? Can you gather about you a capable staff? Do you have friends, relatives, and associates who can help you, by investing money or by contributing their time, their advice, or their professional services toward the realization of your goal?
- What kind of movie are you going to make? Will it be *marketable?* Is there any way to ensure in advance that you will be able to get your movie sold and that it will achieve a wide and profitable distribution?
- What if the movie never plays in the theaters, on the "big screen"? Will it contain elements that appeal strongly to the ancillary markets—

cable TV, TV syndication, and home video—so that you can get most of your money back and maybe even turn a small profit?

- Will foreign sales be an important source of revenue? Or will this area have to be written off because the subject matter of your movie is too colloquial to appeal to a worldwide audience?

These kinds of questions must be answered in advance, with reasonable certainty. You must tailor your concept, your script, your entire project to take full advantage of your particular situation.

SETTING A REACHABLE GOAL

Let's assume that you're a maverick filmmaker who feels he's ready to make his first feature. You've trained and studied and worked hard for a number of years, and now you're champing at the bit. But the bit isn't made of silver; you aren't rich enough to bankroll yourself. And it's a fairly safe bet that nobody is going to give you $10 million to make your first feature just because you feel it's the next logical step in your career.

Perhaps this seems brutally unfair to you. After all, since the majors are squandering $20 million or $30 million on pictures that you often find to be just plain junk, why don't they give you a measly million or so, so you can show them how terrific you are?

The answer, of course, is credentials. You've got to prove yourself on one level before you can advance to the next level. You can't begin to prove yourself until you at least get yourself noticed. So you're going to have to do what many big-name directors and producers had to do before they became big names. Don't go after $10 million, $5 million, or even $1 million. Set your sights lower.

Make a low-budget movie.

That's the best way for you to draw attention to yourself. Make a movie, even if you have to do it on only $100,000.

But that "only" seems a million miles away. And anyway, it's not enough. The way you figure, you're going to need at least $200,000. And you don't know anybody offhand who's going to jump up and plunk that kind of cash into your sweaty little palm.

Take heart. Other filmmakers have faced the same problem, and they've solved it. So can you. Listen to Sam Raimi, director of *The Evil Dead:*

"Originally we were after $150,000, and we met with a lot of resistance because people thought we were crazy to drop out of school to raise such an ungodly amount of money. But I would recommend to a young filmmaker not to give up. Persistence is everything. If you try to make a movie from scratch, it seems an impossible task. But if you just take it one step at a time, one foot in front of the other, like someone learning how to walk . . .

"It's a question of writing the script first, getting together a showpiece, figuring out what the budget of the movie would be, and slowly, dollar by dollar, getting those investments. Just stay on it. It *can* be done."

Yes, it can. So let's start taking it a step at a time, one foot in front of the other.

16

Latching on to a Hot Concept

BEFORE YOU can arrive at a budget, you must have a script. But you also have to tailor your script to the budget that you feel might be within your means.

The script must be based on a marketable concept. Even if you are going to make a so-called "art film," it has to contain elements that are strongly marketable. If you keep making films that don't sell, you won't be making them for very long. As I said before, movies are too expensive to be made only for your friends.

If you are a first-time writer/director making your first low-budget movie, here is what you *won't* have going for you:

- A track record
- A big name
- Stars in the lead roles
- Thousands of extras
- Exotic sets and locations
- Lavish costumes
- Fantastic special effects
- A multimillion-dollar media blitz that predisposes people to want to see your movie and buyers to want to book it

If *you* are not yet a star, and you can't afford star actors, costumes, sets, and special effects, then the subject matter of your movie has to be the star all by itself. The material must be exploitable—in a way that distributors and theater owners will immediately recognize. If it isn't, then no matter how good your movie is, prepare yourself for a tough if not impossible battle to sell it, even if you succeed in making it.

If you want your movie to play on the big screen, you have got to give people something they can't see on television. The major studios accomplish this by making $18 million pictures loaded with elements that TV movies can't afford. The low-budget independents usually accomplish it by featuring sex and violence portrayed more explicitly than what will be accepted on TV.

> "You couldn't do a D. W. Griffith film on a cheap budget, but you could probably do a take-off on Griffith by taking away sound—making a silent picture, in other words; separating image and sound. One of the things that hit me as I began to make my first films was that you could do anything if you took image away from sound, and then you could put it back. You could have moments of contact that would be sync, but for the rest of the film you would operate in a sort of freewheeling space, which was important to me because I couldn't afford always to do sync sound."
>
> Lizzie Borden

Some "serious pictures" like Spike Lee's *She's Gotta Have It* and Lizzie Borden's *Working Girls* gave themselves an edge in the marketplace by choosing to deal with sex, always a subject of vast audience appeal even when it's being handled maturely and philosophically rather than crassly exploitatively. The Coen Brothers' *Blood Simple* had murder as well as sex as its drawing card.

ADVANTAGES AND DISADVANTAGES OF GOING FOR GORY HORROR

The explicit gore effects in *Friday the 13th* were there for three reasons:

1. They were cheap to pull off.
2. They were shocking and horrifying because they went to new heights (or depths) of explicitness.
3. That degree of explicitness would not be permitted on television, so once word of mouth spread about the picture, everybody who wanted to see it would have to go to a theater.

Friday the 13th was a logical progression in the effort to deliver greater and greater (yet inexpensive) shocks that was given new impetus by pictures like

The Texas Chainsaw Massacre and *Halloween*. They were so successful financially that they spawned a rash of sequels, spin-offs, and imitators, the worst
of which are simply very bad splatter movies with little development of plot
or character.

Most of these kinds of films feature a small cast in a confined situation that
is made terrifying by the presence of a monster/madman/murderer. Usually
the victims are young, beautiful women, killed in a state of nudity or in the
midst of sexual activity. Often the murders are filmed from the point of view
of the murderer. For all these reasons, certain critics feel that the filmmakers
must hate women and must enjoy portraying them as objects to be punished
for being sexually desirable. These critics even fear that the adolescent boys in
today's theater audiences must identify with the psychopathic killers portrayed in the splatter movies and like to watch the killers acting out their own
dark fantasies.

But these critics have missed the point.

There are two simple, pragmatic reasons why the victims in these movies
are often filmed from the POV of the killer:

1. It's an easy, effective technique for not revealing who the killer is.
2. It affords dramatically explicit angles for showing the gore effects.

I think the teen-age boys in the audience are mentally healthy, the critics'
fears to the contrary. The teenagers don't take the gore effects seriously;
instead they're entertained and intrigued by how the effects are pulled off.
Furthermore, if someone has visions of someday making his own horror
movie, these types of effects seem within reach—not out of sight financially,
like the effects in *Poltergeist*.

Some writers have called *Night of the Living Dead* the "granddaddy of the
splatter movies." In a certain sense, they're right. It showed other filmmakers
that you could develop a good, tight story involving a small cast in one major
location—and, if the story was exciting enough, you could make a movie with
unknown actors, and it would sell tickets. *Night of the Living Dead* had only a
couple of gory scenes, and they were mild by today's standards, especially
since the picture was shot in black and white instead of color. The splatter
movies escalated the gore. But they retained the formula of a small cast in a
confined situation. The ones that had well-developed plots and interesting
characters made the best movies and were usually more financially successful
than the ones that featured gore and little else.

Lately there has been a movement of distributors against low-budget
"slasher" movies. A key reason for this is that it is increasingly harder to get
an R rating (as opposed to an X) on one of these types of films, and an R is
needed for broad theatrical distribution. However, they still rack up healthy
videocassette sales—it seems there's always a large bottom-line audience for

horror. So making a horror movie of some type can be a relatively safe route to go financially, but nothing is guaranteed. Contrary to popular belief, you can lose your shirt with *any* type of movie, including horror.

Also, when a filmmaker makes a successful horror film, he has a tough time breaking out of that genre. Distributors find it hard to believe that his talents may extend to other areas, and they won't give him a chance to do anything more mainstream. This point of view has always seemed rather narrow and silly to me, but it's a state of affairs that's very hard to buck.

ADVANTAGES AND DISADVANTAGES OF GOING MAINSTREAM

If you can pull off a successful mainstream film, you have a much broader audience for it than you do for horror. So you can make a lot more money. And, once having pulled off this kind of success, you will more easily be thought of as a serious director. So you will be considered for all kinds of projects that would be out of the normal grasp of a genre director.

But when a low-budget mainstream effort flops, it flops miserably. It doesn't have the hard core of loyal genre fans to bail it out with hefty cassette sales. If it doesn't have any name or seminame actors in it, it will probably not land much in the way of TV syndication or foreign sales.

For these reasons, walking the thin line between making a genre film and making a mainstream film can sometimes be a sound strategy. *Blood Simple,* which I mentioned earlier, had sex and bloody murder in it—murders that were about as horrifying and suspenseful as the murders in a splatter movie. Yet because the Coen Brothers' picture had an intriguing plot, excellent character development, and sophisticated cinematic execution, it was accepted by filmgoers and critics on a higher level than what normally might have been expected.

The lesson here is that you have got to have some hook to your low-budget movie. Its plot must be tailored to your available resources. And the story must be a good one, not just one that can be filmed cheaply.

COMING UP WITH A HOOK

Sometimes it helps to come up with a title and a sales campaign (artwork and blurb) before you try to write your script. If you can't envision a title and an ad that will draw people to the movie, then the movie probably shouldn't be made. You probably don't have a good enough handle on what it's *about.* Your concept isn't sharply focused. So it won't sell investors, distributors, and theater owners, and the public will never get a chance to see it.

Here is a list of good, successful titles:

The Evil Dead
Working Girls
The Exorcist
She's Gotta Have It
The Boob Tube

All of these titles conjure up explicit images of what the movies are about. They radiate sex, horror, and/or titillation. *The Boob Tube* is one of the best titles I've ever seen. It gets across the idea that this movie is meant to be a sexy, funny lampoon of programs on TV. It also happens to be a takeoff of an earlier, highly profitable movie entitled *The Groove Tube*. All this is conveyed in three well-chosen words.

Here's a list of bad titles for a low-budget movie:

Terms of Endearment
Ordinary People
The Sunshine Boys
Faces
Dominick and Eugene

These titles fail to telegraph what the movies are about. We'd be totally in the dark if it weren't for the big, expensive promotional campaigns that actually were behind the pictures when they were launched. And of course big-name stars in the casts helped guarantee their success.

Faces was a financially successful low-budget picture, but it was heavily promoted because it was made by John Cassavetes, a famous actor. As I write this, *Dominick and Eugene* hasn't been released yet, but it stars Jamie Lee Curtis and was produced by Mike Farrell, so I suppose that Orion will give it a broad release with heavy advertising and promotion. To my mind, they could also have done themselves a favor by coming up with a title that was less vague.

Another thing: If you take the million-dollar stars out of the casts, movies like *Ordinary People* and *Terms of Endearment* aren't expensive to produce. It's conceivable that a young filmmaker could, by working with a cast of unknowns, make a movie just as good as Robert Redford's *Ordinary People*. But minus the stars, there's an excellent chance that nobody would buy it. It would never get distributed, and people would never get to find out how wonderful it was.

So the issue is not merely whether or not you can make a good movie; it's whether or not you can make one and get it sold—sold to a distributor and sold to the public. For your first effort, make it as easy as you can on yourself. You don't necessarily have to make a genre flick. But neither do you have to make something too esoteric for the marketplace. Try to make a picture that can get a few good reviews, maybe even win a festival or two (this does not eliminate the idea of doing a horror film, because there are horror and sci-fi festivals too). But don't put all your eggs in that basket. Give yourself the comfort of knowing that even if the film misses its mark in some respects, it can still have a chance of making some money and helping to launch your career.

DEVELOPING A SCRIPT

There are three ways of latching on to a hot concept and getting it in shape to be filmed:

1. Buying or optioning an existing property, such as a short story, a novel, or even a finished screenplay
2. Hiring a writer to come up with a concept or to develop your own concept into a screenplay
3. Writing your own screenplay

Buying or Optioning an Existing Property

This tactic has the advantage that the property will come to you whole. If you like the story, you've got it, without a need for costly, time-consuming revisions. Besides, if the property is an already published story or novel, the title and the author already have visibility, market recognition, perhaps even fame. Showing potential investors a copy of the novel that your movie will be based on impresses them. If the novel is a bestseller, so much the better.

You may think that this sort of thing is beyond your reach, but don't be so quick to jump to that conclusion. Many novels, even best sellers, are optioned for $5,000 or less. And often the option money doesn't have to be paid until a production deal is signed. Authors are so hungry to have their books made into movies that they'll option the books for low front money, then take a bigger lump of cash—and sometimes a profit percentage—out of the back end of the deal. Sixty thousand books are published every year in the United States, and only about five hundred movies are made here. A lot of those books would make great movies, but the major studios can't possibly gobble up all of them. This doesn't mean that you, an unknown director, have an excellent chance of optioning a novel. But it does mean that you have *a* chance. So, if you read one that you like, you might as well try for it.

In order to option a novel, a story, or a completed screenplay, you must first contact the author and/or his agent, attorney, or publisher to ascertain that the property is indeed available. If it is, you should hire an agent or a lawyer who is familiar with these kinds of deals to do the negotiating for you and draw up the contract. If you try to do it on your own, there is a strong likelihood that you will neglect some contractual fine point or fail to tie up some rights that turn out to be absolutely necessary down the line in order to secure financing or distribution.

Basically, the rights that you are after are:

- All rights in and to the property in any and all media, including theatrical, nontheatrical, television, videocassette, videodisc, or any other visual or audio device (excluding publication rights, if it is already a published work)
- All remake, sequel, and ancillary rights
- All rights to the title of the property
- The right to copyright the property
- The right to make alterations and changes in the property and to change the title without necessarily hiring the original author or obtaining his consent to do so.

This last clause is very important, since any novel or story that you option will have to be adapted to screenplay form. Even if it is already a screenplay, it may have to be rewritten to please you, your investors, or the eventual distributor. To save money and to make sure the adaptation is to your liking, you may want to write it yourself. Or you may want to work with a writer who you feel can satisfy you better than the original author.

Hiring a Writer

If you decide to develop a screenplay from scratch, and you don't feel competent to do the writing yourself, then you will have to hire a writer. There are many excellent unpublished/unproduced writers who are looking for a break, and if you knock around the movie business long enough on just about any level, you'll probably get to know one or several. Some of them will work very cheaply. Some will even forgo monetary payment up front in return for the prospect of screen credit or deferred payment of one sort or another, including profit participation.

Whatever deal you make with a writer, get it in writing. Get a lawyer or an agent to negotiate and draw up a contract. That way, both you and the writer will feel comfortable working together and sharing ideas, and you won't be suing each other and hating one another when it's all over.

The writing of a screenplay generally proceeds through four stages:

1. Treatment: an abridged exposition of the intended movie from beginning to end, usually fifteen to thirty pages long, with most of the characters and scenes painted in broad strokes and some of the dialogue sketched in so that one can get a good idea of the overall movie without the details.

2. First draft: a fleshing in of all the characters, dialogue, and action; a complete screenplay that may or may not need extensive reworking.

3. Subsequent drafts: revisions in the screenplay based on discussions among the writer, producer, director, and others.

4. Final draft: sometimes called a *polish;* not a complete rewrite, ideally, at this stage, but a fine-tuning of specific scenes to the point where everybody concerned will be anxious to go into production.

If you are *not* happy with the final draft, don't settle for it. Don't call it final. If you have to, look for a new writer. Very few bad or inadequate scripts can be rescued in the filming, any more than a tasty loaf of bread can be baked from a bad recipe. So hold up your production until you've got a screenplay that absolutely pleases you. Sometimes the easiest way to arrive at this point is to opt for:

Writing It Yourself

Many of today's finest filmmakers are also excellent screenwriters. They know how to write cinematically. They can ensure from the outset that each movie project they undertake is an embodiment of their unique personal vision.

If you're that type of filmmaker, you probably won't need me to encourage you to go for it. You'll already have a script that you believe in and want to go out and film. But before you take that step, evaluate your *own* script in the light of the commercial and aesthetic considerations discussed in this chapter. Ask yourself those tough questions and answer them honestly.

If the answers satisfy you, if your confidence level is high and you have no doubt that *your* script is the right one, then by all means . . .

Go for it!

17
Budgeting

NOW YOU HAVE a script that you love. It's going to make a good movie. In conceptualizing and writing the script, you tried to tailor it to a low budget. Did you succeed? To find out for sure, you now have to actually go through the script in minute detail and arrive at some overall figures that will tell you whether the project can in fact be brought in for $200,000 or less. Once you know for sure how much money your project is going to cost, you will also know how much you have to raise.

BUDGETING OVERVIEW AND RULES OF THUMB

Movie budgets are divided into two important categories: *above-the-line* costs and *below-the-line* costs. In the above-the-line category is all money to be paid to the writer, producer, director, and principal talent. The below-the-line category includes all other necessary costs. The first step in arriving at a budget is to figure the below-the-line costs—the unavoidable expenses of making the movie. Then you can add on what you would like to pay and/or what you can afford to pay to the key people performing on-camera and the key people behind the camera, including one extremely important person—you.

Just as the Internal Revenue Service has guideline percentages for tax deductions, the motion picture industry has figured out some rule-of-thumb percentages that can be helpful when you're trying to come up with an "average" budget breakdown:

Story and screenplay	5%
Producer and director	5
Cast	20
Studio overhead	20
Crew and materials	35
Taxes	5
Contingencies	10
	100%

We all know that the IRS gets suspicious when a man earning $20,000 a year claims $4,000 in church donations. Similarly, potential investors may smell a rip-off if a producer has himself down for a $50,000 fee out of a $200,000 production budget. Although the rules of thumb may be stretched to accommodate the special requirements of a given project, if any one category gets way out of line, it will shortchange the other categories, perhaps to the point where the project will be jeopardized.

Time Is Money

Another rule of thumb pertaining to production costs concerns the production timetable: The longer it takes you to make a movie, the more it is going to cost you. You have to pay the people putting in this extra time. Your investors have to pay interest while their money is tied up, which doesn't usually thrill them. Even if you aren't paying *out* anything, you are going without income your picture could have produced if you could have finished it sooner and put it into distribution.

When I make a low-budget movie, I try to stick roughly to the following timetable:

1. Scripting: six weeks
2. Preproduction: six weeks
3. Production: thirty shooting days over a five- to six-week schedule
4. Postproduction: three to four months

By budgeting the time this way, a movie can be made in five to six months. It is tough to cut the scripting and preproduction phases any tighter and still be prepared adequately for filming. And it is hard to reduce the number of shooting days without adversely affecting the quantity and quality of the footage, unless you hire an unusually large crew or even a second-unit crew, which of course costs more money and consequently can be self-defeating if you're hoping to save money by finishing more quickly. Same with postproduction: you can get all the editing and finishing done in a month if you're able to pay a lot of people a lot of overtime. But this kind of time saver is usually unwise or unaffordable when you're trying to work on a low budget in the first place.

I have made five pictures on the kind of schedule outlined above, so I know it works. But it takes thorough planning, accurate budgeting, and shrewd execution in order to *make* it work. Poor planning produces a budget written in smoke, causing the means of execution to evaporate and ultimately converting the smoke to red ink.

Once you've broken down your script to arrive at budget figures tied to a realistic schedule, you should come back and check them against the rules of thumb I've given you. If you find yourself in the ballpark, it will reassure you that your figures are probably good ones.

USING A SUCCESSFUL PRODUCTION AS A BUDGETING GUIDELINE

When I draw up a budget for a film, whether it's a thirty-second commercial or a low-budget feature, I don't have to use reams of paper covered with minute details. I know from experience how to block in fairly accurate ballpark figures for a large portion of the production, and I know that these costs won't vary much from one production to another. Therefore, I can just write them into my budget as a matter of course and go on from there to concentrate on the areas peculiar to the particular production at hand. Once I fine-tune the figures for these specific areas, I add them to my already blocked-in figures to arrive at a total budget amount.

The best way for me to give you some of this experience vicariously, thereby teaching you in a quite meaningful way how to draw up a budget for a low-budget movie, is to take you step by step through the budgeting of one that ended up being brought in on budget and then was sold successfully. I'm talking about my movie *The Majorettes,* which was produced in 1985–86 on about $200,000. Its hook was horror mixed with a theme of teen-age revenge. It was based on my novel of the same title, published by Pocket Books in 1977. I was the producer and screenwriter, and Bill Hinzman (who played the lead ghoul in *Night of the Living Dead)* was the director. We secured financing from Joseph C. Ross, who acted as executive producer, and we went ahead and made the picture without a distribution deal up front. We succeeded in selling it to Manson International Pictures and Vestron Video, and we have raked in enough money in advances that we have already recouped our production costs, and our agents predict that we will make close to $1 million from all markets over the next three years.

So that we have a frame of reference for the discussions to follow, here is the synopsis of *The Majorettes* that was used, not only to help raise investment but also to help promote the picture after it was sold:

Synopsis

THE MAJORETTES

screenplay by

John Russo

A sexy action-suspense thriller, our story takes place in a small town where majorettes are being murdered. The intriguing twists and turns of the fast-paced plot elevate this movie above many others in the overworked "slasher" genre.

Main characters are:

Vicky McAllister. A very pretty seventeen-year-old majorette. Both her parents are dead, and she lives with her invalid grandmother, the grandmother's nurse, and the nurse's slightly weird son. On her eighteenth birthday, coming up soon, Vicky will inherit a trust fund of $500,000.

Elvira Adams. Vicky's grandmother. In a wheelchair, she has lost her speech and mobility due to a stroke.

Judy Marino. A sixteen-year-old majorette, Vicky's best friend.

Jeff Halloway. Judy's boyfriend, the star quarterback of the football team.

Helga Schuler. A sinister woman, nurse to the invalid Elvira Adams.

Harry Schuler. Helga's son. A voyeur.

Mace Jackson. A sadistic drug pusher and gang leader.

Marie Morgan. The majorette coach. Girlfriend of:

Lt. Roland Martell. A county detective, assigned to work with:

Sheriff Mike Braden. A small-town cop who resents Lt. Martell's "interference" on the murder case. He is religious and dedicated, maybe too much so . . .

After finishing their practice at the local high school, the majorettes and their coach are having their pictures taken for the high school yearbook. The photographer is sixteen-year-old Tommy Harvack, who secretly has a crush on one of the majorettes, Nicole Hendricks. After the photo session, while the girls are taking their showers, someone is spying on them and taking photos through a peephole.

That evening, Nicole lets Tommy take her out—a dream come true for him, and a comedown for her. She tries to seduce him but doesn't go through with it; instead she confesses that she's pregnant by Mace Jackson, the drug pusher. While they're talking, Tommy and Nicole are being stalked by a shadowy figure who brutally murders them.

Sheriff Braden, at a church service, finds out about the murders. Lt.

Roland Martell, in bed with Marie Morgan, gets a phone call to join Braden at the scene of the crime. The hunt for the murderer begins.

After a band and majorette practice, Judy and Vicky urge quarterback Jeff Halloway to go to the police with information he has about Mace Jackson beating up Nicole Hendricks. The info causes Mace to get arrested, but Braden and Martell don't have enough evidence to hold him. However, the drug pusher vows to get even with Jeff.

Meanwhile, the sinister nurse, Helga Schuler, is scheming to murder Vicky and her grandmother so Helga can inherit Vicky's $500,000 trust fund. And we have found out that Helga's son, Harry, the high school janitor, is the one who is taking nude photos of the majorettes. Is he also the killer?

Next Judy Marino is murdered, in the high school shower room. Just before the murder, Harry was on the scene taking pictures. But he disappears, and Jeff and Vicky find Judy dead and mutilated.

Helga summons Sheriff Braden to Elvira's estate. Pretending to be upset, she unlocks Harry's basement darkroom and shows the sheriff Harry's nude photos of the majorettes. The sheriff says they don't prove Harry is the murderer. Gloating, Helga tells him, "I *know* he's not the murderer, sheriff. Because, look!" She pops out a photo Harry took from his peephole of Sheriff Braden butchering Judy Marino. Then Harry steps up behind the sheriff and knocks him out. He and Helga tie the sheriff up and blackmail him into killing Vicky next, warning him that Vicky must die *after* she turns eighteen in order for the trust to pass to her and then to Helga after Vicky is dead.

After being grilled by Braden about their discovery of Judy's dead body, Jeff and Vicky are kidnapped by Mace Jackson and his gang of cutthroats. Harry the janitor sees the kidnapping going down and follows, trying to protect Vicky temporarily so she can die after her eighteenth birthday. In an abandoned warehouse, meddler Harry is killed, and in the flurry Jeff and Vicky try to run. Vicky is killed, and Jeff is left for dead.

When he revives, Jeff goes after the thugs, crazed with grief and lusting for revenge. He blows up the gang's trailer, a motorcycle, and a car. He starts gunning down the thugs as they try to escape from the holocaust. Mace gets away, but Jeff pursues and finally kills him. This scene fades as Jeff is putting the gun to his own head.

Her son, Harry, dead and the trust fund lost, Helga flips out and disposes of Elvira with a lethal dose of insulin. Meanwhile, Sheriff Braden sneaks into the house, pounces on Helga, and lynches her, making it look like a suicide. Braden removes the incriminating photos of himself from the darkroom.

Next we see Jeff in a hospital room, in a coma. Lt. Martell and Sheriff Braden visit, and Braden sanctimoniously says that if Jeff ever recovers enough to stand trial, he, the sheriff, will do all he can to see that Jeff gets exonerated.

The sheriff, of course, has gotten away with murder after murder and will probably commit more. CLOSING CREDITS ROLL as he stands in a school yard, watching some grade school girls practicing with their batons, learning to be majorettes . . .

Budgeting According to the Shooting Schedule

If our movie budget is to be accurate, it must be based on a *realistically anticipated shooting schedule.* You must know how many weeks you are going to need the actors, crew, and equipment so that you can figure out how much they will cost you, based on their weekly rates.

A shooting schedule proceeds location by location until all the filming is accomplished; that way, the production doesn't waste time moving people and equipment back and forth to the same locations over and over. Therefore, the first thing we must do is break the script down into locations. For each location, there will be a breakdown of the scenes to be shot there, the cast involved, the estimated number of days to be spent at the location, plus the props, costumes, and special effects or logistical considerations required.

Here is a portion of my location chart for *The Majorettes,* which I made by going through the script very carefully and which you can follow by referring back to the synopsis:

LOCATION	SCENE NO.	CAST	NO. DAYS	PROPS	COSTUMES	SPECIAL CON.
Gym	1	Tommy Marie Vicky Nicole Judy Harry majorettes	1	Camera Batons Broom Record player	Majorettes' outfits Janitor costume	
Locker Rm.	2	All majorettes	1	Batons	Street clothes Towels Soap	
"	15	All majorettes	1	Same	Different st. clothes	Peephole
"	16	Vicky Jeff Braden Judy	1	Knife	Hood, etc.	Peephole Stabbing Body in locker

Once I had a chart like this made for the entire feature, I added up the days estimated for shooting at each location, and I came up with a total of twenty-seven days. This was consistent with my hope for a shooting schedule of thirty days spread over six weeks (to allow for off-days and days used for intermediate planning and regrouping). So far, so good. Also, from this overall chart, I could make up comprehensive cast, prop, and costume lists for estimating those particular costs. But the main point of this exercise is to pin down the shooting schedule to a rather definite number of days.

Blocking in Below-the-Line Costs

Now, as I mentioned before, there are certain below-the-line costs that don't vary much from production to production, so I can block them in without doing much figuring. I'm referring to lab costs, equipment rental costs, and crew costs (wages). When I worked up the budget for *The Majorettes,* I automatically wrote down $60,000 for lab costs because I knew from experience on past productions that $60,000 would cover me. Let's break it down so you can see why. In "lab costs" are included:

- Purchase of filmstock
- Processing of filmstock
- Work printing of filmstock
- Transferring of quarter-inch sound recording tape to sprocket-driven tape for syncing and editing
- Syncing
- Mixing
- Conforming
- Optical printing of titles and credits
- Printing of optical sound track
- Printing of 35-millimeter answer print

Crucial to figuring out what all this will cost is the estimate of *how much film* you plan to shoot, because the lab will charge a *per-foot rate* for each step listed above. Now, *Night of the Living Dead* was shot on 56,000 feet of film, and this was a tight but not unreasonable footage budget for pulling off a successful horror/suspense movie. *Midnight* was shot on 40,000 feet, and I still pulled it off, but less successfully and, frankly, with too much strain on the quality of the production. A ninety-minute 35-millimeter feature is about 8,500 feet in length, and for purposes of figuring out a footage ratio it should be rounded off to 9,000 feet to give leeway for leader wasted in threading up 400-foot magazines. So, dividing 56,000 by 9,000, we can see that shooting that amount of film would give us a little better than a six-to-one footage ratio.

I have always done my editing in 16-millimeter, even when I've shot in 35-millimeter, so the figures for *The Majorettes* were based on doing it that way. It is cheaper to rent 16-millimeter editing, dubbing, and mixing gear than it is to rent the same gear in 35-millimeter format, so I edit and mix in 16-millimeter, then conform the 35-millimeter camera original to the edited 16-millimeter work print to make a 35-millimeter answer print. If you choose to work in 35-millimeter all the way, your intermediate costs will vary from mine somewhat, but you can still figure them out accurately once you understand the procedure. I obtained the exact current price of the filmstock by phoning Eastman Kodak, and I got the current lab prices by phoning WRS Motion Picture Laboratory in Pittsburgh. So, here is the breakdown on my lab costs:

Purchase 56,000'(140 400' rolls) 35mm film	$17,000
Process 56,000' film @ .09 per ft.	5,040
Reduce 56,000' 35mm to 22,400' 16mm work print with inked edge numbers @ .249 per ft.	5,578
Purchase 56,000' 16mm mag. film @ .038 per ft.	2,128
Purchase 100 rolls quarter-inch tape	500
20 hours sound transfer time @ $60 per hour	1,200
60 hours syncing @ $20 per hour	1,200
9,000'one-inch tape for mixing @ .30 per ft.	2,700
40 hours mixing and interlocking @ $90 per hour	3,600
9,000'conforming @ .25 per ft.	2,250
Shooting and processing of titles and credits	3,600
9,000'35mm optical sound track @ .17 per ft.	1,530
9,000'35mm answer print @ .87 per ft.	7,830
	$54,156

It is wise to leave yourself a good bit of leeway in estimating lab costs, because if you go even slightly over budget in filmstock, all the other costs will go up. That's why I always stick with the rounded-off figure of $60,000 for total lab costs. Of course, as lab fees continue to rise, the $60,000 figure will eventually become untenable. Check with your own lab before you go into production; the staff will be glad to help you break down all these costs so they can get the business when you're ready to roll.

Your lab costs will go up if you do things a little differently than I did. For instance, if you don't make your answer print from your camera original, but instead elect to make an interpositive and then an internegative to print from, these elements will cost extra. Again, the lab you deal with will give you advice and cost estimates.

The next big area of the budget that can be blocked in is the cost of renting camera and lighting equipment. For the kind of equipment that I like to use (which may differ from what you prefer), I usually allow $18,000. This breaks down to $3,000 per week over a six-week shooting schedule. The way this works is, you call up an equipment rental outfit, like F&B/CECO in New York, tell them what type of gear you want and for how long, and they give you a quote on a package deal. Don't go by the prices listed in the catalogue. Discount prices are always available for a feature movie because the equipment is going to be rented for a long period, with the ease of shipping it out once and shipping it back once, instead of packaging it and shipping it in and out a dozen times for a dozen little TV commercials.

The gear that we used for *The Majorettes* included:

- A 35-millimeter Arriflex BL camera with six magazines, zoom lens, and a full complement of fixed-focus lenses and filters
- Accessories such as tripod, dolly, shoulder pod, spare battery packs, changing bag, etc.
- Colortran lights, Lowel Soft Lites, cables, filters, etc.
- Nagra recorder with various directional mikes, wireless mikes, fishpole boom, clapstick, cables, etc.

Another very important piece of equipment that we rented for the duration of the production, exclusive of preproduction, was a Moviola six-plate 16-millimeter editing table. Later, we brought in a second Moviola for Bill Hinzman to help in the editing. With all the accessories, the total cost for editing gear was $8,000.

The next big area of below-the-line costs that can be blocked in easily is the cost of the crew. When I'm making a low-budget feature, I use a streamlined crew made up of people who I know from experience will work quickly and efficiently together. Here is the crew that I budgeted for:

Cameraman/editor (twelve weeks @ $1,000 per week)	$12,000
Asst. cameraman (six weeks @ $700 per week)	4,200
Sound engineer (six weeks @ $700 per week)	4,200
Lighting supervisor (six weeks @ $700 per week)	4,200
Gaffer (six weeks @ $600 per week)	3,600
Three grips (six weeks @ $400 per week apiece)	7,200
Two production assts. (twelve weeks @ $200 per week apiece)	4,800
	$40,200

I knew roughly the weekly rates of the crew members, from working with them before. But, since I wasn't sure whether any of their rates had gone up, I called them on the phone to check this out.

Hiring people who can wear many hats saves money and helps ensure the success of a low-budget production. From the outset, I had in mind hiring Paul McCollough to be cameraman/editor. Paul "wears many hats" and wears them well: he is an excellent cinematographer and editor, and he is also an accomplished musician who can write, arrange, and produce musical scores for films. He performed all these functions on my movie *Midnight.* So I wanted him to work with me on *The Majorettes.* It would have cost a lot more than $12,000 to hire separate personnel to film, edit, and score the picture, but with Paul I got a "package price"—and in return, he got a percentage of the profits.

The production assistants are hired for twelve weeks, so they can help out with preproduction. Bill Hinzman and I would be supervising and working with them.

I did not budget any money for a still photographer because I figured someone on the crew already would handle this. It ended up that I took a lot of the stills myself.

Pricing Special Effects and Other Special Considerations

When you have something special in a script, the best way to estimate the cost is to go directly to the specialist who will pull it off for you. *The Majorettes* called for a trailer, a car, and a motorcycle to be blown up, plus numerous murders, bullet blasts, and other gore effects, like the "stabbing" and "body in locker" that you see in Scene 16 in my location breakdown chart. I gave a script to special effects man Jerry Gergely, and he got together with some demolitions experts he had worked with in the past, and they came up with a price of $6,000 for the whole ball of wax.

I also needed a high school band and a high school to film in, including the football field. I figured I could get this stuff for a $1,000 donation to some school, and it turned out when we made the film that Bill Hinzman found a school that would cooperate at that price.

I allowed $1,000 for location fees other than the fee for the school, based on my experience with location fees for past productions with similarly contemporary locations.

I was able to estimate the costs for the rest of the props and the costumes by making lists and assigning ballpark price tags to each item. I rounded off the total to $2,000, but this didn't include the special items that needed to be destroyed—the trailer, the car, and the motorcycle. I allowed another $5,000 for the vehicles.

Blocking in Above-the-Line Costs

Next I had to figure out how much I was going to pay the actors, the director, and the screenwriter/producer. I knew we wouldn't be able to afford SAG rates, so I made my mind up to go with nonunion actors. I knew from the past that I could hire the principals and day players for $100 a day, and extras for $50 a day. My location charts told me how many days each actor would be needed. All I had to do was multiply by the per-diem rates. I came up with a total of $18,000 for the entire cast, but in practice we had to pay out $23,600 because we used quite a few of the actors on overtime, and we decided along the way to pay our leads $150 a day instead of $100.

Bill Hinzman and I, as director and screenwriter/producer respectively, originally were penciled in for higher salaries, but we ended up working for $12,500 apiece plus a percentage of the profits. If *The Majorettes* hits the $1.5 million our agents project, my 10 percent of the gross profit will have been well worth my time.

Now we're ready to add up all our budget categories:

Lab costs	$60,000
Filming equipment rental	18,000
Editing table rental	8,000
Crew costs	40,200
Special makeup FX and demolitions	6,000
High school and band	1,000
Other location fees	1,000
Props and costumes	2,000
Trailer, car, and motorcycle (to blow up)	5,000
Actors (actual figure)	23,600
Director and screenwriter/producer	25,000
	$189,800

Now, if you subtract $189,800 from $200,000, you will see that there was $10,200 left to cover production overhead: costs of operating an office, travel and meals for cast and crew, production insurance, and various other expenses.

Let's see how our budget jibes with the rule-of-thumb percentages laid down earlier:

	RULE OF THUMB	MAJORETTES
Director and Prod./Writer	10%	13%
Cast	20	12
Overhead and Contingencies	30	5
Crew and Materials	35	70
Taxes	5	0
	100	100

We can see that the percentage paid to the director and the producer/writer is in line. Our cast percentage is low, but then we're trying to keep it low by using nonunion actors. I didn't allow anything for taxes because there is not usually any great tax burden on a low-budget motion picture enterprise if it's set up right; I have never found this to be a problem, although presumably the major studios must set aside a percentage of each movie budget to go toward their state and federal taxes.

The category where there is the greatest disparity is "Crew and Materials." We are spending a whopping 70 percent of our budget here, whereas the studio norm is only 35 percent. In other words, *we are putting our dollars where they really count*— into the meat of the production. This leaves only 5 percent instead of the recommended 30 percent for studio overhead and contingencies. I'd rather *not* see the production money go into overhead. And if I've budgeted right, and I spend my dollars wisely, I won't need to put aside a huge contingency.

When we actually produced *The Majorettes,* all the budget categories didn't hold strictly to my preproduction estimates. Sometimes we decided to save money here and spend more there. But we always kept a tight rein on our overall costs. The net result was that *The Majorettes* was brought in on schedule and on budget and is making a tidy profit. If you work hard, your movie can enjoy the same or even greater success.

HOW TO MAKE A LOW BUDGET INTO A HIGH BUDGET

Suppose somebody—perhaps an investor or a distributor—wanted to give us $1 million to make *The Majorettes.* What the heck would we do with all that bread? Isn't it too much, considering that *we* know we can make the flick for $200,000?

Well, we can upgrade the quality of the production, thereby making the movie more marketable. If we produce it on a higher level, we might be able to land a major distributor who will give us a fat advance and a broad theatrical release.

First, we can dramatically increase the below-the-line budget, so we can shoot and process more footage, hire a slightly bigger crew, and add more special effects (explosions and so on, which we can write into the script). Doing all this will mean lengthening our shooting schedule by several weeks, with all the cost increases that *that* entails.

Instead of having Mace's gang living in a cheap trailer, we may want to make their headquarters in a real saloon or an actual farmhouse, which we can buy and then blow up in our action-packed finale. Buying such a place might cost us $100,000. We might blow up expensive vans, motorcycles, and cars instead of the junkers we were going to buy for only $5,000. If so, we could easily end up "wasting" $50,000 worth of vehicles.

We may want to add helicopter shots to the script. We may want to add more slick, time-consuming dolly shots—anything that will enhance the production. It is a question of going through the script and the below-the-line categories to see where the movie can be *improved* by spending more money.

Next we go to the above-the-line category. Now we can afford to pay the director and the producer/screenwriter in accordance with the rule of thumb, 10 percent of the overall budget, for a total of $100,000. We can also afford to hire SAG actors. And once we go SAG, we can put name or seminame actors into our cast. Doing this, plus taking care of SAG obligations, like putting up a completion bond and paying into a Pension and Welfare Fund, could easily cause us to spend another $300,000.

We may want to spend $50,000 producing an original score instead of having Paul McCollough producing electronic music on his own equipment.

Doing all these things could easily add up to another $800,000. It's not too hard to spend $1 million on a movie. If we would add two $1-million-a-picture stars to the cast, we'd have a $3 million movie.

The trick is not just spending money, but spending it wisely—and saving it where it makes more sense *not* to spend—no matter what the budget of your movie happens to be.

18

Raising the Bread

THE ALLURE, the so-called glamour, of show business is what makes it possible to finance movies. Everybody loves entertainment. People who aren't in show business seem to think that the ones who are in it are having more fun. They are willing to put some cash into a movie because they believe there's a chance that it might spice up their lives.

The best part about it is that they're right. We *are* having more fun, and we're willing to let them share in it. Helping to give birth to a movie, whether by writing it, producing it, directing it, or financing it, is a bigger thrill than laying bricks, pulling teeth, or selling insurance.

The fact that everybody who isn't in show business realizes this, or at least has an inkling that it is so, bodes well for your effort to raise enough bread to make your first feature. But you have to do it in a businesslike way. Your project has to seem like an exciting if somewhat risky venture, not pure pie in the sky. In order to set it up right and make people feel like entrepreneurs instead of fools when they put their money behind you, you have to form a company, structure an investment deal, develop sales tools, and make a shrewd, exciting, well-organized pitch to potential investors.

FORMING A COMPANY

There are three main reasons to form a production company. First, it acts as a legal entity to which the production partners all belong and to which they are contractually bound, thereby reducing the chances of antagonism and distrust among the partners. Second, it acts as a legal entity to which the investors will make their financial commitments in return for certain obligations assumed by the production partners, thereby making the partners and the investors more secure and comfortable about the deal and its prospects. Finally, the company, if set up properly, can reduce the financial vulnerability of the partners and the investors, in regard to taxes and lawsuits.

To properly set up a movie company or any other kind of company, one should always secure the advice of good, competent attorneys and accountants. I cannot give generic instructions for setting up a company, as the laws and the loopholes vary too much from state to state. However, I can impart some important guidelines, based on my experience with half a dozen movie companies, several of which I continue to operate in order to dispose of income from the movies produced under those companies.

The legal structures that are often proposed for a movie company are the public corporation, the subchapter S corporation, and the limited partnership.

The only two structures that I have used are the public corporation and the limited partnership. Attorneys and accountants have mentioned the subchapter S to me at the outset of a few projects, but in the end I always rejected it because it would have imposed such severe restrictions on the ways and means of raising money that it would have been an impractical structure for me to use. However, because of the tax reforms of the 1980s, the S corporation is now being used more often by people in the entertainment business. This type of setup is now a viable way to eliminate double taxation —being taxed at the corporate as well as the shareholder level. So, get advice from your attorney and accountant on the new laws. You may end up going with the S structure if you find that it suits your investors' specific needs.

Forming a public corporation is a good thing to do if you are sure that you, your production partners, and your investors want to stick together for more than one production. Under this structure, you will be "married" to one another. All will share in the bounty (or the lack of bounty) of not only the first movie the corporation makes, but of every movie thereafter. If a partner or an investor turns out to be a thorn in your side, you can't get rid of him unless you can buy him out.

Income from a corporation is taxed twice: first as corporate tax, paid out of corporate profits, and second as income tax, paid by the owners and shareholders out of their dividends. For this reason, even when an overall corporation is formed, the limited partnership structure usually is still employed for each individual movie produced under the corporate banner.

The limited partnership is the easiest structure to establish and the easiest structure under which to finance most low-budget movies. A limited partnership consists of limited partners and general partners. The limited partners are the investors; their financial responsibility and liability is limited to the amount of their investment. The general partners are the ones who are responsible for actually making the movie and assuming risks beyond the financial risk taken by the investors; in other words, if the movie goes over budget, the general partners must come up with the additional money and find a way of completing the project. If it is necessary to secure loans, they must sign the papers and pay the interest. They also are the ones at risk if any lawsuits are filed. They must live up to the terms of all the contracts signed by the partnership. When a corporation produces movies under the limited partnership structure, the corporation becomes the general partner for each movie, thus providing corporate protection to the individuals involved in each movie who are employees of the corporation. This reduces the vulnerability of the employees' individual assets (homes, cars, bank accounts, etc.) to lawsuits that may result from the production of a movie.

When we made *Night of the Living Dead,* we were ignorant of the advantages of the limited partnership, so we blundered ahead and set up a corporation, Image Ten, Inc., to produce the picture. But even in our ignorance, we took an important step toward limiting our relationship with and our obligations to our shareholders: we spelled out in the charter of Image Ten that it would exist to produce only *one* motion picture. That way, we wouldn't be tied to our investors beyond that point, and they would have the security of knowing that we couldn't dump the profits of the picture into other ventures of which the original investors might not approve.

The Image Ten situation worked out well because even though we formed a corporation we did not have to make a public stock offering, since we had to raise only a small amount of money from friends, family members, and our own pockets. The total *investment* capital put into our first movie was only $22,000—the rest was in the form of loans and deferments, which brought the eventual total to $114,000. Along the way, we managed to avoid the time-consuming and extremely expensive steps of making a full registration with the Securities and Exchange Commission and developing and filing a complicated prospectus. Legal fees involved in these steps usually come to $20,000 or more—almost as much as we needed to get our movie into production. And it often takes as much as six months to get a full prospectus approved.

After *Night of the Living Dead,* all of my feature movie projects were limited partnerships. Besides having no financial liability beyond the amount of their investment, the limited partners have no obligations or say in the running of the company. Therefore, the general partners retain business and artistic control. Which is not to say that they should just run roughshod over their investors. This is not nice, and it is not practical. The investors might have valuable expertise or advice to contribute to the present project—and cash to contribute to future projects.

To set up a limited partnership, you need a limited partnership certificate and a limited partnership agreement, drawn up and filed by a lawyer. This can cost as little as $3,000 and can be done inside of two weeks. To save even more money, I usually type up the first drafts myself, patterned after previous limited partnerships, then my lawyer does the fine-tuning and filing.

Limited partnerships are not public stock offerings; they are *private placement* investments. They are subject to important restrictions, but they are exempt from full registration with the Securities and Exchange Commission. In each state the law defines the number of potential investors who may be approached for investment and the number of investors who may finally participate in the partnership.

In Pennsylvania fifty potential investors may be approached, and a maximum of twenty-five may participate. This means that if we want to raise $200,000 we must sell the investments at a rate of $8,000 for each partnership share (twenty-five times $8,000 equals $200,000). The small number of investors (fifty approached, twenty-five landed) is what is defined as "private" under Pennsylvania law; if we wish to go beyond that number, it becomes defined as a "public" offering and is much more involved and expensive and minutely regulated by the Pennsylvania Securities and Exchange Commission.

Now, $8,000 is a large amount for a single individual to pop into a movie, and most young filmmakers do not personally know twenty-five people capable of and interested in doing so. That's the principal drawback to the limited partnership, even though it's relatively easy and inexpensive to set up. But the problem can be alleviated somewhat if the investors are willing to band together in groups. For instance, if you have eight friends who will form an "investment group," each one has to kick in only $1,000; they can elect one person to represent the group and sign a letter of agreement with that individual, who in turn signs the limited partnership agreement. I've had several of such groups as limited partners in some of the movies I made after *Night of the Living Dead.*

What if you get lucky and get $100,000—half your budget!—from a single investor? Well, then you need only $100,000 from the other twenty-four. So now you can afford to take less from each one ($100,000 divided by twenty-four) and still raise all your money from the maximum number of investors permitted under the law.

STRUCTURING THE INVESTMENT DEAL

Before you can sell your limited partnership interests, you have to figure out what you're selling. What are the limited partners getting for their money? What are the general partners getting for their work? This deal structure must be incorporated into the limited partnership agreement. It specifies the allocation of income from the movie—how the available dollars are going to be paid out.

A good basic structure is to disperse income in the following order, after first setting up a small reserve (perhaps 5 percent) for continuing to operate the company after the movie has gone into distribution:

1. Pay off all production loans and interest.
2. Pay off all deferments to actors, production personnel, and suppliers.
3. Return all capital to investors ($200,000).
4. Share all additional money (profits) fifty-fifty between general partners and limited partners.

If you really want to land investors, you have to make your deal very attractive to them. You may be tempted to give them back all their money right off the top, before you pay off loans and deferments—because the mere possibility of loans and deferments causes the investors to worry that you might put the movie in the hole through bad management. But if you do get into unforeseen trouble and have to go into hock, how are you going to bail yourself out? Being able to pay off loans and deferments from first income from your movie may end up saving you from personal bankruptcy.

Remember, even though you wait until last to begin raking in a share of the profits, it is a decidedly *healthy* share: 50 percent. And you are getting paid for working on your movie, right out of the production budget. So, all the way around, this is a pretty good deal for you. In fact, it is *so* good that if you really feel that you need an extra incentive for potential investors, you may want to let them make some profit before your percentage kicks in. For instance, they could continue to rake in 100 percent of the distribution income until they've jointly realized a profit of $25,000; then you start getting your 50 percent. There are all kinds of ways to vary the deal structure, but the basic points to remember are not to undersell yourself and not to try to shortchange your investors, or else your partnership will not only be "limited"—it will be stillborn.

DEVELOPING SALES TOOLS

The sales tool that you are permitted to use by law in pitching investors is the investment memorandum. You will need a lawyer to help you write one, but you can save time and money in legal fees by getting the necessary material together beforehand. The investment memorandum is similar to a prospectus in that it contains all the negative and positive factors pertaining to an investment, but it also contains a statement that it is *not* a prospectus. By the technicality of not construing itself as a prospectus or an offer to sell investment, but as a device *purely informational in nature,* it can be rather freely circulated without causing its perpetrators to be accused of exceeding the fifty solicitations permitted a limited partnership.

In structure and content, the investment memorandum is sort of like an expanded, showier version of the limited partnership agreement. It describes the nature of the enterprise to be undertaken by the partnership, the allocation of profits and losses from the enterprise, the tax consequences, the rights and obligations of the general and limited partners, the budget of the project, the anticipated timetable, the prospects for successful marketing, and so forth.

Not only will you help your lawyer by furnishing him your movie's budget, its production schedule, and all the other dry facts connected with it, but when the business of the partnership is to produce a movie, the more intangible aspects of the movie must be described or alluded to adequately. And *that* is where there's room for creative salesmanship. You can give your investment memorandum some glitter by including:

- A captivating synopsis of your movie
- Outstanding credits of actors or production personnel
- Showy newspaper or magazine articles that put movie investments in a favorable light
- Artwork, storyboards, and photos—especially stunning photos of actresses who have already been cast
- Mock-up ads that make it almost seem that the movie is already in the theaters

You could also make a preview trailer of the movie to be circulated on videocassette "for informational purposes." If you don't have sample scenes already shot, an effective trailer might be put together from artwork, narrated, and scored. Or you might want to make a presentation film that includes a profile of you and your key partners and impressive clips from movies—even commercials or industrials—that you have done in the past. Make use of anything and everything that can cause people to sit up and realize that you truly have the ability to turn out a feature motion picture.

Bear in mind that you are not limited to talking about your *own* picture, which after all has not yet come to fruition. You can talk about other low-budget pictures, like yours, that have become hits and returned millions of dollars in profits to their investors. People don't invest in motion pictures because they're looking for a *safe* place to put their money. They might have most of their investment capital in solid, secure, low-risk stocks, bonds, and real estate; but beyond that they may have a percentage of their money set aside as *venture* capital. This is the money that they take chances with, like playing a roulette wheel. They don't want to bet foolishly and lose it all on one spin, but they like the idea that if they do bet big—and win—they can rake in an enormous pile of chips.

Be sure to give them ample evidence of how a low-budget movie can hit the jackpot. For example:

MOVIE	BUDGET	RENTALS
The Graduate	$350,000	$50,000,000
Easy Rider	300,000	19,000,000
Friday the 13th	750,000	17,000,000
Halloween	300,000	18,500,000
Return of the Secaucus Seven	60,000	2,500,000
Working Girls	300,000	1,500,000
Hollywood Shuffle	100,000	1,500,000

Explain to your investors that the "Rentals" column refers to gross monies *returned to the distributor,* not box office gross, which is money taken in by the theater. The box office gross can be a very impressive figure, since it averages three times the rental figure, but the rentals are more meaningful. Your production company will have a share of the rentals earned by your picture, and usually that share will be about 35 percent. In other words, if your picture returns $1 million in rentals, you and your investors will gross $350,000. The distributor takes a larger share because he has to pay for prints and advertising—an enormous expense, which will probably bring his dollar earnings down to a level roughly equal to yours after all is said and done.

Nobody can project what a motion picture will actually earn; any picture can flop or hit big, and nobody has a crystal ball that can "see through" the fickleness and uncertainties of the marketplace. However, you can work up a set of projections as to how much money your investors can earn *if* your movie reaches certain levels of success. Here is the kind of projection table I have used in the past to clearly illustrate a break-even point for my limited partners and to whet their appetites for the vast earnings they may reap if the picture goes through the roof:

Rentals	$600,000	$1,000,000	$5,000,000
Prod. Co. Share (35%)	210,000	350,000	1,750,000
Ltd. Partners (100% of above to $200,000; 50% thereafter)	205,000	275,000	975,000
Gen. Partners	5,000	75,000	775,000

We can see that the movie has to earn only $600,000 in rentals for the limited partners to get all their investment money back, plus a $5,000 profit. If it earns $1 million, they are well on their way to doubling their money— and they can do this inside of two years, from the start of the movie's production to the recoupment of distribution money, if recoupment proceeds according to average industry rates. This is a much larger and faster return than can be gotten from money dropped into "safe" interest-bearing accounts.

It is also important to point out that theatrical rentals are only one source of movie income and may actually turn out to be the *least important* source. Many movies earn many times more from ancillary markets such as foreign sales, TV network sales, pay TV, and home video. In fact, some films that aren't very successful in the theaters become smash hits on home video. *The Texas Chainsaw Massacre 2* disappointed its distributor in its theatrical release, but it went platinum in its home video release, which means it sold $6 million worth of cassettes.

MAKING YOUR PITCH

Once you have gathered together the kinds of sales tools and verbal ammunition we have already discussed, you will have to decide how, when, and where to formally pitch potential investors. You can't just gather fifty people in a room and go all-out to sell them.

You must find some way of narrowing down the investors you actually approach to the few who are most likely to go for your deal. The best way of doing that is to ask them flat out. Once you have made a prospect aware of your enterprise—through your investment memorandum or through casual conversation—ask him if he would seriously consider investing in your movie if he had all the facts. Tell him you don't want to waste his time and you want to adhere properly to the legal requirements that govern the sale of your investment. If, hearing this, he says he would like to meet with you, *then* he is probably a genuine prospect.

The same approach that you use with individuals should be used with venture capital groups. These are groups of investors who have banded together to pool their venture capital. You can get in touch with them by contacting stock brokerages who may supply you with a list of addresses and phone numbers. Also, various venture capital directories are sold in bookstores and carried in public libraries. These groups could be a viable source of money for you, since they already have made it clear that they have money they would like to "venture." By pitching the leader of a group, you are in essence opening the door to a number of investors while only legally "approaching" a single investor. If an incorporated venture capital group signs as your limited partner, it goes on your books as a single entity, still allowing you twenty-four more limited partners.

Some potential investors will insist that you come to their office to talk with them. This may be fine with you, especially if you won't open your own headquarters until your movie is ready to go into preproduction. But if you have your own headquarters, it may be the best place for you to use. For instance, when I was making commercial films, I had a studio/screening

"One big tip I can give is to never, ever leave the home of a potential investor until you either have money or you can get him to squeal—'squeal' in the sense of spitting out the name of another potential investor. They've either gotta 'cough green' or squeal."

Sam Raimi
The Evil Dead and *Evil Dead II*

room that looked very impressive. Movie posters were on the walls. Cameras and lights were set up in a corner of the studio, as if they had just been used for a screen test. I had a soundproof projection booth and a large silver screen that would show my sample films to their best advantage. All this gave me the aura of a successful filmmaker with works in progress.

Naturally, your meeting place should be neat, clean and well organized; that is, businesslike. You should be well dressed and well groomed. This does not necessarily mean that you have to wear a three-piece suit. Some investors will take to you better if you do dress that way, but others actually like the idea that people in the entertainment business can dress more casually— that's part of the aura of freewheeling creativity and lack of regimentation that may have caused them to seek investment activity far removed from normal, stodgier businesses.

When you are talking to investors, be warm and outgoing. Don't be mousy, the antithesis of the dynamic milieu that they expect show business to be. Speak enthusiastically about yourself and your goals. Don't exaggerate your credentials. People want to deal with a sincere person, not a fake.

Usually a pitch should follow this basic outline:
1. A presentation of the movie business in general, highlighting the risks and the possibilities of profit
2. A discussion of your own project and a comparison with similar projects that have been successful
3. Profiles of you and your partners, telling why you have what it takes to succeed
4. Showing of sample films
5. Answering investors' questions
6. Asking for the sale

Don't forget to *ask for the sale.* It's the reason you're there. Most people will vacillate if they aren't asked to make up their minds. Ask the investor for a check right then and there. If he doesn't have his checkbook with him, phone him or, better yet, go to see him the next day. Pursue him until he signs. Then ask him to recommend someone else who he thinks may want to invest in your movie. That way, he becomes your ally in more ways than one. He might want his friends to invest along with him so they won't accuse him of not turning them on to a good thing—and also won't be able to razz him if it fails.

WHAT IF YOU RAISE ONLY PART OF THE MONEY?

As you collect money from investors in a limited partnership, it must be placed in an escrow fund for safekeeping until the full amount of the budget for your project is raised. Only then is the partnership officially formed. You cannot spend *any* of the investment money beforehand. And if you fail to raise all the necessary capital within a specified period—one year, in many states—you must dissolve the partnership and start over.

However, to circumvent this dire possibility, you can give yourself a loophole. You can build into your limited partnership agreement certain conditions under which you may proceed with your production even if the full amount of the budget is not raised. Here is how this can work:

Remember, our budget of $200,000 was for shooting in 35-millimeter and taking the production all the way to a 35-millimeter answer print. We don't necessarily have to go that route. What if we were to shoot in 16-millimeter? It would cost much less. Furthermore, what if we were to take the movie only to interlock stage (an edited work print synced with a 16-millimeter mix) instead of making a composite print? The savings would be greater still. What if we worked with a smaller crew? What if the director, producer, and screenwriter took lower salaries? With budget cuts in various categories, we might be able to make a movie on $100,000 or less. Distributors *will* look at unfinished movies. If they like the interlock, they will often assume the cost of a blowup and a finished print.

Sometimes going to a distributor with a film that is unfinished is to your disadvantage because you won't get a big advance, or you'll get no advance at all, or the distributor will ask for a bigger percentage than he would otherwise. *But* the unfinished film cost you less, so you have less money at risk. And in the final analysis, if you hadn't taken the shortcuts, you might not have made any film at all.

Therefore, if you spell out in your limited partnership agreement and investment memorandum your intention to produce your picture on either a "first-class level" or a "fallback level"—depending on how much investment is raised—you will have given yourself an ace in the hole. You don't even have to permanently sacrifice your full salary; if the movie is made on the reduced budget, payments to production personnel—even actors or crew members, if they're willing—may be deferred until after the picture is sold and starts to generate income. (The Appendix contains a sample limited partnership agreement, set up to incorporate a fallback strategy.)

Sam Raimi directing *Evil Dead II*. *Photo by Mike Ditz.*

Sam Raimi dropped out of college in Michigan to make a thirty-minute 8-millimeter sample film so he could show potential investors he had a good idea for a horror movie and the ability to pull it off. Shot in 16-millimeter on a budget of $375,000, the sample became *The Evil Dead,* termed by Stephen King "the most ferociously original horror film of 1982." Dino De Laurentiis gave Sam $3.5 million to make *Evil Dead II,* and it won the 1987 Golden Unicorn—the grand prize at the Paris Science Fiction & Fantasy Festival.

19

Sam Raimi
From Super-8 to Super Hit

★ I became interested in movies when I was six years old and my father would shoot 16-millimeter movies of our family and project them on a wall in the basement. I was always amazed—it was incredible to me that my father could actually capture reality and then replay it for us.

My friends and I started making movies in high school. We'd make mostly comedies. We'd all do everything; we didn't have individual titles like producer, writer, director. We'd pitch in leaf-raking money and snow-shoveling money and go to the local K mart and buy a few rolls of Super-8 film, put it in the old camera, and start making pictures.

I recommend that young filmmakers make films in Super-8 (film, not videotape) because it's a great training ground. You have all the same basic elements that are used in professional filmmaking, so it's a chance to refine your skills and techniques. You've got to write a script, deal with camera placement, movement, angles, and lenses. The actors have to be directed and orchestrated in the same manner as in 35-millimeter filmmaking. Same with the lighting and editing.

At Michigan State, my brother Ivan and I and our friend Robert Tapert decided to make Super-8 movies and market them on campus. We would shoot a Super-8 movie, edit it, and score it, then take out ads in the student newspaper. We would then show the movie in a room that we'd rent from the University. Ivan and Robert would sell and rip the tickets and I would run the projector—we had our own little movie company. We were actually making some money doing this, and Rob said, "Hey, let's try it on a big scale; let's do it like the big boys and make a professional feature film." Bruce Campbell joined the effort, and in August of 1979 we formed the limited partnership Renaissance Motion Pictures.

DROPPING OUT TO MAKE *THE EVIL DEAD*

We did some research and decided to make a horror movie because we figured horror movies, no matter how badly made, could always find a market in some drive-in somewhere. We looked and said, "Yeah, they did it right with *Night of the Living Dead* and *The Texas Chainsaw Massacre*—now if we can make one that really works, we could make our investors money." We didn't know if we could make them rich, but we figured that if the investors believed in us enough to finance the project, we had a responsibility to make a good enough picture that would break them even and hopefully make them a profit.

Because we had never made a horror movie, our first step was to learn *how* to make one. We sat in the drive-ins for a summer, and I made a couple of Super-8 horror movies with Bruce and Robert to try to figure it all out. The first ones were very, very poor—I didn't quite understand what it was all about—but finally we decided that we had the formula down. We dropped out of school and got jobs as busboys, custodians, and cabdrivers to gather seed money and begin this great undertaking.

How $150,000 Was Raised from Doctors and Dentists

I took the script for *The Evil Dead* and rewrote it to ten pages and entitled it *Within the Woods*. Robert, Bruce, and I filmed it for $1,600—a thirty-minute horror movie in Super-8 to show to potential investors as a sales tool. It showed people that we knew the horror movie basics and could scare the audience in a minor way.

The Super-8 movie crystallized exactly the type of picture we intended to make in the minds of the investors. This Super-8 showpiece was probably the biggest help toward raising the money. We also created a prospectus to enable us to sell shares in the movie legally. We took the Super-8 movie and showed it to doctors, dentists, lawyers, and anyone that might have a few extra dollars.

The fact that we wore suits and ties and had matching briefcases helped us as much as anything, I think, because an "official" image helped to instill confidence and project respectability. The venture seemed so wild to people that we needed every bit of evidence of a businesslike attitude we could muster. People thought we were crazy to drop out of college to raise such an ungodly amount of money.

There are many miserable moments for the independent filmmaker trying to raise a lot of money. Where will the next investor come from? *Where?*

But persistence is everything, and it often pays off. In Detroit, for instance, people were interested in investing in a movie because it seemed exciting and different to them. High rollers who might otherwise have put $10,000 into a trip to Las Vegas decided to take a gamble on us.

During the money-raising process I ran into plenty of con men. Most were so crooked you'd have to screw 'em into the ground to bury 'em. Watch out for the ones who say "You need $385,000 for your movie? No problem!" *Of course* $385,000 is a problem! Leave quickly. They are full of hot air. No money will come from them.

Renaissance Motion Pictures was lucky to find Irvin Shapiro of Films Around the World, Inc., a rare breed of honest man. Through his international sales of *The Evil Dead* we were able to return almost all of our investors' money.

Irvin is the man responsible for naming *The Evil Dead.* The picture was originally titled *Book of the Dead,* but Irvin tore into it a word at a time. He said, *"Book?* That'll scare off the kids. *Book*'s a nasty word to the horror crowd. They don't want to know about reading. *Of the?* That doesn't say anything. That's out. *Dead?* Hmmm. That can stay. We'll call it *The Evil Dead."*

Irvin is pure businessman. He has a very hard time believing in movie deals. His motto is "It's not a deal when they tell you it's a deal. It's not a deal when you sign the contract. It's not even a deal when you get the check. It's only a deal once you've spent the money."

That's why Irvin Shapiro is the sales agent we needed.

MAKING *EVIL DEAD II* FOR DINO DE LAURENTIIS

The biggest reason Renaissance Motion Pictures made the sequel to *The Evil Dead* was to finally throw our investors into profit. We owed them everything. Also, we wanted to star Bruce Campbell in the film without fear of studio replacement. Embassy Pictures removed Bruce from our second feature, *Crime Wave.* We knew that if we made *Evil Dead II,* no one would remove Bruce because he's the only actor who survives in the original *The Evil Dead.*

We worked with quite a few people from *The Evil Dead* on *Evil Dead II,* including cameraman Tim Philo, animator Tom Sullivan, optical effects specialist Bart Pierce, and composer Joe LoDuca. Joel Coen, who was the assistant editor on *The Evil Dead,* went on to make two successful films, *Blood Simple* and *Raising Arizona,* with his brother Ethan.

Working with DEG (De Laurentiis Entertainment Group) on *Evil Dead II* was great. Dino and the boys had some very good script comments, so we made some changes, but after that they left us very much alone. When we delivered a picture that was potentially X-rated, they said, "Okay, we realize that the strength of the picture lies in its current form; we won't go for an R rating; we'll just release it as it is." So we were able to preserve the integrity of the picture. We did go out with a disclaimer on the film saying that the picture contains "scenes of violence that may be too intense for persons under the age of seventeen."

But the lack of an R has slowed up distribution of *Evil Dead II.* Without an MPAA rating, many theater chains won't show the film, and lots of newspapers won't carry the print advertising. But I still believe we did the right thing. The original versions of *The Evil Dead* and *Evil Dead II* remain intact, and I'm very pleased about that.

My aspiration is to tell entertaining stories through the medium of film, stories that are as visually exciting as possible and that hopefully will create an experience that is uplifting for the audience.

PART V

GETTING IT IN THE CAN

"The audience, individually, is an idiot. Collectively, it's a genius."
SAM GOLDWYN

"You've got to keep attacking the audience and their values."
JACK NICHOLSON

20

Gearing Up for Production

EVEN BEFORE YOU raised your production money, your movie was technically in preproduction. You have already accomplished several important steps that cost little or no money. You have a polished script, a finalized budget, a production timetable and shooting schedule. You have gathered key props and costumes, built sets, and scouted locations. You have a pretty good idea who will be on your production staff. You have lined up a place you can use for a production headquarters—even if it has to be in your own office or your own home. Either you have already started casting (by using a casting agency if you can afford it, or perhaps by going to community theaters to scout talent if your movie's budget is too low to afford professional actors) or you have at least developed an idea of the type of actors you would like to cast. It surprises you that you have gained such a head start on all these tasks, but now you must carry them to completion before you can start the camera rolling. Now that your escrow funds have been released, you can go full steam ahead on:

- Finalizing casting and signing contracts
- Hiring the crew
- Hiring specialists
- Renting and buying equipment
- Building sets and scouting locations
- Gathering props and costumes

CASTING AND SIGNING CONTRACTS

The actors to be used in any particular film can be broken down into three basic categories: principal players, supporting players, and extras. The principal players are the ones with big parts, key roles; these are the roles that are filled by big names or stars if the production can afford them. Supporting players have the next biggest or next most demanding parts. And extras appear in only a scene or two, very briefly, usually without any lines.

How well or how poorly you cast your movie is one of the most important factors in determining its chances for success or failure. It is unwise to start shooting unless you are fully satisfied with the actors who will play the key roles.

Even if you think you are pretty sure of whom you want to cast, you still should probably have a general casting call. Many times it will result in the discovery of people who can do the job better than the ones you previously had in mind. When we cast *The Majorettes,* we didn't even pay for an ad; instead I called the entertainment editors of the major newspapers in Pittsburgh, and they wrote a few lines about our movie and the fact that we would be casting during certain hours. Over three days, 180 actors showed up. We talked to all of them, gave them a chance to read, and asked the most likely candidates to come back for screen tests, which we videotaped. Then we reviewed the tapes to finalize our cast.

Even though you are making a nonunion film, you will still need to have freelance players contracts and/or Talent, Services, and Advertising Release Forms (see Appendix for samples) signed by all the actors you cast. Usually the principals and supporting players sign contracts and releases; the extras sign only releases. A contract spells out in substantial detail the terms and conditions for employment. A release is a short-form contract basically giving the production company the right to use the voice and likeness of the actor not only in the movie to be produced but also in any publicity materials relating to the movie. When you sign a distribution contract, the distributor will require you to provide evidence that you have secured these rights from the actors, for he does not want them to sue him after the picture is released.

HIRING THE CREW

On a low-budget production the crew members do not usually sign contracts. You just talk with them individually, letting them know what the production entails and how many weeks of work will be involved, and then you settle on a weekly rate for their services. They are usually paid at the end of each working week. It isn't such a bad move on your part to give them a week's pay in advance; there are so many low-budget productions that go bust owing the crew money that you will gain much goodwill and enthusiasm by demonstrating that your production is going to be honest and aboveboard.

HIRING SPECIALISTS

People who perform special, time-consuming work behind the scenes should be hired as early as possible during preproduction to give them an opportunity to make their best contribution to your movie. Talk to your music producer, animator, costumer, and special effects expert as soon as you can. If you don't, you may cast your movie and still be unable to start shooting.

Costumes have to be made, bought, and tailored to fit the people who are going to wear them. Obviously this is a bigger problem if you're doing a period piece than if you're making a movie that takes place in a contemporary setting. In a low-budget production you should strive to have the actors supply their own outfits as much as possible. As long as the clothes are not going to be ruined during the movie's action, most actors would rather wear their own things anyway. But they will still have to bring in several choices of apparel for you to select and approve, because you might want a certain look or you may need to make sure that the costumes of various actors don't clash.

Music might have to be written and recorded for use during filming, especially if the actors are going to be shown dancing to a portion of the score so that their movements must be shot in sync with the actual piece that will be on the sound track. Even if this is not the case, you still have to start producing the music early enough for it to be ready at the same time that your scenes are ready to edit.

Casts and molds might have to be made from the bodies of the actors so that certain special effects can be pulled off. In slasher films this often involves making phony but realistic-looking arms, hands, torsos, or heads that match those of the live actors. So the actors have to be hired in plenty of time to be available for sessions with the special effects expert.

If an animated figure is going to substitute for an actor at any point in the movie, that figure has to be sculpted so as to create an accurate likeness of the actor. This can involve time-consuming posing and mold-making sessions.

Animators, costumers, special effects experts, and other specialists usually work without contracts on low-budget productions, although sometimes they may require you to execute a simple letter agreement briefly outlining what they will do for you and what the payment schedule will be. However, you will have to sign a more complicated contract with your music producer (a sample Music Agreement can be found in the Appendix).

Many times it is possible to obtain movie rights to music for free or for merely covering some of the expenses involved in producing the music. For many musicians, especially relative unknowns, having a movie score to their credit is a big career boost, and it makes the music more valuable. It may open the door to a sound track album release, release of a single that may become a hit, or a lucrative deal with a music publisher. Even if none of this happens, the public exposure that the musicians gain can lead to other jobs. Therefore, in order to gain these advantages, musicians will often make deals in which they grant the movie sound track rights, commonly called *synchronization rights,* to the movie producer free of charge, as long as they retain all other rights to their music. Sometimes the musicians are even willing to give up a percentage of these other rights to the movie producer because of the leverage that the movie producer may exert in having a sound track album produced.

RENTING AND BUYING EQUIPMENT

The main concerns pertaining to equipment, other than pricing and paying for it (see Chapter 17) are to make sure you get it in on time, that it is the *right* equipment, and that it is functioning properly. Rental outfits will usually ship the equipment package a week early on a feature production at no extra charge. This gives you time to check it out and familiarize yourself with the operation of any gear that you have not used before.

Also, your cameraman and assistant cameraman will usually want to come in a week or at least a few days prior to the first shooting day to inspect the camera equipment, clean and oil it, and run a camera test. Running a camera test involves shooting a couple hundred feet of film to make sure camera registration and lens settings are accurate. The cameraman and his assistant will screen the test footage right away. Then, if it isn't satisfactory, there is still time to order replacement equipment.

BUILDING SETS AND SCOUTING LOCATIONS

Set construction has to start in plenty of time to have the sets ready according to the shooting schedule. The locations have to be scouted and reserved, which may involve negotiating location fees. You may have to go through a lot of red tape to obtain permission to film in hospitals, military installations, public or private parks, or government buildings and offices. Don't take anything for granted. Start early in securing your clearances.

These are the main considerations in choosing locations:

- They must satisfy the aesthetic requirements of the movie.
- There must be enough room to maneuver the camera, tripod, dolly,

etc., even when the location is crowded with actors, crew people and their paraphernalia.

- It must be possible to record clean, sharp sound.
- It must be possible to light the scenes properly without blowing fuses and without wasting time trying to overcome lighting problems.
- If takes are blown and have to be reshot at a later date, it would be nice if the location will still be available in its present form. You wouldn't want to come back and find that the walls that were green in the footage you already have are now painted brown. So it would be wise to inquire to some extent about the future of the locations that you wish to use.

GATHERING PROPS AND COSTUMES

You will have to start making or ordering some props and costumes well in advance so they will be ready for the shooting schedule. Many of these items will have to be made or bought in duplicate, triplicate, or even quadruplicate if they are going to be seen in several different forms or conditions during the movie. If a blouse is to get ripped and bloodied progressively from scene to scene, and those scenes are not going to be shot in script sequence, then quite a few different versions of the blouse will be needed. You might even need several fresh blouses in order to film the effect of the blouse being damaged in more than one take.

Obtaining realistic military or police gear can present special problems. There are laws that prevent the indiscriminate sale or rental of such gear. Therefore, the producer must submit requests in writing to the officials and the outlets where military and police insignia and uniforms are to be obtained. This takes time and can be very frustrating, so don't put it off until the last week of preproduction.

Blank ammunition—something we all tend to take for granted because we've seen it used in countless movies—is not always easily accessible in every caliber. None of us had expected that buying blanks for the .30/.30 Winchester rifle in *Night of the Living Dead* would be a problem, but we had put off buying the blanks until we needed them, and they were not immediately available. Because we had already shown the rifle in scenes where it was not being fired, we felt we had to either make our own blanks or reshoot a lot of the scenes using a different rifle—and we could not afford to do that. So it ended up that all the blanks we used had to be made from live cartridges by our ammunition and demolition expert—something I would not advise anyone to do.

In movie production, perhaps more than in any other endeavor, anything that can go wrong will. So, if you have the slightest suspicion that a difficulty may be encountered here or there, tend to it right away. Make sure you have some way to back yourself up if things don't go exactly the way you would like, because they almost never will. Keep your wits and your good humor about you, and keep telling yourself that without the hassles maybe this business of making movies wouldn't be so much fun.

21

Putting the Bucks on the Screen

WHEN MOVIE PEOPLE talk about "putting the bucks on the screen," they mean that, to the fullest extent possible, the dollars spent on a production should produce visible results in the finished movie. Dollars that don't "show" on the screen are dollars wasted.

I have another way of putting it. I often say that our job is to "pull the production up by its bootstraps"—to try to make every dollar count for *more* than it's worth. You have to make people believe that your $200,000 movie might have cost $.5 million or even $1 million.

In a way, this is not as hard as it sounds, because Hollywood budgets are so bloated—loaded with dollars that don't show up on the screen—that studio executives look at every movie with an inflationary prejudice. My movie *Midnight* was made for a total of $71,000. Yet when a vice president of RKO Pictures screened it, he estimated the budget at $1 million. This is of course a compliment to my ability to get the bucks up on the screen. But it is also a wry commentary on the inability of the major studios to *think* any lower than a million.

The Majorettes cost $200,000, but it looked good enough that distributors assumed the budget must have been much higher. This helped us get enough money in advances to "make us well"—in other words, to cover our production costs. It's pretty tough to land a big advance if the distributor can tell that you're asking for more than you shelled out to make your movie. Why should he "get sick" to the tune of several hundred thousand dollars for prints and advertising after he's already coughed up a couple hundred thousand to make *you* well?

To pull a production up by its bootstraps, you can (1) tailor your script to available low-cost or *no* -cost resources that look expensive; (2) incorporate those kinds of resources into the production if you stumble onto them during the shooting, whether they were written in or not; (3) use all the free or low-cost talent that you can get; (4) wear many hats well and hire other people who can do so; (5) sweat out every detail of the production, from start to finish.

Low-cost or no-cost resources might come from your limited partners. In the case of *The Majorettes,* our executive producer, Joe Ross, came into the project wholeheartedly, not just by putting up all the cash, but by committing himself, his family, his business employees and associates, and his business property to the making of the movie. Joe had a lovely building, ideally situated in the heart of Pittsburgh, that we were able to use rent-free for our production headquarters. He owned a yacht club whose buildings and environs were perfect for about half our locations. The chef at the yacht club was persuaded by Joe to let us use his $3 million home as the Adams Estate—the swanky old mansion where majorette Vicky lived with her invalid grandmother and the sinister nurse, Helga. We were even able to situate Mace's trailer in the woods near the yacht club and to have the nearby volunteer fire department standing by handily when we blew up the trailer, the van, the motorcycle, and the car in our big wrap-up. All this represents a lot of bucks on the screen for a $200,000 movie.

Remember, once your investors sink their money into your movie, they have a huge stake in how well it turns out. Plus, they probably invested in the first place because the idea of making a movie excites them, so they'll love becoming more involved. Ask them. You have everything to gain and nothing to lose.

Many people long to be in a movie or just hang around the set, even if they don't have a nickel invested. Some of them will work their butts off for free simply for the opportunity to learn the business or to earn some sort of low-level screen credit. Use these people where you can, but don't depend on them for anything crucial until you find out how reliable they are. Some volunteers don't figure that volunteering obligates them in any way. If you ask them to make some props, they figure somebody who's getting paid will take over if they happen to slack off a little; meanwhile, the people who are getting paid are tied up on something else because the prop-making job was supposed to be covered. You're ready to shoot, and you're stuck without the props. So, make sure to use only the volunteers who understand that volunteering to do something on a movie is a commitment.

By the time you set out to make your first feature, if you've paid your dues and learned the business from the ground up, you'll be accomplished at many aspects of it. Ideally, your whole production team will be that way. I mentioned before that Paul McCollough, who worked on *Midnight* and *The Majorettes,* is a person I always like to work with, because he can light, film, edit, record sound, compose, and produce music. I'm a writer, producer, and director, as well as a cameraman-editor. I understand the whole production process, plus marketing and distribution. Paul and I together had so many areas covered that we were able to make *Midnight* with basically a four-man crew—ourselves and two others—for most of the shooting schedule. We did all the editing and finishing ourselves, too.

I'm not telling you this to brag; I'm just illustrating what you might aim for. But don't try to cut the corners too close. Even though we were able to pull it off, *Midnight* suffered considerably from lack of money. If you have the money, and it needs to be spent, spend it.

There are ways that you can put dollars on the screen by not spending anything but time. Time in preproduction. Time in casting your movie properly. Time in rehearsal. Time in going over production details with your staff and crew. Time in paying attention to fine points of makeup, set dressing, lighting, camera technique, sound recording technique, etc., that many productions—even high-budget productions—have a tendency to neglect. *Nothing* about your movie should be slipshod if you can help it. Do all that you can afford to do, and do it with professional competence and thoroughness. If your movie looks completely professional, the lack of lavish production values will not be a major handicap in landing a distributor and pulling people into the theaters.

THE DIRECTOR AS RINGLEADER

Putting the bucks up on the screen depends on everybody connected with the production, but the main responsibility is that of the director. As the director, once there is a script—whether or not you have written it yourself—you are the person who must cause it to be *realized*. In that sense you really are the creative force behind the movie. When you are successful as director, you get the lion's share of the glory. When you fail, you take most of the bad raps.

Ideally, the line producer and everybody else in the work force, including the actors, should support you, the director, to their utmost in giving birth to the movie. But it is up to you to help focus the energies and talents of everybody around you, to set a tone that enables all the rest of the people to make a solid contribution. To do this, you have to involve them to the fullest extent possible in the task at hand.

Before production begins, you should read through the script with the principal actors and key production personnel so that everyone has an overview of what must be filmed and how you envision pulling it off. If possible, these people should visit sets and locations together to discuss shot setups and special logistical considerations and to get a good idea of how the scenes will be lit and where the mikes will be placed. Doing this together will stimulate enthusiasm. It will help mold everyone into a team. Your cast and crew will come up with good ideas, and they'll help each other anticipate and avoid problems.

Even if there isn't time for a lot of rehearsal on the set, you can encourage the actors to rehearse together in their spare time. Most of them enjoy doing this. They love the idea of doing anything that will ultimately make them come off better on film. In *The Majorettes* we had some rather accomplished actors and actresses as well as some who were totally inexperienced. So we asked the experienced ones to teach the others and help them practice their lines. This considerably improved the overall quality of the acting.

A film crew is very much like a family for the duration of a motion picture production. They can either be a squabbling family or one that gets along splendidly. You, the ringleader, set the tone. And the fortunes of the production rise or fall according to your ability to get everyone to chime in and play on key.

HOW A SHOOTING DAY SHOULD PROCEED

The planning and preparation for a shooting day actually starts months ahead of time, because if this isn't done properly, the day will almost certainly be a disaster. Someone won't show up. Someone will show up in the wrong costume. The set or location won't look right. There won't be enough power for the lights. A vital piece of camera equipment will be missing. A prop won't be there when needed, or it won't function properly.

Once you're actually into the shooting schedule, each day starts the day before. At the end of each shooting day the producer and/or director have to meet with key members of the staff to go over who and what will be needed tomorrow. Failing to do this has a tendency to produce unpleasant surprises of the sort mentioned in the preceding paragraph.

A shooting day should start *very early.* On a thirty-day shooting schedule, you must get an average of three finished minutes of screen time per day to come up with a ninety-minute feature. *The Majorettes* had thirty scenes spread over sixteen locations. We had to crank out about one scene per day and still allow gaps of time for breaking down and moving from one location to another. This is not a piece of cake. Most scenes require numerous camera setups. Sometimes it will take hours to set up and light a single shot. Therefore, shooting days routinely are ten, twelve, fourteen, sixteen hours long.

Another important reason for starting very early in the morning is that it often takes an hour or two to get all the actors made up and in costume—if there is no *special* makeup like wounds, scars, black eyes. If an actor has to be rigged with squibs—exploding devices that simulate bullet blasts—then it is going to take even longer. The crew should be setting up for the first shot while the actors are being readied. If you're lucky, everybody will be ready to go at about the same time.

It is wise for the producer and director to have some fill-in or pickup shots for the crew to do just in case something fouls up and everybody *isn't* ready to go at the same time. For instance, it may be that "approach shots" are needed

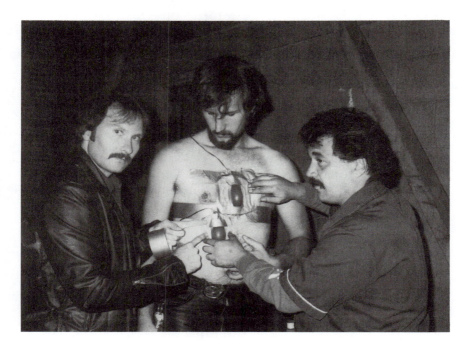

An actor being rigged with squibs—explosive blood packets to simulate gunshot wounds. The rigging and filming of even the simplest special effects take much time and careful planning so the shooting schedule won't be blown. *Photo by John Russo.*

of one of the actors driving to the present location. If he's ready to go and the other actors aren't, a skeleton crew can be dispatched to get those shots instead of sitting around doing nothing.

To give a practical example of a day in the life of a shooting schedule, let's pull some sample scenes from my location breakdown chart for *The Majorettes:*

LOCATION	SCENE NO.	CAST	NO. DAYS	PROPS	COSTUMES	SPECIAL CON.
Barbara's house	11 and 12	Barbara Braden Martell Coroner Cops Morgue attendants Jeff Judy Crowd	1	Baton Knife Note Body bag Coroner's bag	Shorts and halter Swimming suit Cop outfits White coats	Heat pool for stabbing Fake torso and blood, etc. Morgue wagon Cop cars Jeff's car

Note: You can see that Scenes 11 and 12 were to be shot in one day (actually a night shooting). The location chart doesn't list anybody to play the killer because Sheriff Braden *was* the killer, so he'd be playing a double role.

Now, because we were late in getting all the production money together for *The Majorettes,* instead of being able to shoot in the middle of summer, as planned, we couldn't get started until almost fall. We had two weeks of exteriors that had to be shot in the front part of the schedule, even though logistically it would have been better to shoot some of those exterior scenes later. But if we waited, the leaves might start to change to their fall colors—giving the lie to the summer setting of the screenplay.

The late start meant that we had to shoot Scene 11, a nighttime swimming pool scene, on September 24. We were hoping for Indian summer weather, but we didn't get it. It was only forty degrees that night when Dana Maiello, playing the part of Barbara, had to go into Bill Hinzman's swimming pool. She was okay while she was in the heated water, but every time she got out into the cold air she just about froze to death.

In Scene 11, Barbara, one of the majorettes, gets murdered in her swimming pool. A hooded murderer yanks her out of the water by her hair and stabs her. This shot DISSOLVES to Barbara being zipped into a body bag. The coroner is on the scene with Sheriff Braden and Lieutenant Martell. Barbara's mom and dad are there crying as the morgue attendants carry her body away.

Scene 12 picks up as the morgue attendants carry the body around to the front of the house, where there is a crowd of onlookers. Quarterback Jeff Halloway and majorette Judy Marino, his girlfriend, are among the onlookers. Jeff and Judy are both broken up over Barbara's murder, and as the cops try to push them aside, Jeff insists on talking to Sheriff Braden and giving his testimony about the gang leader, Mace Jackson.

Since these were night scenes, obviously we had to wait until dark to start shooting. But we still asked everybody to be at the location at four o'clock. There was plenty to do before nightfall:

1. We had to set up the cop cars, Jeff's car, and the morgue wagon in the front of the house.

2. The actors had to rehearse their lines. Since I was playing the coroner, and I'm not an accomplished actor, I was in dire need of the rehearsal time.

3. All the props had to be checked out, and the camera placements and other important details of the gore effects had to be discussed with special effects man Jerry Gergely.

4. The extras for the crowd scene had to sign releases. The scene had to be explained to them, since they were novices. The ones who were selected to be cops or morgue attendants had to be given their costumes, and the costumes had to be pinned, stitched, or adjusted to look right.

We shot Scene 12 ahead of Scene 11 so we would finish as early as possible with the mob of extras and then could concentrate on the actual murder with its special effects. Then we filmed the aftermath of the murder—after taking a break for the dead Barbara to be made up as a corpse so that I, as the coroner, could deliver a little speech about autopsies and so on to Braden and Martell.

We blocked the action for Scene 12 to consist of:

1. A PULLBACK SHOT from the strobing lights of the sheriff's car to ESTABLISH THE CROWD as the morgue attendants bring the stretcher and body bag around the side of the house.
2. A MEDIUM SHOT of Jeff and Judy, both sobbing, as he tells her he can no longer keep silent.
3. A PANNING SHOT of Jeff and Judy approaching one of the cops and asking to see Sheriff Braden.

With one problem or another—neighborhood traffic noise spoiling our sound takes or nosy kids peeping into a shot—it took us from dark until about ten o'clock to knock off Scene 12. Then we got rid of the extras, and Jeff and Judy took off, and we started on Scene 11. It wasn't just a straight-up-and-down murder. The killer had to toy with Barbara first, stalking her, building suspense. Some of the key episodes within the scene were these:

1. Barbara comes into the kitchen and reads a note from her parents telling her they'll be out. She hears a noise—a door? Who is it, if her parents are out? She shrugs and goes into her bedroom, where she strips and puts on her bikini.
2. The murderer watches her as she strips. His knife glints in the foreground of the shot. As she goes out to the swimming pool, he follows her. We employed numerous additional techniques to build suspense—a phone call, disturbing noises, movements of Barbara and the killer back and forth around the place—before she actually dove into the pool. All this business involved different camera, lighting, and sound setups.
3. Finally, she started swimming. We took plenty of shots here to stretch out the suspense.
4. The actual murder took several hours. Jerry Gergely had made an appliance that would spurt fake blood when slashed with the knife, and he had also made a replica of Barbara's torso that would spurt fake blood when stabbed—but this had to be filmed in extreme close-up so the edges of the prop wouldn't be seen inside the frame line. All of these gore effects are very

messy to work with. Numerous takes and various angles have to be shot for adequate coverage. And, *of utmost importance,* cover shots have to be taken that are not so gory, in case the gore shots wouldn't be passed by the MPAA Rating Commission for an R rating. Cutaways that are entirely free of gore must also be taken for television release.

5. Once Barbara was sufficiently "dead" for cinematic purposes, Jerry Gergely had to make her up as a bloodless corpse. This took a couple of hours. So, in the meantime, we shot the part of the conversation among the sheriff, the lieutenant, and the coroner that takes place after the body bag is already zipped up. We did this with a dummy in the bag, made up of wadded-up rags and newspapers and so on. Then we got the close-up of the corpse as I zipped the bag shut.

It was almost dawn before we could say "It's a wrap!" As the crew broke down the equipment and loaded the truck, I met with the director and the production assistants to go over last-minute details for the next scene on our shooting schedule. Since we had just worked all night, there would be no filming tomorrow. But that didn't mean we could sleep all day. We had to meet at the production headquarters to screen the dailies from our previous day's shooting. We also had phone calls to make to actors and extras, costumes to clean, and props to tinker with, to make sure everything would be ready next time the director yelled "Action!"

22

Editing and Finishing

ONCE THE FOOTAGE is "in the can," we move into the part of movie-making that I like best—the postproduction phase. I don't like shootings very much. They are full of hassles and worries and have a tendency to wreck your health because you're going for days and days working at full speed with barely enough sleep to keep your brain cells alive.

During postproduction, unless you're on some kind of insane deadline (like the film is already booked into theaters and the first playdates are only a month and a half away), you can get some decent rest and at least show up fresh each day to do your syncing and interlocking. Here is where you'll experience the thrill of seeing what you filmed start to come together for the first time. To me, this is the real fun of filmmaking. All the rest up to this point is like gathering clay. Now the clay is in your hands, and you can mold it and play with it without worrying about an airplane flying overhead and screwing up the sync sound.

Postproduction proceeds in the following stages:

1. Syncing and interlocking
2. Making a rough cut
3. Making a polished edit
4. Cutting music and effects tracks
5. Making a final mix
6. Building in titles and optical effects
7. Conforming
8. Making an answer print

SYNCING AND INTERLOCKING

If you can find enough money in your budget, it's a good idea to pay an assistant editor to have your takes synced while you're still shooting. You can make an arrangement with your motion picture laboratory to do the actual syncing, and if the lab is close to where you are shooting, you can stop by to screen the picture-and-sound takes in sync on a special projector designed for that purpose, called an *interlock projector*.

If you can't afford to pay extra for syncing, try to make the time to do it yourself. That way you get the jump on the job of editing your picture, and you can shoot with confidence, knowing that everything is in sync and is looking and sounding good.

To sync takes, you work from camera-and-sound logs kept by the crew during shooting. Here is the way a sample log sheet might look:

CAMERA/SOUND LOG

Date _9/12/80_   Title _THE MAJORETTES_
Company _MAJORETTES, INC._
Director _HINZMAN_   Cameraman _McCOLLOUGH_
Magazine # _1_   Roll # _1_   Emulsion _5247_

SCENE NO.	PIC. TAKE NO.	SOUND TAKE NO.	REMARKS
1	1	1	N.G.
"	2	2	N.G
"	3	3	GOOD
"	4	4	GOOD SAFETY
"	5	W/LD	GOOD
"	6	W/LD	GOOD

Special Lab Instructions _PRINT ALL TAKES_

Good Footage _273_
N.G. Footage _127_
Total Footage _400_

Date, company, title, director, and cameraman are self-explanatory. The magazine number was important, because if the footage had been scratched during filming, we would have known to look toward that particular magazine as the possible culprit, and we wouldn't have used that particular magazine again until we knew for sure that it was okay. The roll number helped us keep track of our footage budget during shooting, and now it helps us find a particular scene if it needs to be examined or even reprinted for any reason. The emulsion, 5247, is the Eastman Kodak code for 35-millimeter color film-stock, which told the lab how to process what we had shot.

Note that the lab was instructed to print all takes, whether good or no good (N.G.). Sometimes you can save money in work printing by printing only the good takes. But when I'm making a low-budget picture on a low footage ratio, I like to print and screen *everything*. (Because of the low footage ratio, we couldn't have saved much money by printing only selected takes anyway.) Sometimes a piece of a supposedly N.G. take can be used to "save" a scene in editing, so I like to have that freedom. Sometimes a take that was labeled "good" does not look so good when it is screened. A continuity blivet might be spotted that was missed during shooting. Or, because of that magic we call *screen presence,* a take that was previously rated second best might turn out to be the one that shines.

The takes for each scene are synced in the order in which they were shot, and the wild takes for each scene are spliced together on separate rolls. Then all this material is screened, scene by scene, so that the first editorial decisions can be made.

All the material pertaining to a particular scene is always kept together (for instance, in a single box or plastic bag) in a well-organized editing room so that whatever is needed can be found immediately. All we have to do is look in the bag marked "Scene 1," and we will find the Scene 1 sync rolls, wild footage rolls, wild sound rolls, camera logs, and anything else pertaining to Scene 1.

MAKING A ROUGH CUT

During screening of all the sync and wild takes, the editor takes notes, marking down the director's final choices of best takes and participating in a discussion with the director and producer as to how the scene should be put together. Then the editor, on his own or with the director, can put together a first edit, called the *rough cut.* This is a stringing together of most of the shots in the approximate order that they will appear in the finished movie. Certain cutaways and inserts might be missing at first. Certain shots might go on too long, to be trimmed and shortened once the overall rough cut can be viewed and a good idea of screen time and pace can be established.

In rough-cutting *The Majorettes,* we let all of our murder scenes play very long at first, going for the maximum of screen time. Because of the low footage ratio while we were shooting, the relatively short shooting schedule, and so on, we were not entirely sure that we had enough stuff in the can to make a tight, suspenseful 90-minute movie. We thought we might have to "stretch" certain scenes merely for screen time. So we wanted to see how the overall movie played and how much running time we actually had before we made our final editing decisions and shortened those scenes to a more effective pace.

"When you're shooting a film, you're constantly surrounded by people and exhausted from not getting any sleep. Then production finishes, and you can just take all your footage and go into a room and send everyone away and do anything you want with the stuff. In other words, you can experiment with it. That's why I like the editing part of filmmaking best—the cutting and chopping."

Lizzie Borden

MAKING A POLISHED EDIT

To me, it is imperative that the director work closely with the editor throughout the entire editing process, from rough cut to polished edit. I have found that some editors forget that the scenes were blocked and shot a certain way in order to be edited a certain way. In other words, an editor often will, for one reason or another, fail to reconstruct the director's thinking and will put the scenes together in an entirely different way than the director envisioned. He will do this even when given copious notes, storyboards, and shot breakdown lists. The only way for the director to make sure that the movie comes together the way he wants it is to be present for the entire creative process.

The director is the one who, above all, must have an accurate overview of the movie and the weight and importance of each shot, each scene. He must evaluate the pacing. He must be able to tell a cinematic story with unity, coherence, and emphasis. By screening and evaluating the rough cut, he knows which scenes have to be shortened, which ones lengthened, and which ones drastically reedited or even eliminated. He can determine where a proper musical score can rescue a scene and where music should be dropped in favor of unenhanced dialogue and/or sound effects.

Little by little, by painstakingly cutting, trimming, and reediting, the polished edit starts to take shape. From a technical standpoint, the objective is to get the dialogue to play crisply and interestingly and to get the nondialogue scenes to seem to play well even without scoring or SFX. It is unwise to rely too heavily on the ability of music and SFX to rescue a scene. If you can get it to play well without these embellishments, *then* you can be sure you have a good scene, which will only be enhanced when the rest of the sound track is added.

The dialogue is not usually edited end to end on one sync roll. Instead it is "laid up" (edited) in the synchronizer on two synchronous rolls, called *A&B rolls*. By doing it this way, if certain dialogue overlaps other dialogue, or if dialogue needs to be segued from scene to scene, this can be done in a preliminary mix, called a *premix*. During this premix, any dialogue that must be treated with special attention (for instance, altered in volume or timbre) is given that treatment by the sound engineer.

CUTTING MUSIC AND EFFECTS TRACKS

There may be scenes in your movie that must be carried by music or SFX. For instance, right after our title and opening credit sequence, *The Majorettes* opened with a dance number performed by the majorettes, which we shot in sync to music produced by Paul McCollough. There was dialogue leading into the number and dialogue afterward.

Because this was a key scene, designed to introduce the girls in a favorable light and make them look attractive, charming, and sexy, all the editing, including the editing to music, was started right away, along with our dialogue editing. Usually, though, all the dialogue is edited first. Then music and effects are added. Generally there are at least two rolls of music, called *A&B music rolls.* The music is laid up in the synchronizer on two rolls to allow for overlapping and segueing (fading one piece of music out and another in) when the two pieces of music are mixed together. When music has to be mixed this way, it is done in a premix. Sound effects are handled the same way, in A&B sound rolls, which are mixed down to one SFX roll in a premix. The objective is to end up with one roll of dialogue, one roll of music, and one roll of SFX, all in sync with each other.

When sales are made to foreign countries, the music and effects tracks (M&E tracks) are vitally important. They must be as polished and complete as possible, without gaps where SFX are noticeably missing. The foreign distributor will dub in actors speaking in the language of his particular country, and this will replace your English dialogue track. Then the foreign postdubbed dialogue track will be mixed with your original M&E tracks to make a finished sound track for your movie that is suitable for release in the foreign country.

Don't scrimp on sound effects. Even when you think a scene is carried by music, it will generally still be better if sound effects are added. The lack of a full and complete SFX track is a sure sign of amateurism—it's one way to get your movie labeled low-budget, which is exactly what you don't want. Taking the time and trouble to do the SFX track right is one important way to pull your movie up by its bootstraps. Be inventive and creative. For example, if you're doing a horror movie, you can experiment with weird, eerie sounds of your own creation. In *Night of the Living Dead* there are reverberating drills and ratchets and screams played backward through our mixing gear. We had a ball getting together in our studio and inventing unique sounds for our first feature.

Before you do any of your premixes, you must make a mixing log. In the log, for each and every roll of dialogue, music, and sound effects, including all the A&B rolls, you must list the footage counts where each sound occurs and where it ends. If you are mixing onto 35-millimeter tape, your footage counts must be in 35-millimeter, even if you did your editing in 16-millimeter. You have to use a 16–35 synchronizer to figure out where each sound will occur when your 16-millimeter rolls are mixed to 35-millimeter format for final printing, because that is the format your sound engineer will be working in.

Below is a sample mixing log for reel number one of my movie *Midnight:*

TITLE __MIDNIGHT__ DATE __JUNE 1980__ REEL # __1__

DIAL A	DIAL B	FX A	FX B	MUSIC A	MUSIC B
22½ BEEP		22½ BEEP			22½ BEEP
			25 WIND	25 MUSIC IN	
		45 SCREAMS			
82½ MAMA		88½			
		91½ SCREAMS			91½ FI
114 MAMA					
				126 FO	
	132 GIRL				
	150 MAMA				
154 MAMA					
160		160			
		162 HIT	162		
	163		163 BODY FALL		
	165 HIT IT!				
		166 HITS	166 LAUGH		
			172 WIND		
		174		174 FI	
	177 GROUP				

Note that even the beeps are logged—the frames where a high-pitched tone is placed on the tracks so we can hear where to sync them up. On the A dialogue roll, the first sound we hear after the beep is Mama talking; the log shows that this happens at 82 1/2 feet. On the A FX roll, the first sounds after the beep are some screams, at 45 feet. They stop at 88 1/2 feet and start again at 91 1/2 feet. On the A music roll, the first music cuts in at 25 feet and fades out (FO) at 126 feet. There is a music segue here, because on the B music roll we can see that another piece of music is fading in (FI) at 91 1/2 feet as the piece of music on A is fading out.

By scrutinizing the mixing log, you can tell where all the sounds occur and how they overlap. This guides you and the sound engineer through the entire premix. Once you have dialogue, music, and sound effects each on their own separate tracks, you are ready for:

MAKING A FINAL MIX

The whole process of mixing is truly enjoyable, because you are seeing all the pictures and sounds of your movie working together for the first time. As you mix, you are watching the edited picture in sync with all the A&B rolls of edited sound. Along the way, the sound engineer is making numerous improvements, working with the track ingredients electronically to make them sound their best.

As you work toward your final mix, you can even add sounds that may have been forgotten or overlooked in the editing stage. Professional mixing studios carry an unbelievably extensive library of sounds on reels and cassettes. When we mixed *Midnight,* at Magno Sound in New York, engineer Aaron Nathanson helped us improve our tracks immeasurably by dubbing in wind rustles, footsteps, and numerous other ambient sounds from his own library. It was this process that reinforced the aforementioned credo for me: no matter how good a movie plays without certain effects, it will almost always be enhanced if you take the trouble to add them.

Paul McCollough and I greatly appreciated the opportunities to make our tracks better. For example, there was a scene in *Midnight* where some teenagers were chased by cops in a patrol car. But the start of the chase seemed dead, even though the music and SFX came in on cue. So I went into the recording booth right there in the mixing studio and dubbed some ad-lib lines from a "police radio dispatcher" onto our final mix. As I dubbed the lines, Aaron electronically gave them a tinny "squawk-box" sound that lent them authenticity.

Take full advantage of the embellishments that a professional mixing studio can offer. But don't go in there expecting the studio to bail you out. We mixed *Midnight*—a complete feature—in only three days, and the mix cost us $6,000. Can you imagine the expense had we gone in there unprepared and had wasted a couple of days just fooling around and getting our premix tracks and log sheets in the proper order?

BUILDING IN TITLES AND OPTICAL EFFECTS

Many times you can have the lab or the animation house design and shoot your title and credit sequence and other special sequences even while you are editing and mixing. For instance, we gave a dub of a piece of eerie music that

Paul McCollough produced especially for the opening of *The Majorettes* to Bob Wolcott of The Animators, Inc. before we even began editing the rest of our picture, so Bob could get started right away making us an animated opening. He used the artwork that was on the cover of my novel *The Majorettes:* a skeleton with a twirling baton. On the animation stand he did smooth camera moves on aspects of this artwork, shot exactly to the beat of the weird music. He made the title of the movie "materialize" out of the skeleton's eyes. Each time the skeleton twirled the baton, one of the opening credits would appear. We ended up with a suitably creepy, impressive opening to *The Majorettes,* and all we had to do, other than supplying the artwork and the clearance from the artist, was to cut Bob's negative into the place slotted for it at the beginning of reel number one.

Even if you don't have elaborate matte effects, animated creatures, and so on in your movie, you will still have, at the very simplest level, titles and credits that must be shot and supered over your live action scenes. This stuff needs to be shot on an animation stand, and your lab needs to do special types of printing to make a composite title-and-credit sequence. Start this work as early as you can and communicate fully and effectively with your suppliers so you won't lose time down at the end of the production schedule.

Very important: When the title of your movie appears on the screen, the COPYRIGHT NOTICE must appear, too. Make sure that this notice is built into your printing negative. (See Chapter 25 to learn how to register your movie with the Library of Congress and furnish deposit copies to the Register of Copyrights in order to secure full protection of your ownership rights under the law.)

CONFORMING

Once you approve a final mix and a final picture edit, your camera negative must be conformed (matched) to your edited work print. If you have shot in 35-millimeter and edited in 16-millimeter, the job of conforming involves using a 16–35 synchronizer. Conforming 16-millimeter to 35-millimeter is a painstaking process but is not too difficult to learn. The first time I did it was with *Night of the Living Dead,* and I pulled and spliced more than a thousand shots without cutting in an incorrect shot or scratching the negative.

Damaging the negative is the single greatest worry in conforming. If you are not going to handle the job on your own, make sure that you hire a fastidiously dependable conformer. If your lab is a good one, it should be able to provide this service satisfactorily, but don't take anything for granted. If possible, use only a conformer you have used before or check with other filmmakers to get recommendations.

It usually takes about three weeks to get a feature movie conformed. But it can take much longer, depending on the speed and proficiency of the person doing it, so get a tight estimate beforehand. And don't expect the job to be done overnight.

MAKING AN ANSWER PRINT

Once the negative is conformed, the mix is finished, and all title and credit sequences or other special sequences are cut into your 35-millimeter negative, you are almost ready to have your very first print, the answer print, made. Before this can be done, the negative will be "timed." *Timing* is a process by which the scenes in a movie are closely examined to determine any color or exposure corrections that should be made in printing.

I would advise the director to sit with the timer during this entire process. There may be a scene that was underlit for a spooky effect, and without knowing this the timer would brighten all the shots, inadvertently destroying their impact. The timer's notion of "correct" flesh tones might not jibe with the director's notion; left to his own devices, the timer might add too much red to flesh tones that were perfectly natural in the first place, giving all the actors a rosy, Christmassy hue. Don't laugh. I have seen this kind of thing happen again and again.

If you have tons of money in your budget, you can afford to leave the timer alone and wait to see how the answer print turns out, then screen it, ask for adjustments, and have still another print pulled. And so on, until you are satisfied. But most low-budget productions can't afford that sort of luxury, so sit with the timer all the way through. Then your answer print will probably be quite usable.

Screening the first print of your movie is a thrilling moment, the culmination of months, even years, of hope and hard work. You deserve to relax for a bit and enjoy the feelings of pride and satisfaction. Don't forget the cast and crew—and the limited partners who put their faith and trust in you. Invite all of them to a special screening. Let them join you in celebration. At last you have a real movie to show and sell!

PART VI

THERE'S MORE TO MAKING A MOVIE THAN MAKING A MOVIE

"We are not limited to just the so-called 'formula' pictures, but are willing and eager to be associated with the 'challenge' picture, that project that challenges all the creative resources of the New World production and marketing team."

ROBERT M. CHEREN
New World Pictures

"I'm not in the art business. I'm in the 'ort' business. As in, 'Your movies ort to make money.'"

EARL OWENSBY
E. O. Pictures

23

Understanding the Pipeline: A Distribution Overview

BEFORE YOU SET out to sell your movie, you must understand what rights you are selling and whom you are selling them to. You must also understand how and when to sell the various rights in and to your movie so that they can be exploited to their utmost value. In other words, you must have a knowledge of the distributors and the distribution pipeline.

THE RIGHTS TO YOUR MOVIE

You and your partners financed and produced your movie on your own, without any help from a distributor. At this point you own it free and clear. What exactly do you own? You own *all* the rights. Here is how *all the rights* was defined when all the rights to *Night of the Living Dead* were sold to the Walter Reade Organization:

> Licensor does hereby give, grant and assign to Reade the sole and exclusive right, license and privilege to distribute, exhibit, rent, advertise by any means, sell, exploit, transmit, perform, release, rerun, subdistribute, sublicense and otherwise market all parts of the picture in any and all languages and versions, in all sizes and gauges of film for all purposes and by every means, method, medium and process and device now or hereafter known, invented, developed, contemplated or devised and to use, perform, publish, record and otherwise exploit any and all music and musical compositions contained in the picture. . . .

Quite a mouthful. You can see that even though video cassettes weren't invented yet, Reade got the rights to them by means of the clause "any process and device now or hereafter known, invented, developed, contemplated or devised." We sold all the rights to *Night of the Living Dead* to a single distributor. You don't necessarily have to go that route with your movie. But usually if a distributor is going to pay you a healthy advance and then plunk a huge amount of cash into prints and advertising, he *will* demand a share of all the rights, including (in layperson's language):

- Domestic and foreign theatrical rights
- Domestic and foreign nontheatrical rights (distribution to ships, airlines, hotels, military bases, colleges, clubs, nonprofit organizations, etc.)
- Domestic and foreign television rights
- Domestic and foreign home video rights
- Ancillary rights such as the right to develop and produce remakes, sequels, TV series, or stage plays based on the original movie or screenplay
- Merchandising rights, such as novelizations, sound track albums, music videos; also, tie-in items like T-shirts, toys, and other specialty goods featuring the movie's title, logo, characters, story content, or spin-offs (new concepts or creations inspired by the original movie) thereof.

If you land the right distributor, it can be a good move to let him market all aspects of your movie. This gives him such a big stake in its success that he can ill afford to distribute it halfheartedly. With more than one market to help him amortize his investment, he may be able to justify paying you a substantial advance and putting a sizable chunk of cash into prints and advertising.

THE DISTRIBUTORS

Motion picture distributors can be divided into four basic categories:

- Majors
- Mini-majors
- Independents
- Producers who elect to distribute their own product

The *major distributors* are of course the big studios like Paramount and Columbia Pictures, who not only produce major motion pictures but also maintain their own distribution offices in most of the thirty-two territories or "exchanges" that the United States has been divided into for purposes of marketing motion pictures. The majors spend an average of $20 million per picture. And each major may make eight to fifteen pictures a year. They have the clout to put those pictures into the widest possible distribution. When a bigger-than-average picture gets a major send-off, it may open in one thousand or more theaters all at the same time. That means one thousand prints will be pulled, at a cost of $1,500 apiece, for a total of $1.5 million. Another $5 million to $8 million will be spent on national advertising. So, all told, it can cost up to $30 million to make and successfully launch a major motion picture.

The *mini-major distributors,* like New World and Orion, may maintain offices in the key exchanges only and rely on subdistributors to handle the other territories. The "subs" are paid a percentage of the box office, usually 15 to 25 percent. In general, the mini-majors are not as heavily capitalized as the majors and don't spend $18 million or more to make a picture. Instead they are likely to spend $3 million to $5 million when they produce and finance a picture in house. Sometimes they make special arrangements with a major studio to give a major release to a picture that seems especially promising. But, even operating on their own through their own exchanges and subs, they are quite capable of engineering a wide national release.

The *independent distributors,* like Troma, Inc., and Independent-International Pictures Corporation, generally do not maintain offices in any of the exchanges outside their home base. Within the home base they may handle all distribution on their own, but outside of it they rely entirely on subdistributors. The smaller independents usually launch a picture on a sort of "tryout" basis. *Night of the Living Dead* was launched this way. The Walter Reade Organization initially pulled only fourteen prints of the picture and opened it in Pittsburgh in fourteen neighborhood and drive-in theaters. When it played to packed houses, they pulled a few more prints and moved the picture to Philadelphia, then Cleveland. Eventually, by continuing to pull prints as money came in, and moving the picture around territory by territory, most of the available theaters in the United States were covered, and we racked up about three thousand playdates. But it took a couple of years to do so, and it took longer than that to collect most of our money. I say "most" because the rest never was collected. Like many independents, The Reade Organization lacked the money and manpower to take legal action against the theaters that didn't want to pay.

The *producer who distributes his own movie* is in effect acting as a first-time independent distributor. In his home city he can probably do a fairly good job, but outside of it he is dependent on subs who will have little inclination to give his picture their full attention or to pay him fairly or on time. He is in an even worse position than the established independents in this regard, because he has no track record, no experience, and presumably no future product line to motivate the subs and the theater chains to treat him respectfully. Sometimes the only reason an independent distributor collects any money at all is that the people who owe it are entertaining hopes of booking more of his pictures at some later date.

THE PIPELINE

The distribution pipeline—the network of outlets for marketing motion pictures and their ancillary rights—is hungry for product. But it must be the right kind of product; in other words, it must be product that the distributors feel can be resold successfully to the public. Let's assume that your movie fits the bill and the pipeline is anxious to gobble it up. If you have retained rights to certain territories, or even if you simply wish to understand what the distributor is doing and aid him in marketing your picture, you must know how to line up the various outlets and feed them on the proper schedule to maximize the dollar return on your movie. For instance, you will not want it to be shown on network TV before it opens in the theaters, because people won't want to come out and see it after they've already seen it. And you won't want it to play on cable television before you've had a chance to sell cassettes, because by then anybody who wants a cassette of it will have already made himself a dub from the cable broadcast.

Generally, the best order in which for you to feed the pipeline is as follows:

1. Play your picture in the theaters. This is not only a major source of revenue; it is also a major source of publicity. Even if the picture doesn't do tremendously well, millions of people will find out about it through the distributor's promotion campaign and through cooperative advertising, which is advertising whose costs are shared by the distributor and the theater owners and recouped by them right off the top of box office receipts.

2. Go for a network television sale. If the picture is very successful theatrically—or even if the network executives anticipate that it will be—you might make a big score. The likelihood of doing this on a low-budget movie is not too great but is not entirely out of the question either. *Prom Night,* a modestly budgeted horror flick, landed a network sale of $3 million.

If you fail to sell to the networks, don't sell *any* further TV rights at the moment (or, if you do sell them, don't allow them to be exercised for twelve to eighteen months after the date that the contracts are signed). The money you can gain won't be enough to justify crippling your ability to:

3. Exploit home video rights. The video distributor will love the free publicity your picture has already gotten through its theatrical release. This huge amount of regional or national promotion is usually a guarantee of a substantial number of videocassette sales, both to individual purchasers and video rental businesses.

4. Exploit TV syndication and cable rights after you have sold as many videocassettes as you can.

5. Clean up on nontheatrical sales.

I left out foreign sales. That's because the foreign markets can be sold before and during the time that you are doing any or all of the above. But *within* each foreign country or territory, the best marketing plan will generally proceed as I have outlined: the picture will be moved from a theatrical release to a network television release to a home video release and so on.

I also left out ancillary sales. These can also be sold while your movie is being distributed as I have outlined. But certain tie-ins, like novels and sound track albums, ideally should be landed well before the movie's release if at all possible. That way, the book publisher or record company has a chance to coordinate his efforts with the launching of the movie and contribute in a big way to the media blitz. However, even if it is not possible to land ancillary sales beforehand, if your movie is successful at the box office these types of sales will later become possible. My novelization of *Night of the Living Dead* didn't come out until 1974, six years after the release of the movie, but by that time it had become a so-called cult classic, and Warner Books paid me a hefty advance for writing the book.

If you sell all the rights to your movie to an overall distributor, ideally he will know how to play all the potential markets for maximum revenue. But your best bet is to negotiate a distribution contract that allows you a voice in the decision-making process, which is not always as clear-cut as I have outlined. For instance, the possibility of a fat home video advance may arise, tempting you to forgo theatrical distribution entirely or to settle for a moderate, abbreviated theatrical release. You can make these kinds of choices wisely only if you truly understand the distribution pipeline and are not completely dependent upon the whims of the distributor.

In the next chapter you'll hear from Christopher and Linda Lewis, two filmmakers who decided to control both the making *and* the distribution of their movies by producing them for the home video market and tailoring the budgets accordingly. The exciting thing about this style of production is that it is probably the easiest and cheapest way for the young, under-financed movie-maker to break into his first feature.

Linda and Christopher Lewis review production reports at their studio in Tulsa. *Photo courtesy of The Entertainment Group.*

Christopher and Linda Lewis shot their first movie on videotape for a measly $27,000, and it grossed $1 million in video stores. Their new company, The Entertainment Group, in Tulsa, Oklahoma, is now turning out a series of made-for-home-video movies, each budgeted at $250,000 to $300,000.

24

Christopher and Linda Lewis
Movies for Home Video

★ CHRIS: My mother is the actress Loretta Young, and my father is a producer, Tom Lewis, so at an early age I kind of got inundated with the movie business. When I was sixteen, my father told me that if I wanted to get into films I had to learn from the ground up, so I got a job as an assistant film editor in a commercial production house in New York called Farkus Films. They did TV commercials and industrials. And then in college I went to the University of Southern California cinema school and happened to be in the same class as George Lucas, Randal Kleiser, and John Milius. Lucas, Kleiser, and I had a little company together. While in college, we made little music videos and inserts for a local television show in Los Angeles. So aside from learning how to edit film and all that, while we were at school we got some practical experience in the television business. After graduation I stayed in television as an associate producer, while Lucas, Kleiser, and Milius went on to great success in the motion picture end.

Linda and I met in 1973, when she came to Los Angeles to work as a researcher on documentary films. We were married in 1976, and at that time there was a recession in the movie business. So we worked in TV for a while, then moved here to Tulsa, where I worked for the ABC affiliate as a news reporter. That eventually grew into my producing *PM Magazine* here as well as co-hosting the popular show.

MAKING *BLOOD CULT* ON $27,000

Linda had an advertising agency here in Tulsa with a show where she did movie reviews. She also did a travel show that was aired on several local cable systems. Around 1984 or 1985 our *PM Magazine* was canceled, and instead of going back to doing news, Linda and I talked to a friend, Bill Blair, who owned a film distribution company called United Home Video. He was having a difficult time getting enough product to distribute to the home video market, so we decided to try to make a low-budget movie together going straight to video distribution and bypassing the theaters altogether. We felt that the home video market, with its fast growth, was the market of the future for movies. Bill Blair invested $27,000 in us, we made *Blood Cult,* and it sold fifteen thousand cassettes and grossed about $1 million.

LINDA: After that, we made *The Ripper* and *Revenge,* then *The Terror of Tenkiller.* With *Blood Cult* our timing was right because in about November 1984 the covers of both *Time* and *Newsweek* talked about the VCR revolution, and Bill Blair had the ready-made network for distributing to video stores, and Chris and I over the years had been talking about marrying television techniques we had learned with the production values associated with making a movie. On *Blood Cult* we got our friends together from the TV stations here in Tulsa. We all took vacation time to make a short-order picture and shot it in nine days, very much like a television show or soap opera.

CHRIS: We talked Sony into leasing us a couple of Betacams at a reduced rate, so our first feature was shot basically with the same equipment you'd do a news program with. You can shoot and edit on Beta equipment, and the other thing that's so good about it is you can run a really small crew because the recorder and camera are all in one unit, and you don't have a lot of wires going all over the set. Plus, the cameras work very well in low light conditions.

LINDA: *Blood Cult* and *The Ripper* retailed at $59.95, and *Revenge* went out at $69.95. They sold very well, considering they had never been shown in theaters, and proved to us that films can be made anywhere in the country now. Hollywood and New York are not the film centers anymore. And if you have an inventive attitude, with this kind of camera equipment you can make a successful movie. Video may not be the most acceptable format for making movies today, but it is a way, and for a reasonable amount of money, anywhere in the country you can make a movie. Several other people right here in Oklahoma have done it since we did. That was our point with *Blood Cult.* We know it's not an award-winner, but it's a financial success.

CHRIS: When you work on a low budget, you have definite limitations— you don't have access to big names or big special effects. *Blood Cult* was an experiment for us to see if a picture could be made and marketed without going into theaters, and if it could make money.

So this is a glimpse at what I think is the future of the business. The studios can't afford to squander money on things like *Ishtar.* They should have learned that lesson with *Heaven's Gate.* Everyone wants to make a big splash, but most of the people working in the business in the future are gonna be doing small movies. And the same with television. The networks can't spend

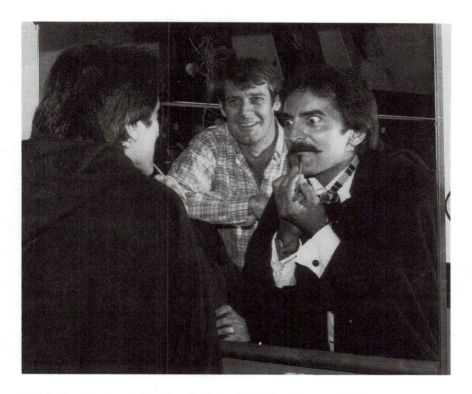

Christopher Lewis watches Tom Savini making himself up as the Ripper.
Photo by John Southern.

$4 million for Movies of the Week anymore. They're all cutting back, and hopefully it'll make room for a lot more product and put a lot more people to work.

In our case, with *Blood Cult,* we were out to make something marketable to get our start, and a lot of people were entertained by it, and I got a chance as a director to prove that we could do it with a crew that, for the most part, had never worked on a feature film before. But, ideally, as a filmmaker, you learn from these kinds of projects, and you go on to do the next one with a little bigger budget and so on—you graduate to a higher level. You learn what works and what doesn't, and you also find out which people are going to work well with you and which ones aren't.

HOW TO MAKE LOW-BUDGET VIDEO HITS

CHRIS: The last picture we did for United, *Revenge,* was in 16-millimeter instead of videotape, and it starred Patrick Wayne and John Carradine. Now all our pictures are being shot in 16-millimeter.

LINDA: We shoot in 16 and transfer to videotape for editing. We off-line edit a picture in about two weeks, on three-quarter inch, and then we mix everything on one-inch. For budget reasons and for expediency it's very effective for us. I think that many people who are in film school now and are used to working with videotape as well as film can see that it's a great system.

CHRIS: We do what a lot of television shows are doing: we shoot on film to get the "movie look," but then we transfer it. And since we never have to make a theatrical film print of our movies, by shooting 16-millimeter and transferring directly from the negative, you can't tell the difference between that and 35-millimeter that has been transferred to one-inch tape. So that's basically the first step. And then we edit everything on video because it's much quicker. Sometimes you can even have a complete rough cut before you finish shooting your film, if your editor's a fast worker.

Another advantage of *shooting* in 16-millimeter is that if later on there comes a chance for a theatrical release, you can conform your negative and blow it up to 35-millimeter, and the picture quality is pretty good. There is a software package in the video editing system that will in essence give you a sprocket-hole-accurate negative-cutter's list, time-coded frame by frame. But this is not primarily in our equation. Before we went into this, we did a lot of research, and we've done cost analysis, and to make a long story short, the cost of going for a theatrical release, when you add up prints and advertising and all those figures, you're talking two-and-a-half million bucks, over and above your production costs.

Our pictures now have budgets of $200,000 to $250,000, and our research has shown that normally with a picture like *Revenge,* if you went theatrical, you'd make about two-and-a-half times your investment. But on our system, where we bypass theatrical and just go to home video, and do an advertising campaign *just* for home video distribution, we make about four-and-a-half times our money. So for sound business purposes, we've decided to forgo the kind of thrill most filmmakers get by seeing their pictures on the silver screen.

At the moment we are preparing a package of six more pictures for a new distribution company—a company we hope to own a part of. We're not really in the distribution business, but we have discovered, like every Hollywood producer, that unless you control your own distribution your future as a filmmaker is uncertain at best.

A good example of that happened after *Revenge,* when we formed The Entertainment Group here in Tulsa and made a production/distribution deal with one of the biggest home video distributors for a film called *Death Drive-In.* We literally, as producers, tailor-made a film for them from original idea through shooting script and casting. We spent a lot of our own money on development and came right down to the start of production before we discovered that they might be in financial trouble. They finally backed away, but not before we both wasted a lot of time and money. I can show you twenty Hollywood producers who will tell you similar stories. So we'd like to control our own distribution, if at all possible, as Roger Corman did with New World.

But for most producers and directors that's impossible. You have to get to a certain plateau before you can even think of doing your own distribution. Most of us have to deal with established distributors. For me, I'd rather make a straight-across-the-board deal and have a distributor take all the rights. It makes a much cleaner deal. We get paid for the production cost of the film and retain a percentage, but they control the rights and can sublicense if they wish. Your only problem then is collecting what you are owed.

As far as the delivery elements are concerned, it's possible to make a 35-millimeter blowup even from a one-inch videotape master, although the quality is not as good as in going film to film. And we can easily deliver music-and-effects tracks for overdubbing with foreign languages, since we mix on a twenty-four-track machine, with English dialogue on its own separate channel.

Different distributors have different requirements, however, depending on whatever route they decide to go.

LINDA: An excellent tool for a new filmmaker is a ten-minute trailer, a preview, that shows what the movie is going to be about. A distributor can look at it and see if it's going to make a salable product, and you don't have to risk everything up front. You can shoot it on videotape. It's a visual tool to sell with.

CHRIS: Distributors don't seem to like to read. If something's put on a platter for them, maybe they'll buy it. But to have to use imagination—that's the filmmaker's job. The more graphic and the simpler that you can make your presentation, the better off you are.

LINDA: We feel that it's almost imperative to get your distribution deal up front, if you can do so without risking your own assets and going into the hole financially. That's the biggest lesson we've learned. It's extremely tough to make a deal after the fact, because you're not in the driver's seat.

CHRIS: If you go to film school, often you can make your films under the umbrella of a school and lessen the risk that way. Spielberg, Lucas, and Kleiser all did it that way, so the recommendation speaks for itself.

We get a lot of films from high school kids who have gone out with their friends and made a movie to show us what they can do, with an eye toward maybe getting hired to do effects or something on one of *our* films. But the thing is, as long as you're not risking a lot of money—and it's getting cheaper and cheaper to make films—you should just go and make one. And if that doesn't get you a distribution deal, it will show the work you can do, and it will get you into a film school, and to me one of the most important things to do to get a break is to get into a film school *somewhere.* Most universities have them now, all around the country. In my case, when I went to USC I was lucky enough to be in a class with a bunch of people who became extraordinarily successful in the movie business. But the point is, one makes a lot of contacts there with people who are your peers, who might get a job and then help you get a job, or you may all end up working together. Much of the movie business, from what I've seen, is connections.

25

How to Sell Your Movie

THERE ARE A large number of potential buyers for your movie even if you don't land a deal with one of the majors or mini-majors. The pipeline is out there. Now, how are you going to tap into it?

Just as you got your picture made starting from scratch, you can get it sold starting from scratch. Let's take it one step at a time. The usual steps in selling a motion picture are:

1. Hiring an agent
2. Developing a marketing package
3. Contacting distributors
4. Negotiating and signing a deal

HIRING AN AGENT

It is not absolutely necessary to hire an agent to help you sell your film. In fact, there are important advantages to handling the job yourself. For one thing, the agent will charge you 10 to 15 percent of your take. For another thing, if you use an agent, you will miss out on the wonderful opportunity of using your movie to give yourself a firsthand education about the selling and marketing of motion pictures. You will also miss out on the opportunity of making numerous contacts for financing and distributing future projects.

On the other hand, using an agent also has certain advantages. The agent thoroughly understands the movie business and already has friends and associates in high places. Because he works within the industry every day, he knows the potential buyers well, and he often has the inside scoop when the buyers' needs shift from day to day. Thus he presumably can target your

picture toward the distributor most likely to make a deal. And he can probably negotiate the deal more shrewdly than you can. He's wise to the loopholes
and pitfalls of distribution contracts.

A very important function that an agent will perform, other than helping
you sell your movie, is to scrutinize and evaluate all the reports and payments
(or lack of payments) from the distributor to make sure the count is honest
and you are receiving your fair share. If you have to audit the distributor's
books or take legal action of any kind, your agent will know when to recommend these steps and will supervise their implementation.

Agents, also known as *producer's representatives,* generally fall into two
categories: attorneys who specialize in the legal aspects of the entertainment
industry, primarily motion pictures, and distributors or ex-distributors who
have taken their thorough knowledge and years of experience in distribution
to the other side of the fence. In other words, instead of representing movie-
buyers, they are now representing movie-*makers*—the very people they used
to negotiate "against."

There's a good chance you will end up hiring an agent even if you start out
selling your picture on your own. Along the way you will get some discourag-
ing rejections, and you will very likely meet an attorney, a distributor, or an
ex-distributor who offers to agent your picture for you. So at that point you
might make that move. Or, even if you take the job right up to the point of
getting some offers, you may feel that you need an agent/attorney to negotiate the fine points, scrutinize the contract, and close the deal for you.

If you decide up front that you must hire an agent, and you don't know
any, you can get some recommendations from a distributor or from your
attorney, who will know how to contact other attorneys who specialize in the
entertainment business. The distinction between distributors and agents is so
blurred that it's hard to tell the difference from their ads in motion picture
trade publications. This is because the same company often performs both
functions. So go ahead and start making your contacts, and you will soon find
out whether these companies will offer to agent and/or distribute your picture.

When you hire an agent, the best way to set up the deal is to specify that
you will collect the money from the distributor and then pay the agent his
commission. The agent will want it the other way around. But do your best to
prevail on this extremely important point, for reasons of self-protection.

DEVELOPING A MARKETING PACKAGE

Whether you are using an agent or selling your movie yourself, you will
need to develop a marketing package to present to distributors. You should
begin to develop this package even before the picture is made. It can include:

- An open letter to distributors, announcing the picture
- Artwork
- Synopsis
- Profiles of key production personnel
- Profiles of key actors/stars
- Press clippings
- Stills
- Preview trailer or sample scenes

For *The Majorettes* we produced a folder with a cover illustration based on the cover art of my novel (the skeleton twirling a baton). Inside the folder we enclosed our profiles, press clippings, etc., introduced by the following letter, which was mailed to distributors while we were still finishing our editing:

THE MAJORETTES, an action-suspense thriller, is now in post-production. We will have a finished print in February 1986.

WORLDWIDE DISTRIBUTION RIGHTS ARE AVAILABLE.

John Russo wrote the screenplay for THE MAJORETTES based upon his popular novel, which was published by Pocket Books and will be rereleased as a tie-in. Russo was co-author of NIGHT OF THE LIVING DEAD and writer-director of MIDNIGHT, currently in release through Independent-International Pictures. He has also produced and/or directed two other feature films and has published ten terror-suspense novels. The director of THE MAJORETTES is Bill Hinzman, who was director of photography and second-unit director on two George Romero pictures, THE CRAZIES and HUNGRY WIVES. Over a twenty-year film career, Mr. Hinzman has directed hundreds of commercial motion pictures, including many documentaries for national television.

For further information, please contact producer John Russo or executive producer Joseph C. Ross at the above address and phone number.

By mailing your marketing package to distributors even before your movie is finished, you will alert them in a very positive way that the movie is coming, and you may even begin to receive tentative offers. At the very least, certain distributors may leave room in their thinking for your picture. If they have reservations about spending acquisition money on some other picture, they may hang on to that money until they have a chance to evaluate *your* movie.

Of course your marketing package can be used not only to interest distributors but also to interest an agent in representing your movie. If you strike up a deal with an agent early enough, his input can help shape the marketing package and the marketing strategy.

The three pictures that I produced between *Night of the Living Dead* and *The Majorettes* were sold without the help of an agent. During that time I had met two excellent agents, Chuck Gelini and Charles King, of Silver King Pictures. They had important contacts at the executive level of most distribution companies, and they had successfully sold hundreds of pictures. So we hired them to agent *The Majorettes*. I became the key liaison with Chuck and Charles, because my experience had taught me enough about distribution to make good decisions on the various deals and offers that Silver King developed.

Our agents advised us to make a twenty-minute sample reel comprised of five or six of our best scenes, so Bill Hinzman and Paul McCollough selected and edited those scenes ahead of all others. We made six three-quarter-inch videotape dubs and six half-inch dubs for Silver King to use in its initial screenings for distributors, to whet the distributors' appetites.

After we had our 35-millimeter answer print, we again made a half-dozen three-quarter and a half-dozen half-inch dubs of the entire feature. Your movie in its entirety is your single best selling tool. The other elements of the marketing package can embellish and entice, but the movie itself ultimately has to be good enough to land the deal.

Very important: Now is the time to file your copyright registration, before you send your movie to other people, where it may fall into the hands of film "pirates" who will duplicate and distribute it without paying you a red cent.

Movies are copyrighted on Form PA, available from the Register of Copyrights, Library of Congress, Washington, DC 20559. You fill out the form (your attorney can help you) and send it with a check for $10, a synopsis of your movie, and a copy of the entire movie in its best format. Your copyright will be secure as soon as the copyright office receives your material, even though you may not receive the certificate for a few weeks.

"Best format" usually means 35-millimeter, and that is why I did not register *The Majorettes* when we had only one 35-millimeter answer print. Instead, I waited until we could make videotape dubs of the picture, for a very important reason: the Copyright Office will grant "special relief" from the expense of depositing a copy of 35-millimeter format if you write and explain that virtually all the funds you were able to raise went toward the production of the movie, and it would be a hardship to have your only 35-millimeter print languishing in the Library of Congress. I wrote such a letter, the special relief was granted, and I was able to obtain a copyright certificate for *The Majorettes* by depositing an inexpensive half-inch videotape.

CONTACTING DISTRIBUTORS

Anybody who is in the motion picture business should subscribe to trade publications, *Variety* and *Boxoffice* in particular. In addition to letting you in on what's going on throughout the industry on a daily, weekly, and monthly basis, the trades are excellent reference guides for reaching agents, distributors, financiers, etc. *Variety* annually publishes thick special issues pertaining to the film festivals that take place all over the world, international film markets, and international home video markets. *Boxoffice* publishes an annual *Buyers Directory,* listing names and addresses of distributors, subdistributors, manufacturers, dealers, and suppliers; and an annual *Guide to Independent Distribution,* the current issue containing addresses and phone numbers of sixty independents.

Getting your movie into a showplace like a credible film festival could expose it to dozens of American and overseas theatrical, home video, and television buyers, sales agents, and festival directors in a span of only a few days.

Festivals of this sort can be excellent places to have your film seen by distributors and agents, because when so many of them view it at once a bidding war may be launched. Each attending distributor knows that he is not the only one to have seen your movie, and if he wants it he had better beat the others to the punch.

If you have an agent for your movie, he should do the job of taking it to the various festivals and sales conventions. He will have a number of pictures on his slate besides yours, so even if yours doesn't get any offers some of the others probably will, and his expenses will be covered. You will be welcome to go to Cannes or Milan or Las Vegas or wherever one of these events is taking place, if you want to fork out the money. But if you don't go, the agent will be there working for you.

If you are working without an agent, don't be afraid to approach distributors. They will want to screen your movie because *they* will be afraid of snubbing a possible hit picture. They can't afford not to look at movies; buying and distributing movies is what keeps them financially viable.

NEGOTIATING AND SIGNING A DEAL

If you want your picture to be distributed theatrically, in most cases you will not be able to land a distribution deal unless you are willing to offer the distributor a share of all markets. This is the only way he can protect himself against the enormous losses he will suffer if he invests in prints and advertising and the picture fails to perform. This is why it is not a good idea to sell off some of the markets (foreign or home video, for example) before you approach a distributor. You would be extremely fortunate if a distributor agreed to take your picture on with some of the markets already closed. He would have to believe in your picture very strongly indeed to take this kind of chance. So, for all intents and purposes (and especially on your first film), you should go in offering worldwide rights.

In an ideal distribution deal you get a huge advance, you get a big percentage of the profits, the distributor commits to releasing your picture immediately, and the distributor commits to a wide theatrical release, with a big advertising campaign. Here's a closer look at that ideal deal. Let's say a major studio buys your $200,000 picture, and you have succeeded so well in putting the bucks on the screen that the studio thinks the budget was $1 million. The best advance that you can realistically hope for is probably around $1 million. More likely, you will get $500,000 to $750,000.

The distributor will probably take 35 percent of the rentals as a distribution fee—a rather standard figure. It sounds wonderful to you at first. But wait. Your advance will be recouped out of your 65 percent. So will all the advertising and print costs. Unless the picture is a blockbuster, your percentage may not ever bring you another dime. But still you have made a hell of a profit, and you have launched your career. The studio may bankroll you to the tune of $5 million or $6 million for your next movie; this is what happened to many of the people whose stories are in this book—people like Monty Ross, Sam Raimi, and Tobe Hooper.

It is extremely important to get a commitment from the distributor to release your movie by a specified date or else pay a penalty. He may be required to pay you some cash or else forfeit certain rights. You must have a guarantee against the possibility—it happens all the time—that the distributor will lose faith in your picture or promote some other picture instead of yours, letting yours sit on a shelf.

The widest kind of theatrical release is of course a major release in a thousand theaters or more, as we discussed in a previous chapter. If your movie gets that kind of release, a huge promotion will be virtually automatic. The next highest level is a release that involves pulling three hundred to five hundred prints and moving them quickly through the theater chains.

Believe it or not, a pretty exciting distribution can even be accomplished with about one hundred prints, if the distributor works his playdates shrewdly and energetically. I have seen this done so smoothly and successfully that it fooled me into assuming that somebody else's picture was getting a major release until I later learned the inside story. The distributor in this case made a deal to have the picture played by a huge theater chain on the eastern seaboard, a chain of fourteen hundred theaters. He kicked off the picture in New York City, booking most of the one hundred prints and spending $125,000 in advertising, which included a heavy schedule of TV spots for maximum impact. He got the hoped-for big box office grosses and high visibility for his picture, and he used this as a springboard into the rest of the fourteen hundred playdates that the theater chain had promised. By scheduling these theaters in blocks of one hundred and playing the dates in a rapid, carefully calculated sequence in a number of cities on the East Coast, the picture seemed to be everywhere at once. It went into all the major cities and surrounding territories on a similar basis, and within a year or less the whole country was covered. Meanwhile, since audiences loved the picture, it was a genuine hit, and word of mouth among theater patrons made continuing huge expenditures for advertising unnecessary. Thus the box office take was enormous, but the overall cost for prints and promotion was especially low. The picture reaped huge profits for the distributor and the production company.

Now, you may have to settle for the kind of distribution deal that isn't so hot: You get a low advance or no advance at all; You get 50 percent of the profits, and the distributor gets the other 50 percent; the distributor uses his "best effort" to release your picture; either the distributor makes no specific commitment as to how much he will spend for prints and advertising or else the commitment is a low-level one involving twenty to thirty prints and $20,000 to $30,000 for initial promotion.

Even when you believe it's in your best interest to go ahead with a less-than-wonderful deal, there are points on which you should not compromise. When you get no advance or a low advance, say $30,000 to $50,000, by contract you should not have to pay for prints and advertising out of your share. Instead the distributor should front these distribution costs and then be paid back out of the first of the gross rentals so that you and the distributor are in effect sharing them equally. Then you split the rest of the income fifty-fifty. You must also stipulate in the distribution contract that *none* of the distributor's overhead costs are to be charged to your picture. Otherwise he'll charge you for his phone bill, his secretary, a portion of his rent, etc. It cost you more to make your picture than he is risking to open it in theaters, so he can cover his own overhead.

A small, poorly financed distributor (perhaps one of the less established independents) might counteroffer to take only a 30 or 35 percent distribution fee *provided* that you pay for prints and advertising out of your percentage. Avoid this kind of deal. Knowing that you are paying, once the picture looks like a success, the distributor will be inclined to keep spending promotion money, reducing your take and maximizing his own.

Warning: Here is a scam that you *must* watch out for if a distributor offers you a deal like the one above and you are giving him a 50 percent share of worldwide rights. Remember, he is making no commitment to release by a certain date, probably by plying you with the argument that he must go by "market conditions" and use his professional judgment and "best effort" to give your picture its best shot against the big boys and their heavily promoted blockbusters. If you fall for this deal, you will be signing away 50 percent of the profits of your picture *in all markets.* The distributor can give it a token theatrical release or *no theatrical release at all* and immediately sell off *all the other markets.* You could have done this on your own and kept *all the money.* Instead the distributor is taking 50 percent without risking any of his own capital. Nice going, sucker.

On the positive side, the standard "fifty-fifty split after advertising and prints" deal can be highly profitable if the distributor is honest and energetic and your picture turns out to be a sleeper. When the picture opens big in its initial twenty or thirty bookings, the playdates will start rolling in from all over the country, and you can step up your promotion effort and pull more prints to meet the demand.

HOW *THE MAJORETTES* WAS SOLD: AN OBJECT LESSON

Now that you have an overview of the various distribution deals, I want to use the marketing strategy behind the selling of *The Majorettes* to give you an inside look at the deal-making process. We did not land a deal with a major studio, but we certainly tried. If we had not tried, we'd still be plagued with the notion that maybe we could have lined our pockets with a $1 million advance if we had had the guts to ask for it.

Our strategy was to start at the top, asking for big money, then work our way down until we found out what the market would bear. We told our agents to screen the picture for all the majors and if they got any interest to ask for $750,000 to $1,000,000. When they were dealing with a mini-major or a major independent, maybe the asking price should drop a notch or two, to around $500,000.

To make a long story short, over a period of months we came close to getting some offers from the biggies, but we couldn't sew up any of the offers. It looked for a while that Vestron Pictures, Vestron's theatrical division, would give us a good theatrical release, but they backed off finally, mainly because their theatrical branch was just getting started, and they wanted to kick things off with a bigger-budget picture with name actors.

We got offers from some of the smaller independents, which would have included small advances of $30,000 to $60,000. But we were leery of giving up a share of worldwide rights without a higher advance. We had to consider the fact that Vestron was offering us $100,000 just for domestic home video rights, and Manson International was offering another $60,000 for foreign rights. It would be nice for us if we could sell U.S. theatrical rights *only* to some distributor, but we couldn't find one who would invest in prints and advertising without demanding a share of video and foreign.

Our agents were high on the Vestron and Manson deals because, they said, Vestron could easily move 50,000 cassettes, and Manson was a big, important overseas distributor that could turn over as much as $500,000 worth of sales for even the "low-end" pictures that it included in its package. With $160,000 from those two companies right off the bat, we'd recoup most of our production budget. And if things went well at Cannes, which was in the offing . . .

Things did go well. Manson racked up more than $200,000 in foreign sales at the Cannes Film Festival and at the Milan Festival and the American Film Market that immediately followed. Manson expects to add another $300,000 to this total. But even if Manson never collects another dime, our picture is already in the black by means of the prerelease advances. Vestron hasn't released it for home video yet. And we still have TV syndication and cable rights to sell. So that's why our agents are projecting that our $200,000 picture will return up to $1.5 million to us over the next several years.

To fully understand why we went for the Manson and Vestron deals, there is something else extremely important that you must recognize about today's theatrical market. With the demise of the drive-ins and the neighborhood theaters, it is more and more true that, as most distributors will tell you, "Either you have a hit picture or you have no picture at all." This means that there is almost no market for middle-level pictures. If a movie can't bring in tons of money, nobody will book it. Instead they'll book some reasonably dependable rerun onto one of the screens of their ten-screen multiplex.

If we had given *The Majorettes* a low-level release and it had failed to take off, we'd have been in the hole for prints and advertising, and we'd be giving the distributor half the "good" money from the other markets. Rather than take that risk, we bit the bullet and went without the thrill of seeing our picture on the big silver screen.

26

Reaping the Rewards

NOW THAT YOUR picture is sold, the ball game is far from over. Get ready for the extra innings. They're going to determine whether you rack up a winning score or play to a disappointing loss.

In this chapter we will discuss how to light up the screen—and the cash register; in other words, to get your picture played everywhere and collect from everywhere possible. Even though you have a signed contract, you won't collect a dime unless you comply with certain clauses in that contract. The distributor won't even pay you your full advance until you give him what are referred to as *delivery items*. Once you do, the distributor's marketing team will pay your advance and go into action full-force, pulling prints and dubs of your movie and landing sales. Then you will start to receive producer's reports detailing the results of the sales effort, and you'll have to know how to monitor and evaluate those reports and make sure that you collect your fair share of the royalties.

DELIVERY ITEMS AND DEADLINES

After we signed the Vestron and Manson contracts on *The Majorettes,* producer's rep Charles King told me, "You have to make sure you comply with delivery. If you don't, the picture may never be distributed. But, if you *do,* promptly and professionally, the next time you come to these people with a picture you want them to distribute, you might get another $75,000 to $100,000 in advances, based on their faith in your ability to actually *deliver.* Delivery is the single biggest thing that kills most producers and takes them out of the business, even if they know how to make a decent picture."

The delivery section of your contract will be about five pages long, spelling everything out in excruciating detail. The distributor should have personnel to help you comply, explaining anything you don't fully understand and doing their best to help you fulfill the requirements. After all, they aren't rooting for you to screw up—they want to distribute your picture. I'm going to leave out the fine print here, but remember when you get *your* particular deal you should check out the fine print very thoroughly with your agent and attorney, and work hard to comply absolutely. Delivery requirements usually encompass the following items:

- A 35-millimeter low-contrast positive print of your movie
- A one-inch videotape master
- M&E tracks
- A dialogue-and-action continuity script (for postdubbing into foreign languages)
- Music cue sheets
- A complete employment list of everybody who appeared in or rendered services toward the movie
- Copies of all contracts, agreements, and releases relating to the movie
- Copyright certificate
- MPAA rating certificate
- Insurance policy
- Certificate of origin
- Still photographs (as many as fifty may be required)
- Biographies of principal players, writers, producers, and director
- Synopsis
- Advertising materials
- Credit list and logo art
- Cast list with character names and character descriptions

Some of the items on this list might not be as straightforward as they seem. For example, you might not realize that most foreign countries require a different type of one-inch master, called a *PAL master,* than what is required for broadcast or duplicating within the U.S.—and this is just one of the many things that can trip you up when you're trying to comply with delivery.

One of the single biggest stumbling blocks is often the MPAA rating. In order to have your picture rated, you must get the proper forms from the MPAA Classification and Rating Administration, 14144 Ventura Blvd., Sherman Oaks, CA 91423. The fee is based on the production budget. Currently, on a $200,000 picture the fee is $1,500. You submit your film, and they screen it and either approve or disapprove the rating you request. Sometimes you must edit and resubmit several times and even submit to the Rating Appeals Board. Often you must end up butchering your picture, which is why cover shots are so important during filming.

In the case of *The Majorettes,* we had to come up with an R rating even though the picture wasn't going into theaters in this country. While there is no rating system overseas, many countries have censorship boards that are much stricter than the Motion Picture Association of America (ironically enough, South Africa's board is one of the most straitlaced).

Anyway, Manson International told us that acquiring an R here in the U.S. would make it easier to get approval from the various foreign censorship bureaus. Plus, Vestron told us that in many states the sale of videocassettes would be hampered if we went out without an R, for many stores won't carry X-rated or unrated product. Then, complicating everything even further, when I told Vestron the extent of the changes the MPAA demanded we make in order to obtain that R rating, I got the impression that Vestron might back out of the deal, because they said that one of the things they loved about the picture was the shock effect of the violence, and it was very important to them to retain those scenes intact. However, after some consideration, Vestron decided to release the picture in two versions, an R version and an unrated version for places where the violence wouldn't be objectionable.

Without our cover shots, we would never have gotten our R certificate and our distribution deals would probably have fallen through. The cover shots will come in handy again, when we sell TV rights, because the TV censors will require still other modifications of our murder scenes.

PROMOTION AND PUBLICITY

While you're racking your nerves complying with delivery, you'll also be having the fun of seeing the distribution campaign kick into gear. If your movie is getting a theatrical release, the distributor will develop a full range of promotional items and gimmicks, including:

- A press book, which is a showy pamphlet displaying ads, promotional quotes, publicity stills, profiles of actors and production personnel, and general information about the movie like running time, cast of characters, etc.
- A one-sheet, which is a twenty- by forty-inch poster, usually in full color, lavishly portraying the movie, for use in theater lobbies
- A preview trailer
- TV and radio spots
- Fliers, standees, banners, giveaway items, and various supplementary advertising gimmicks

As the campaign goes into action and the initial bookings are lined up, you can bolster the impact of the distributor's effort by sending out your own press releases and lining up interviews for yourself, your cast, and your production partners. Your contributions can be particularly powerful when your movie plays your hometown. When the Walter Reade Organization chose to use those meager fourteen prints to open *Night of the Living Dead* in Pittsburgh, we realized that our future as filmmakers was on the line. If we opened big, the distribution would be continued. If the box office grosses were low, the picture would probably be pulled.

Just as we always went all-out for every little $300 TV spot, we decided we weren't going to sit by idly and let our futures be decided by the winds of fate —not if we could help the winds blow in a favorable direction.

Two weeks before the picture opened, we mailed press kits to more than fifty newspapers, from the major publications to corporate newsletters. Almost all of them ran articles, interviews, and pictures, making a big deal out of "the first feature movie ever produced in Pittsburgh by Pittsburgh people." We held our own premiere at one of the biggest downtown theaters, complete with limousines, klieg lights, and an elegant cocktail party. We plastered our own posters all over the place—in corporate offices, on bulletin boards, in stores, and on telephone poles.

Night of the Living Dead opened to packed houses. For the first time in its history, the Associated Theater chain had to take out ads in local newspapers apologizing for turning patrons away. Thanks in part to our own efforts, our first movie was off and running!

RAKING IN THE CASH—AND THE GLORY

As soon as you have a successful movie, even a moderately successful one, ride those coattails for all they're worth. Use the notoriety to build yourself a name, meet important people, develop key contacts within the motion picture industry, find new investors, and push for new projects. Ideally, you should have several new scripts or treatments ready to produce. Don't wait for distribution to run its course, because even an auspicious opening can degenerate to the point where there's not so much to brag about. Make your moves while the timing is right.

Don't forget to let your cast and crew bask in the glory with you by including them in interviews, screenings, parties, etc. They deserve to enjoy these "glamorous" affairs. And they'll respect you and treat you well on future ventures if you show that you are willing to share the accolades as well as the hard work.

Keep your investors happy, too—fully inform them about your movie's progress, let them participate in the decision making, and show them that you welcome their advice. Remember, they put up their money because they imagined that investing in a movie would be more fun than playing the stock market. Don't disabuse them of that notion. Give them an accurate account

IMAGE TEN PRODUCTIONS

AND

THE WALTER READE ORGANIZATION

cordially request the pleasure of your attendance
at the world premiere of a feature motion picture

Filmed in Pittsburgh

NIGHT OF THE LIVING DEAD
WORLD PREMIERE

FULTON THEATER   8:00 P.M.
TUESDAY   OCTOBER 1, 1968

*reception immediately following
cocktails and hors d'oeuvres*

10-12 P.M.   WILLIAM PENN HOTEL

—— Present to Doorman ——

An invitation to the world premiere of *Night of the Living Dead.*

of the cash flow and pay them as soon as possible. If you make sure they get their money back, they'll be anxious to invest in your next picture.

In order to do this, you and your agent are going to have to ride herd on the distributor. That means you must understand how the cash flows from the theaters to the distributor and to you. So, let me give you another lesson in the peculiar economics of the motion picture business.

MOVIE MONEY

Sometimes movie money seems just as unreal as the phony bills that are used in the movies. It's unreal for some big star to get $5 million per picture. And it's unreal for somebody like you to make a hit picture and never see any of the profits. Unfortunately, it happens all too often.

There are three basic categories of movie money, and the category your

> "To my surprise, *Texas Chainsaw* was a hit, and it really didn't make things very much easier. Whereas today when that happens, when a sleeper crosses over and breaks through, Hollywood takes great notice, even if the films are really not that impressive. In a way, I feel like the ground-up cement helping to make the path easier for people a decade later. They do one picture, and the next thing you know somebody gives them $6 million for their next thing."
>
> Tobe Hooper
> The Texas Chainsaw Massacre

share comes out of helps determine how much you will probably get. The categories are:

1. Box office gross—the money taken in by the theaters from ticket sales
2. Returns in rentals—the share of the money that goes to the distributor
3. Producer's share of profits—paid to the producer if the movie makes enough money to cover prints and advertising and there is still cash left over

You've seen how the producer's share of profits can turn into "funny money" when the wrong kind of contract is signed with the distributor, and when the term *profits* is defined to your disadvantage—whether it's gross profit, net profit, or something else. Here is how the profits can start turning into funny money before the cash even gets from the customer to the theater owner, and can keep turning into funny money all the way down the line:

• Ticket sales go unrecorded. Some theater employees, instead of ripping up tickets and giving customers the stubs, will sell the same tickets over and over. For example, if a ticket costs $6 and an employee sells the same ticket to five customers, he can tell the boss there was only one customer, plunk $6 into the till, and pocket the other $24. The distributor never hears about this money because the theater owner doesn't know it exists.

• The employees may be honest, but the theater owner himself may underreport ticket sales. Porno theaters have turnstiles to guard against this practice, but regular theaters for the most part have no such deterrent.

• The subdistributor may be taking kickbacks from the theater owner so they can jointly rob the distributor.

Only about 30 percent of the box office gross ever gets back to the distributor on average—*if* he's a big distributor with a lot of clout. The independents are lucky to see 15 percent to 25 percent of the box office take, because the kinds of deals they can make aren't nearly as favorable as what the majors enjoy.

But anyway, let's assume that a large amount of cash finally does make its way back to your distributor. You'd better hope he's honest, because here are a few of the ways that *he* can rip you off:

- Underreporting collections
- Padding expenses
- Charging bills from other pictures to *your* picture
- Giving your picture a low percentage of the package price when it is part of a slate of pictures sold to overseas markets or to TV
- Double-billing your picture with a dog picture that he owns and attributing the lion's share of the rentals to the dog even though your picture was the draw
- Playing your picture in theaters that he owns and then running the same game as the dishonest theater owner, giving your picture a small percentage of the actual box office gross
- Paying you extremely slowly or simply not paying you at all

How do you think I learned about all these scams? The hard way. So pay attention and don't make the same mistakes. Make sure your agent and your lawyer build the proper safeguards into your distribution contract.

One of the most important safeguards is the contractual right to audit the distributor's books. If you have a strong suspicion that you're being cheated, pay a motion picture auditor—$3,000 to $15,000, depending on the complexity of the job—to go in and audit right away. Don't wait for a year to go by; the money might be spent by then, and you'll never recover it. If you feel you have sufficient cause and don't hesitate to do an audit, the distributor will be put on notice that you are not going to let him get away with anything. But don't audit frivolously. You'll wind up with egg on your face, and the distributor won't be anxious to take on your next picture.

Even though you have to watch out for the many rip-offs in this business, it is still a fine place to have fun and make a good living. So don't let the pitfalls scare you off. Take the proper steps to protect yourself. That way, when you make a hit picture you'll line your pockets with more than just great press clippings and marvelous reviews.

PART VII

GOING ON TO BIGGER THINGS

"Your ace in the hole is really knowing how to make movies. But until you make a few, you haven't any proof that you can do what you think you can do. Much less what you *say* you can do. This town is pitch city. Sit in a restaurant for five minutes, and you'll bump into four people who are in development, three who are directing, and six who want you to cast them."

KAREN ARTHUR
Director, *Lady Beware*

27

Making It as a Maverick

EVEN AFTER YOU'VE enjoyed some success, the life of a maverick film-maker isn't exactly a romp in the meadow. It's more like a wild, whirling gallop—you keep your eyes on the next hurdle, the next goal, try to pick out the best place, the best timing, for your next leap. It's exciting but also hazardous.

No matter what level of success you reach in the movie business, you still have to scramble and work hard for your next gig. You can't take anything for granted. The bigger the name you make for yourself and the more money your pictures make, the more your services will be in demand. But if you have a few flops the demand may evaporate.

Often, the major studios will bombard a maverick filmmaker with offers after he hits it big as an independent. Suddenly finding money is no longer a problem. But other equally difficult issues must be addressed. If an independent allows Hollywood to entice him, can he maintain his innovative spirit, his creative vitality? Will formulized, bureaucratic thinking force him into a mold, or will he be able to retain the spark of originality that got him noticed in the first place?

In this final section, you'll hear from mavericks who've hit these questions head on. Some have found a magic land of opportunity accompanying recognition; some have found frustration and disheartening constraints. I hope you'll find their experiences both sobering *and* encouraging.

Tom Savini's excellent work in his specialized field of makeup special effects has led to opportunities for him to direct movies. He will share the joys and challenges of his unusual, multi-faceted career.

Tobe Hooper's movies have grossed more than $450 million, yet he has faced and still faces some of the studio system's toughest obstacles. He'll tell you what it's like to move from independence to the wheeling and dealing world of Hollywood.

Oscar-winning director Oliver Stone had his maverick status thrust upon him—it was either get out of the system or get out, period. He, too, chose to fight to get to the top against those heavy odds. He'll take you along as he traces his climb, and you'll see how struggling and hard determined work come with the territory.

No true maverick is perfectly happy working *for* somebody instead of *with* somebody. We like to call our own shots. We might end up working harder and making less money than many of the folks who have sacrificed their autonomy. But we like to think we're happier than they are.

As for me, although I have agents who sell my work in Hollywood, I've chosen to live and work mostly in Pittsburgh, my home town, where I feel comfortable working with a talented group of friends and associates. All of my feature movies have been filmed right here. But they've been sold in every country in the world.

In my twenty-two years in the business, I've always either been self-employed or banded together with a few other mavericks like me in small companies free of the strictures and restraints of corporate America. Free of many of the perks and safety nets too—like solid pension plans, stock options, guaranteed pay raises, and retirement benefits. If I take a paid vacation, the pay is coming out of my own pocket.

To maintain the independent lifestyle that I enjoy, I have to keep lots of balloons in the air and irons in the fire. In freelancer parlance, a "balloon in the air" is a project or an idea for a project that you hope will eventually develop to the point where somebody might actually pay you some money for it. An "iron in the fire" is a project that may be on the verge of a green light (money on the table so you can go ahead)—except the fire might still go out, or someone else might get hired instead of you.

So I keep plugging away. At any given time, I may have a screenplay or two in development, a novel half written or almost finished, a movie ready to go into preproduction or negotiation with financiers and/or distributors. When you're hot, you're hot—when you're not, you're not. So you've got to keep working, or the irons might stop glowing and the balloons might fall out of the sky.

It's rough. It's tough. Sometimes it's a laugh and sometimes it's a scream. It's disappointment mixed with joy.

There's nothing else I'd rather do.

Tom Savini in his studio. *Photo by Bob Michelucci.*

Tom Savini used to steal makeup from his mother's purse to make himself up like Lon Chaney. Even in Vietnam, he had his makeup kit with him and tried to keep practicing. He was the special makeup effects artist on movies like *Friday the 13th, Dawn of the Dead,* and *Knightriders,* and managed to land acting roles in the movies as well. Directing his effects scenes got him noticed by high-level producers, and now he's become a director of feature movies.

28

Tom Savini
How One Dream Leads
to Another

★ I was twelve, a little Italian kid loafing on the street corners, and one day I went to see *Man of a Thousand Faces,* starring James Cagney in the story of Lon Chaney. It was the first film I had seen that actually showed you how to *make* a film—you saw actors behind the scenes, cameras and stuff, and you saw Cagney putting on makeup and becoming the phantom of the opera and the hunchback. This really flipped me out. Wow! Somebody has to make these movies; they don't just pop onto the Earth! I started collecting makeup out of my mother's purse, and I used to shine shoes in the neighborhood so I could buy makeup. I started putting together a kit and reading books about makeup in Carnegie Library, and I no longer hung out on the corners; I had a motivation, a goal in life—to be a makeup man, to be like Lon Chaney.

I got the acting bug in grade school, too. One of my friends and I started creating skits, making ourselves up, and making the whole class laugh—getting our acting rewarded, in other words. And then when I was in high school I got interested in the plays there. That's when George Romero came and picked me and some others to read for a screen test for a movie called *Whine of the Fawn,* which ended up not being made. So I was doing high school plays, and I was a makeup person, and I was also dancing. I had no formal training, but one of my older brothers was a fabulous dancer. I had another brother who was studying to be a mortician, and I would see him in the basement practicing sculpting in case he had to repair a damaged head or whatever. So my brothers had a big effect on me.

I studied acting in college and kept on doing makeup. Then I went into the army. I was a combat photographer, but I spent most of my time processing the reconnaissance films from the airplanes. I'd develop the film and make prints, and the intelligence people would analyze it for troop movements. If there was an attack, I'd have to go out and film the blown-up machinery and the blown-up people. And when I was there, looking through the camera, it was a safety for me: my mind made me think—not really, but almost—like it was special effects I was looking at.

In Vietnam obviously I couldn't keep up with my acting, but since I had my makeup kit with me I kept practicing making scars and fangs and beards and whatnot. And when I got back to the states, I went right to the Fort Bragg Playhouse in North Carolina and to the Fayetteville Little Theater, where I was involved as an actor and as the makeup director. So I played Ben Franklin and Thoreau and King Arthur in all these plays, and I also did all the makeup. For Ben Franklin I would do my own four-and-a-half-hour makeup, then assist other people with theirs. Then, when I started in the movies—with *Deathdream* and *Deranged*—I started as a makeup artist, but I would always try to play some small part in the films to satisfy that part of my passions. With George Romero it was easy to get to do it. With *Martin* I did the makeup and the stunts, getting hit with a car and so on. *Dawn of the Dead,* same thing. I did the effects and improvised a part that's not in the script. And I did about sixteen stunts. I went off the balcony at the Monroeville Mall into the fountain. I got hit by lots of trucks and cars. Lots of falling stuff. In *Friday the 13th* I did a stunt, too—I went through a window.

I've taken bad raps from certain critics about my contribution to gore and violence on the screen. But, although I have a reputation for making this stuff very realistic, there's still a difference between the real stuff and the fake stuff. And you know, *I* don't write the stuff. I'm not saying those who do write it are demented or anything—and those are the tags I get; people tell me I'm sick or demented. But when I'm hired to do a job, it's already written. Sometimes the script is pretty explicit; sometimes it isn't. As far as the effects go—my feeling is that if it's in the script, I should make it look as realistic as possible. When I was just starting, with films like *Maniac,* I'd say, "I don't think you guys are gonna get away with this on the screen. How can you possibly think you will? I mean, we'll make it, we'll create it, but I don't think you'll get away with it." Then every last second is in the final film, and I still don't know how they got away with it. But it was okay, to me, because I had to get my name out on *something.* So I got my name out by doing the splatter films and doing those effects as realistically as possible. A lot of people don't understand how much sculpture and mechanics and making lifelike replicas of people is involved in making the splatter films. It's not just pumping artificial blood through fake knives.

I turn down almost all those slasher films now to take on something that involves creatures. And I keep saying to people, "Well, I'm making the transition from blood and gore to the creatures." Then a movie like *Friday the 13th*

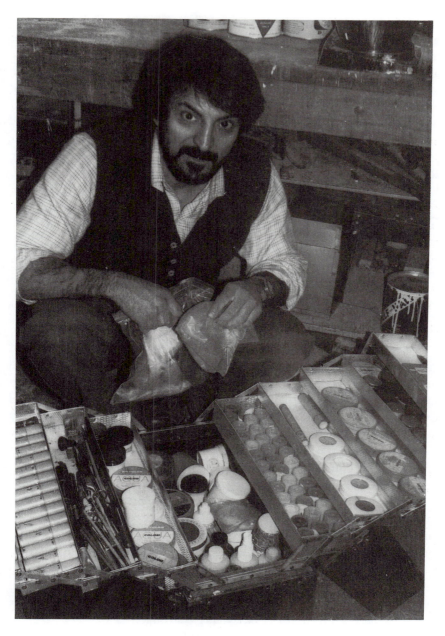

Tom Savini peers into his bag of tricks. *Photo by Bob Michelucci.*

Part IV comes along, and I felt I had to do that one because I did the first one. Plus, I got to kill Jason. Plus, it was called *The Final Chapter*—I wanted to be the one who did the first one and the last one. But then they went ahead and made Part V and Part VI afterward.

I did a movie in Hong Kong with lots of creatures and *Creepshow* with lots of creatures. And then of course *Day of the Dead* came around. Well, I had to do that one. It meant a lot of money, and it's a sequel to *Dawn of the Dead,* which I did, so there you go: it's a cycle.

I think to some people, I hope to most people, when one of my movies or Rick Baker's movies or any of the top artist's movies comes out, it's like, "Let's go see the latest exhibit." At least the makeup fans think that way.

ON TO DIRECTING

When I was in the theater and watching directors work, I always thought, God, why didn't he do this? It'd be much better if he did that. Then when I was doing special effects for movies, in some cases it was in my contract that I would get to assist in the directing of my effects scenes, but only as a magician, only as an effects artist.

Then, all of a sudden, to my surprise, cameramen, directors, whatever, would come up to me and say, "You should direct something. When are you gonna direct?" I kept hearing this over and over again, and I wasn't out there promoting myself as a director, but people would say this to me, and it got me thinking, it got me going. And then I was offered directing work by Laurel Entertainment for *Tales from the Darkside.* I grabbed it and loved it, and they liked my work. My experiences in makeup, acting, and doing stunts probably were the best teachers I could have had. They've given me great insight into what I seek in a director, and into what kind of director I intend to be.

George Romero is the kind of director that actors love because he lets his actors improvise. And when an actor improvises, you're getting a more natural performance out of him. He's drawing more out of himself. He's drawing on his own experiences to create something fresh. And the same kind of thing George lets you do as an actor he lets you do as a makeup artist. He lets you think of things on your own. You don't have to adhere strictly to what is written. The main goal is to follow his instructions, but when you get a signal from George that it's okay to go further, you can improvise with the effects too. And that's great. You feel like you're contributing more. For example, for *Dawn of the Dead* we'd sit around and think up ways to kill zombies. I mean, there were lots of ways in the script, but we wanted to think of some more. It was like a three-month Halloween. The fun was to sit around and think of things to do and then to actually be able to do them in the film. George would let you do them.

During *Creepshow* we had Fluffy, the creature in the crate, and Steve

Tom Savini with Fluffy, the monster he designed for George A. Romero's *Creepshow.*
Photo by Bob Michelucci.

King's script said we see a blur of fur and some teeth—so it was totally open for me to create a monster. When Fluffy first appears, there's six of us operating Fluffy's facial expressions, aside from the actor, who is opening the jaw and making the eyes move himself—and one of the six people is George. I handed him a control and said, "George, you operate this," just to get him in on it, you know, and I'm talking everybody through it—"Okay, Bruce, pump the lines," "Daryl, move the mouth"—and we're going on, the camera's rolling for five or ten minutes, and I think an assistant director said, "George, you wanna cut the camera?" He forgot! We were all having so much fun making this creature's face move, he didn't even think about yelling, "Cut!"

At this moment there are about seven scripts that people want me to direct, some from big companies and some from people I've never heard of. In fact, New World Pictures just flew me out to Hollywood a week ago to talk about some of the projects that are coming to them with my name on them as the director. They wanted to meet me and see how I felt about the projects, and they said they wanted me to direct for New World. I ended up signing a two-picture deal with them.

It came as a surprise to me that without my being out there pushing myself as a director, but simply going about my business doing the best I could, directing my own special effects, people began to think I would be a good director for an entire movie. It was a seed that was planted and grew during my theater days, and now it's blossoming.

But I would never stop doing effects work. Let's say I directed a film tomorrow and it was a big success. If there were effects in it, I'd still be supervising and designing as well as being a director and having a crew execute them—just like I do now. I go in there, and I do get my hands in the clay and my hands in the plaster and stuff, but in essence I'm conducting a group of artists who execute my designs. As a director I would still do that, and who knows, I might take on a directorial job just to do the effects! The more you do, the more you get to do. Acting, stunt work, special effects, and now directing.

Tobe Hooper directing *Invaders from Mars. Photo courtesy of Tobe Hooper.*

Ever since his stunning debut with *The Texas Chainsaw Massacre,* **Tobe Hooper** has been providing electrifying thrills for audiences all over the world. With movies like *Poltergeist* and *Salem's Lot* he won critical as well as popular acclaim. His avid fan-following pushed *The Texas Chainsaw Massacre 2* and *Invaders from Mars* to the top of the home video charts, both movies going platinum just a few days after they were released and earning more than $18 million in cassette revenue. Tobe has been working on major projects with budgets up to $30 million (in the case of *Life Force,* for example). Yet, like everybody else working in Hollywood, he still has to fight hard for enough creative control over those projects to bring them to the screen the way he believes they would best entertain an audience.

29

Tobe Hooper
Making It in Hollywood

★ When I was a child, I wanted to be an actor for the recognition, but something happened, and I got behind the camera instead. The acting urge went away when I made my first sound movie at age seventeen and starred in it. Not only did I dislike myself on the screen, but I didn't like trying to film myself. Since I was shooting the picture and didn't trust anyone else to frame it, I'd frame up on someone about my size, then I'd get on the mark and do my lines without letting anyone even pan the camera, because in my small group I was the only person who could operate it.

At the University of Texas film school, I got to work with people who knew how to make movies. After that I took a chance and went into business for myself, making documentary films. I guess I made at least 60 documentaries, and probably that many special education TV spots.

My first feature movie, *Egg Shells,* was an art house picture, a well-intended film about the end of hippiedom. It got about fifty playdates at most, and I was looking for something else to do on a low budget. One of my close friends said I should go see a film playing at the University of Texas student union, called *Night of the Living Dead.* I went to see it, and I knew then what I was going to make. That picture just flipped me out. I had grown up a horror fan, but those kinds of movies were delivering nothing in comparison. *Night of the Living Dead* was a true inspiration; it made me see how the horror genre could be given new life. I'd already been working on a story about kids in isolation, and after seeing *Dead* the rest of it just fell into place one evening in about thirty seconds, while looking at the chainsaws in the Montgomery Ward hardware department. It was over the Christmas holidays, and the crowd was packing in, and it just occurred to me that a chainsaw could get me out of this crowd. So when I got home, the story came to me—something I could mix with this story of isolation. I had been going in a totally different direction, using fantasy and other devices that actually came into their own many years later.

USING MPAA HELP TO GET AN R

The Texas Chainsaw Massacre got an R, but the only things you really see are the hitchhiker cutting his own hand with his knife and the screamer, the Sally character, getting her finger cut. One drop of blood wells up, and Grandpa sucks it off her finger. Leatherface falls on the chainsaw and cuts his leg, but that's always been okay—to see the bad guy get it. Yet people talk about the movie as if it's so awfully gory.

During shooting I was calling the MPAA every week. I'd say, "Look, I want to get a PG, and I need to hang a girl on a meat hook. How can I do this?" And they'd say, "There's no way you can do it." And I'd say, "What if I don't show penetration? If you just see her hanging there?" And that would be okay with them. In all my conversations with them I was talking PG; of course there was no way they would give it a PG, but at least if I was working toward it maybe there would be a compromise and I would get an R. And that's exactly what did happen. When the girl is hung on the meat hook, before she hits the meat hook you see blood on the wall behind her, and then I pan quickly down her body to a big washtub below her to catch the blood. There's no blood running in it, but it makes the connection in your mind, and you think there must be a gallon of blood running down her legs.

We shot 16-millimeter ECO, low-ASA Ektachrome commercial filmstock, and when we made the blowup I tried to mute the color to give it that *Godfather* quality. The first print was just beautiful, and even though it suffered when they took the negative to New York and struck all the release prints, very few people noticed that it was a blowup. In filming it, I got heavily into all the characters and action, hoping the story would be strong enough to transcend the 16-millimeter format and a print that might look like it had been hit by a truck.

WHAT SUCCESS DOESN'T MEAN

To my surprise, *Texas Chainsaw* was a hit. But it really didn't make things very much easier. Plus, I was pigeon-holed as a horror director.

About a year after *Chainsaw,* I came to Los Angeles to do an alligator movie that's had about a dozen different titles. It's been called *Eaten Alive,* and it's been called *Starlight Hotel Slaughter.* It was originally called *Death Trap,* but the producers didn't think that was a commercial enough title. They figured I had a name that would sell on the international market, so they got in touch with me in Texas, and I wasn't in the Directors Guild yet, so I got screwed financially. I had already gotten screwed on *Chainsaw* but

Tobe Hooper and co-writer Kim Henkel adjust a corpse atop a tombstone for the opening scene of *The Texas Chainsaw Massacre. Photo courtesy of Tobe Hooper.*

had kind of expected it to happen. Back then I just figured it was a natural part of the stepping-stone process that would lead me to being screwed on a much higher level.

I was out here three years before *Salem's Lot* happened. Bill Friedkin took me under his wing for a bit, and I went to work for Universal on a five-picture development deal, but nothing took off. Kim Henkel was with me—he was my writer from *Chainsaw*—and back then we were looked at a little bit askance. People thought we were so-called rebels. And that's so far from me, it's absurd, but people had a tendency to identify me with the madness in my movie.

Then, when Bill Friedkin left Universal and moved his office to Warner Brothers, he asked me if I'd like to do *Salem's Lot*. I have a real feeling for Stephen King's work because his writing touches me right down to nerve central. At first Jon Voight was supposed to star in it as a theatrical movie, but it didn't get off the ground until finally it went to television as a miniseries with David Soul. TV was actually a good home for it, despite the censorship problems, because of the sheer volume of the novel. It needed the four-hour format. The character relationships were so important that making it in a two-hour package for movie theaters would have been very hard to do. There are three versions of it—the four-hour version, which was cut to three hours, and then an under-two-hour version for European distribution. The more characterization that gets lost, the less effective the story is.

AFTER *SALEM'S LOT*—GOING AGAINST THE FLOW

I hate to say some of the things that I've turned down as a director, and in doing so I didn't endear myself to the system. The whole system was relatively new to me, and a whole game of its own outside filmmaking. *Salem's Lot* got me critical acclaim and attention, and instead of going with the flow I was turning down things like *Piranha* and *Wolfen*. Just because I'd been making films for ten years and was an accomplished cameraman, makeup artist, set designer, screenwriter, even a music composer didn't mean I was automatically going to make it in a business sense. Meanwhile, the producers of *The Funhouse* kept talking to me, and it had a weak script, and that was a big drawback, but I went into the production thinking I could do something about that. I should have waited longer to make my next picture, but instead I made a picture too quickly. I ended up in a hectic seven-week shooting schedule, under really tough conditions, and had to go to Florida to do it, because a lot of it was night shooting and I had to go to a state where the child labor laws were compatible. The whole carnival setting of the film interested me, but the script was never quite right, so I feel that I rushed into that picture and dented the image I had coming off of *Salem's Lot*.

THE HOLLYWOOD SCRAMBLE

When I wasn't making a picture, I was working with writers, developing properties. For instance, I was connected with *Motel Hell* for a while, then someone else went off and made it, and there have been countless stories like that. It takes so long, usually, to develop a film inside this establishment that everybody is mind-blown when a studio gives something a green light. The studios are like the banks, tightfisted with money for pictures, and you have to do endless paperwork and budgets, as well as the writing and the rewriting. The executives all have ideas they prefer to yours, and the president of the studio has a whole array of predetermined reasons not to like your proposal, like a picture in the same genre didn't do well, or the script can't be any good, or maybe he just doesn't have the vision to see beyond the printed page. In fact, trying to break new ground here is one of the frustrations—it's actually easier to get a copycat picture made, because you're ripping off a concept that has been proven to work. There are some brilliant people in this business, and then there are some who don't know what they're doing and can't believe anybody else can know or that anyone can predict a hit picture.

At one point Steven Spielberg took an interest in me (he's a *Chainsaw* fan), and he introduced me to John Milius, and Milius and I decided to do *Chainsaw 2* together, and we were trying for only a million-dollar budget. We went all over town looking for a measly—I'm speaking in Hollywood terms—a measly million dollars from one of the majors to do *Chainsaw 2*. But we simply couldn't get it off the ground. And it's strange, because a genre piece especially has worldwide built-in guarantees. It's often hard to get a package off the ground. And then there are times when it comes perfectly naturally. And sometimes the easiest ones to get made are the ones nobody ever sees.

Later on, of course, we got a deal from Cannon on *Chainsaw 2*—with a higher budget, because it was part of a 3-picture package they wanted.

GOOD SCRIPTS AND CONCEPTS SHINE THROUGH

My favorite film that I've made is the original *The Texas Chainsaw Massacre,* then *Salem's Lot, Poltergeist,* and *The Texas Chainsaw Massacre 2.* If you look at my films, it's easy to see that the ones that have a good story and a good script are the ones that shine through. I've really had only those four that were good scripts, and without a good concept it's sometimes a futile exercise.

Very few directors get final cut here in Hollywood. The distributor will cut your movie as he sees fit. He will take out what he wants out. A problem some guy had with his wife a week ago may enter into an alteration of your movie.

Lifeforce (the first of the three Cannon films) had everything going for it visually, with Alan Hume as my director of photography. It was a beautiful idea of Colin Wilson's, the idea that vampires on this planet had their genesis in outer space. Had it just been left "space vampires" in concept, it would have been okay. But twenty minutes were cut out of it. The first edit of the picture turned out to be two hours and seven minutes long, and the distributors said it was too long because theaters want to show pictures at two, four, six, eight, and ten o'clock. So I cut it down to 1:47, and that was still too long for them. In the meantime, they had started having allergic reactions to the title, *Space Vampires.* But "space vampires" was the picture I was making, and it was a little bit on the tongue-in-cheek side: the humor was a springboard into the rest of the picture. But they cut those moments. They were the first moments to go, because they were character springboards, and the distributors wanted to condense the film down to the most dynamic scenes. They were very insecure about even leaving the word *vampire* in the picture. I managed to save it a couple of times, but in the body of the film the lines were literally lifted. They wanted to remove the whole concept of "vampire" from the film. I think they were trying to manipulate the footage into another genre. And once they changed the title and did an ad campaign around *Lifeforce,* the picture was totally not what it was meant to be.

Sometimes it's impossible to change the shape of a film when the spirit is already built into the celluloid. If you try to alter its spiritual essence, cinematically and storywise, it loses its hook.

Almost the same kind of thing happened with *Invaders from Mars,* the next picture I directed for Cannon. All three pictures dovetailed one on top of the other. When I went back to England to help the distributors take twenty minutes out of *Lifeforce,* I was already prepping *Invaders*—sets were being built, and I was working with Dan O'Bannon's screenplay, which outlined a really good way to do the remake of *Invaders from Mars.* It had some of the same conceptual guidelines that the original *Invasion of the Body Snatchers* had. On page one, you had the teacher and the little boy in a Jeep screeching up to the general's office. The kid is trying to get to see the general, and he's trying to tell this story, and about midway through the movie, through combinations of flashbacks and present time, the story comes up to date. And so the last half of the film is in present time. It was an exciting way to transpose information through the flashbacks, with a progressive build.

Two weeks before I started shooting, an executive at Cannon who was the head of its literary department called me in London and said he hated the script, so they threw it away. I had actors committed, and I had to start shooting in two weeks. I went back to L.A., and they had a new script for me that they had whipped out over the weekend. So here they gave me a script and said I had to do it, and a lot of what was good in Dan's script was no longer there—the characters were there, because the actors had already been cast, but it was a totally different picture. I had arguments with them on the phone from London, and finally this guy said, "Why do they have to come from Mars? I don't like the idea that they come from Mars." And I explained, "You know, we're remaking a picture that was a famous cult picture called *Invaders from Mars,* so unless we change the title, where do you want them to come from?"

Tobe Hooper (with bullhorn) and director of photography Daniel Pearl (seated on crane) during filming of *Invaders from Mars. Photo courtesy of Tobe Hooper.*

After all these hassles, even though my original intention was just to be producer on *Chainsaw 2,* I decided to also direct it to finish off my commitment to Cannon. And I had only twelve weeks from the start of principal photography to the release date of the movie, because it was already scheduled to go into fifteen hundred theaters. I figured at least there wasn't much time for them to screw *this* movie up, and I *had* to get one good picture out of this three-picture deal. So *Chainsaw 2* was the least affected by their "wisdom." But even though it was the least tampered with, some of the Dennis Hopper stuff was removed, and I hated to see that happen, because it was the stuff that showed you that he was nuts—and you needed to know that or else his motivations didn't make enough sense. That put a dent in the movie, but luckily it didn't totally blow it, and I can still watch that picture. But just so you readers will know, the Lefty Enright character, that crazy Texas Ranger that Hopper played, actually was an old boyfriend of Stretch's mother, and he had sent Stretch's uncle to prison ten years before the movie started. So there were scenes of Stretch remembering Lefty Enright, and that is why she comes to him in the first place—she reads a newspaper story about "COWBOY CHASES CHAINSAWS." And they get to know one another a lot better. That's all out of the picture now. They just lifted pieces right out of the scenes. But I ended up feeling grateful that I was able to get one good picture out of the situation, and I do feel that people are rewarded when they see it.

OWNING THE PICTURE

The idea of ownership of a picture is very intriguing to me right now, especially after seeing what this comedian, Robert Townsend, did with his credit cards. I just got my platinum awards on both *Invaders from Mars* and *Chainsaw 2*. Platinum is $6 million, but *Chainsaw 2* went double platinum— $12 million worth of business on its first day. It's very exciting to think about making and owning a picture and bypassing this whole system of getting a green light and going into profit turnaround and spending part of your life being irritated and not in a good mood. It's really fun only when I'm saying "Action" and "Cut," and everything else is just space in between.

Had I stayed in Texas, the only things I would have really missed are *Salem's Lot* and *Poltergeist,* and I might not have missed those. At times, instead of focusing on the thing I really want to do, I'm juggling three or four projects at one time, in various stages of development. Sometimes it's a fluke, the ones that get a green light. There are quite a few films that I've developed that I wish I had made. They would have satisfied me, things that I approached with the kind of passion that the audience would definitely have felt. But the pictures just never got made. Now it's too late to make them, because there's a new audience out there, so some of these properties that were very good will never come to be.

I believe that a filmmaker has to keep up with his audience, and continue to *be* audience, which is very hard to do from inside the industry. Being objective about a film isn't the same as when you're a fourteen-year-old kid out in the middle of the country. In the nucleus of the industry one's values can be altered frightfully. And I've been in and out of the audience mode several times over fifteen years. And now in the past couple of years I've stopped watching films at home so much, and I'll go out to a theater, or I'll fly back to Texas and go to the theaters around the University of Texas to hear the audience. I can usually be fairly anonymous, but when I went to Tokyo I was mobbed—it made me feel what I imagine somebody like David Lee Roth must feel. It was kind of wonderful in a way.

Oliver Stone directing *Wall Street. Photo by Andy Schwartz.*

When **Oliver Stone** couldn't land directing jobs after graduating from NYU's film school, he kept on writing instead. His screenplay for *Midnight Express* won him his first Academy Award. After that, he worked on a string of big, successful projects such as *Conan the Barbarian, Scarface,* and *Year of the Dragon.* Finally he wrote and directed *Salvador* and *Platoon,* which landed him a total of ten Academy Awards. Shot in the Philippines on $5 million, *Platoon* grossed more than $140 million and won four Oscars—including best picture and best director.

30

Oliver Stone
Underdog Victories

★ I graduated from New York University Film School in 1971 with a B.F.A.; I had directed three shorts, and I thought I was a pretty good director, but nobody else thought so. Nobody would give me a job. It was a very tough business when I got out in the 1970s; the directors were mainly established people like Franklin Shattner and George Roy Hill—there was really very little fresh new blood. Each studio was doing only about six pictures a year. Coppola and Scorsese were just getting their breaks. But it was a very desolate period. I wrote eleven screenplays. No agent would represent me. I couldn't even get an agent to read those things. I was writing about Vietnam, and the doors were all closing in my face. Essentially New York was a very hard, cold experience. I drove a cab, and I got married. I was a messenger for a while. My wife helped support me, and I had a rough time. Now of course in the 1980s you write a script and it seems agents are falling all over themselves to read it. The emphasis is *on* youth, whereas this was not so in the 1970s.

FIRST MOVIES

Nobody was buying what I was writing, so I raised some money through private sources with some partners and directed a film in Canada on a very low budget, called *Seizure,* or *Queen of Evil,* with Martine Beswicke and Herve Villechaize. We shot it for about $200,000, and it was released very badly by Cinerama Releasing Corporation; then it was buried and forgotten. To this day, I'm still trying to get the video rights back, but it looks bleak.

Anyway, that was my first film, and it was done very cheaply with a lot of headaches and nightmares, and after that I went back to struggling and finally got a break in 1975. Robert Bolt, who's a great screenwriter, took an interest in a script I wrote called *The Cover-up,* which was never made, but through his efforts I got an agent for the first time. And that agent was a good one; he eventually got *Platoon* read by a lot of people, and although nobody wanted to produce it at that time, my writing talent was recognized, and I was given the chance to write *Midnight Express* in England. It was made on a very low budget, and it was a surprise hit. So, my cab-driving days were suddenly over. My price went up, and I was considered successful.

In 1981, I directed *The Hand,* a horror film with Michael Caine. It had some good things in it. It was a bit like *Blue Velvet,* but seven years too early. It wasn't a hit, because people wanted something like *Friday the 13th,* and we just couldn't deliver that. *The Hand* was a psychological movie about mental blackouts, so we were neither fish nor fowl; we fell between the cracks. And it was a very disappointing experience to me. It was my second horror film, and I sort of learned my lesson and walked away from horror films at that point in my life, and I'm never going to do another one, because I just don't have the horror film director's sensibility. It's a very specific sensibility. You have to almost in a sense be a master sadist to be a good horror film director. You have to be able to drive a nail right in through the forehead of the audience. You have to be willing to do that. You have to be a visual sadist. I'm sure John Carpenter's a nice guy, but he's also an excellent sadist in that sense. So is De Palma—he makes it work for him. Hitchcock too. He tortured Tippi Hedren to death in *The Birds.* Those are most effective films, but I don't have that capacity. So I learned my lesson.

SWORDS, SORCERY, AND GANGSTERS

Of the scripts I've written, I don't have any favorites. I look at them as children. Each one is a different type of child, and I have an affinity for each one in a different way. Some I would say have been less successful than others. *Eight Million Ways to Die* was truly botched in its making, but it was a good script.

De Palma did a hell of a fine job with *Scarface.* I loved that movie! I almost got killed researching it. I was in Bimini, hanging out with some Colombian drug dealers—middle-management types in this big smuggling haven—and I got into a party scene with them and almost got blown away one night. The critics were shocked by the violence in the film and repulsed by it. But the violence was based on truth. It was a great film, ahead of its time. It certainly was the basis of *Miami Vice,* which ripped it off. It never died, because the intelligent people who saw the movie—and I include street people in that— knew the dialogue was right on. It was the bluenoses who resented the movie. But there were some good reviews. Vincent Canby of *The New York Times* said that this was one of the most effective gangster movies since *The Godfather.*

I guess *Conan the Barbarian* was botched to some degree, but there are things I like in it. I took Conan very seriously and spent about six months working on it very hard. I had been a Robert Howard fan for many years. I really was pushing to do it, and Ed Pressman and I got together. He wanted me to direct my script, but I was unfinanceable at the time, and we turned it over to John Milius, who rewrote my script. But I thought Conan was very important work, and seminal work in the sense that it was one of the first sword and sorcery films—probably *the* first. He was a new kind of hero. I really believed in that script, and I don't think it ever really got to the screen in the form I intended.

I was very disappointed in that experience. But I never took one writing job for money alone; I always got involved in screenplays because I really believed in them. I've written many other scripts that haven't been produced, and I like them all for some reason or another. But I have no favorites.

UNDERDOG VICTORIES—*SALVADOR* AND *PLATOON*

The same with my movies. I love them all. I mean, *Salvador* to me is sort of a prodigal son because it was a movie that was made against overwhelming odds, on very little money. And it was a very radical look at American foreign policy in Central America. For that reason it was turned down for distribution by all the majors. Very few people knew my work, so I didn't get too much in the way of offers from talent. The agents weren't too hot on the idea. But I made the picture anyway. I got James Woods. I got John Savage. Jim Belushi. It was distributed by a small British company. But ultimately it found its success on video and was nominated for two Oscars. So that was an amazing underdog victory for me.

So was *Platoon.* All the circumstances in making it in some ways were much easier than *Salvador* because we had a few more bucks. But *Platoon* was also an enormous underdog and an outdated script that had been written in 1976 and forgotten and looked down upon, but it came back out of nowhere.

I think I was in a position where I had given up on that script, and I put it on the shelf. My feeling was that nobody in the movie business cared about Vietnam or wanted to make a realistic movie about it, so it was forgotten. And I was working with Michael Cimino in 1983 and 1984 on *Year of the Dragon,* which he wanted me to write with him, but I didn't want to get involved, and we made this elaborate business deal where I would go ahead and write *Year of the Dragon* and he would produce *Platoon* with De Laurentiis. He convinced me that *Platoon* was still doable in the 1984 period, when I

really doubted it. He said, "You'll see, the climate is going to turn around."
He was prescient, and I wasn't. But he convinced me, and I took it off the
shelf. Cimino never ended up producing it, but he got it off the shelf, and at
last it got made.

ON TO *WALL STREET*

My main reason for making *Wall Street* was to take a look at the 1980s era
in terms of Yuppies living in urban centers. It reflects a reality wherein money
has become the sex of the eighties. Net worth equals self-worth. And these
protagonists represent a valueless system. I want to shed some light on their
life-styles and the reality of money. I think what's going on on Wall Street is
to a degree an extension of the combat in Vietnam. There are certainly a lot of
veterans in the Street, and these guys look on their job as a life-and-death type
thing. It's a dog-eat-dog thing to survive. They're just highly attuned animals,
quite ready to slash and burn, like everybody else, to make a buck. I think
that once you work inside that system you have to go along with those values.
Those values are money, money, money. Nobody cares. Nobody gives a shit.
It's like a basketball game, you know—who scores the highest points.

Wall Street has a great cast—Charlie Sheen, Hal Holbrook, Daryl Hannah,
Michael Douglas, Terence Stamp—and I've always done the same thing in
every film, as far as casting goes, which is to try to get the best actors I can
get, whether they're big names or not. I've worked a lot with non-SAG people
because I like to try to use real people in my movies, and sometimes it works
and sometimes it doesn't. There's no formula on it. I'd say it has a fifty-fifty
chance of success. It's a question of your individual inclinations. But I always
feel it makes things much simpler on the set if you can get a good actor to do
what you want to do, because it saves a lot of time. If you cast correctly, you
are going to lick a good portion of your problems up front.

31

Coming Attractions

THIS BOOK HAS taken you all the way from the basics of movie-making to the pinnacle of success. It is now up to you to turn the vicarious into the actual—to make your own dream come true. Your "coming attractions" are waiting for you, somewhere in your own future. Since I love to watch movies, I'm as anxious to see what kind of picture you will make as you must be to get it into production.

HOW TO HANDLE SUCCESS

No matter what level of success you attain, you'll still have to work hard to continue to grow. You've already seen how hard people like George Romero, Tobe Hooper, and Oliver Stone had to work to make their mark in the industry and to keep their careers moving. You've gotten some insights into the pitfalls and the seductions of the movie world. How well you are able to handle these webs and snares when it's your turn to face them depends on your own strength of character. It also depends on your shrewdness—your ability to negotiate deals or to land agents and lawyers who will do it for you honestly and adeptly.

Always be on your guard. Remember that you are in the entertainment business, which many people regard as fun but not exactly *serious*. Therefore, in their eyes, you are not quite a serious person. If you were, you'd be in accounting, law, bricklaying, or plumbing. Money is not a serious matter to you; art is. That's what many people think, especially the con men. Since they don't believe that money is as important to you as it is to them, they don't even feel guilty when they cheat you out of it. You're an artist, they figure. What do you care about money?

Even as you learn to look upon these kinds of people and their glowing promises with skepticism, even cynicism, you have to remain open to fresh ideas. You have to preserve your "touch"—your ability to create awe and magic through cinematic art. More importantly, you have to preserve your ability to *be* awed and enchanted. That's what Tobe Hooper means when he talks about flying back to Texas to become part of the audience once again instead of just a cog in the motion picture establishment.

WHEELING AND DEALING

One of the stifling paradoxes of this business is that sometimes the deals you *make* slow your career down more than the deals you're still chasing but can't land. Oh, boy! you think. If I could only get that! Then it comes through, and you're on cloud nine. But then nothing happens. The project evaporates. You've got a signed contract, but you can't collect any money on it and you can't get started making the movie that the contract calls for.

A distributor I had sold scripts and movies to in the past called me on the phone and asked me to write a screenplay for a horror movie that could be produced on $200,000 or less. He offered to pay me $15,000 against a percentage of the movie's profits. I already had some partially developed ideas in my file along the lines of what he was looking for, so I knew I could write the script in four weeks, which would make the $15,000 a decent sum for the amount of my time involved. The distributor was all fired up, saying he had to get rolling on the movie right away.

We worked out a contract whereby I would get $5,000 upon delivery of the script and $10,000 upon commencement of principal photography, which I was *told* would take place within ninety days. However, the distributor said he would need to tie up the rights to my screenplay for three years to make his investors happy, in case something went wrong and they couldn't start shooting as planned. I figured, What the hell? Even if they never shoot the thing, I've made five grand for a month's work. So I didn't push to get the clause eliminated, because most of the time when you push a small distributor too hard he backs off and the deal falls through.

What happened was that the movie did *not* go into immediate production. Two of the distribution partners got into a hot dispute about the story and the director, and it's been almost three years now, and they're still fighting with each other. The net effect is that I let them *option* my property for three years for only $5,000. I may never collect the other $10,000, and I can't get my property back either, until the term of the contract expires. By that time, the story may be so shopworn that I can't sell it anywhere else.

No matter what financial level you're working on, projects still have a tendency to fall through, seemingly without any rhyme or reason. I once optioned a screenplay for $7,500 against a payment of $125,000 upon commencement of principal photography, and the deal looked like almost a sure thing—because investors had already deposited $3 million into the producer's bank account so he could get started making the movie. It was already cast, and the director and crew were hired. Even the music was already produced. But the producer decided not to make the picture anyway. He chose to forfeit the option money and all the preproduction expenditures. I've never been able to find out exactly why.

No matter what kinds of safeguards you build into your contracts, your objective is still to make movies, not to get paid little chunks of cash for *not* making them. So, remember to keep plenty of balloons in the air and irons in the fire. Just like all the other people who are succeeding in this business, you'll have to have a dozen projects in various stages of development and wheeling/dealing at all times.

KEEP ON LEARNING

Stimulate your enthusiasm by studying the work of others, whether they are gifted amateurs or noted professionals. Go to see films of all types, from the artistic to the crassly commercial. Study the trade publications to find out which films are drawing people into the theaters. Figure out *why*. Keep trying to get a handle on what *moves* the audience. You can build these ingredients into your own worthwhile work, no matter what kinds of themes and subjects you want to explore.

If you have a feeling that your knowledge of any part of the movie business is shaky or incomplete, there are many good books that can help you. Two of my favorites are *Independent Feature Film Production,* by Gregory Goodell, and *Making Films Your Business,* by Mollie Gregory. You may also wish to subscribe to some of the excellent movie magazines, like *American Film* and *Premiere.*

You can get a subscription to *American Film* by joining the American Film Institute, which conducts wonderful workshops and seminars on all aspects of movie-making, from the creative to the business and legal. The seminars are held in major cities all around the United States, so you don't have to go to New York or Los Angeles to attend if you happen to live far away from those two major motion picture centers.

Don't study only film. Study everything around you. Learn to communicate verbally as well as visually with your fellow man. Movies have contained dialogue even before human voices were put onto film in 1927. Before that, the dialogue was printed on cards, but it was still there. Not only are love, hate, humor, and violence important potential movie themes, but also politics and philosophy and the history of our striving for human progress and dignity. Oliver Stone proved this when he made *Salvador*. So, learn as much as you can about everything going on in the world. Build your craftsmanship around a solid understanding of the human condition. Then, maybe you'll become an important filmmaker.

2. *Contractual Arrangements.* The General Partner has made the following contractual arrangements with respect to the Motion Pictures: The General Partner has entered into employment agreements with John A. Russo & R. Paul McCollough, pursuant to which they have written original screenplays for the Motion Pictures. John A. Russo has written an original screenplay for a motion picture tentatively entitled "MARCY GIRL" and R. Paul McCollough has written an original screenplay for a motion picture tentatively entitled "BROTHERS IN BLOOD". All rights, titles and interest in and to such screenplays have been acquired by the General Partner. All of the rights of the General Partner pursuant to the foregoing agreements shall be assigned to the Partnership upon its formation.

Other than the foregoing, no definite arrangements have been made, as of the date hereof, by the General Partner.

3. *Services of General Partner and Payments to It.* The General Partner shall serve as producer of the Motion Pictures. In consideration for such services, and of all rights in the screenplays written by John A. Russo & R. Paul McCollough (to be assigned to the Partnership upon the formation of the Partnership), and of furnishing the services of its key personnel toward the production of these Motion Pictures, the General Partner shall be paid *$20,000* by the Partnership.

4. The General Partner may hereafter, prior to the formation of the Partnership, pay preproduction expenses in connection with the Motion Pictures. The General Partner shall have the right to be reimbursed therefore by the Partnership upon its formation.

5. *Estimated Production Requirements.* The estimated production requirements ("Production Requirements") for the production of the Motion Pictures shall be *$50,000* except that the General Partner shall have the right, in its sole discretion, to increase the Production Requirements by an amount not exceeding *$10,000* (to a sum which shall be not more than *$60,000*).

6. *Raising of Production Requirements.* The Production Requirements shall be raised, contributed or arranged for, as follows:

A. The General Partner shall have the right to make arrangements for loans ("Loans") to be made to the Partnership to be applied to the production costs of the Motion Pictures. No such Loans shall bear interest at a rate in excess of 13% per annum.

B. The General Partner shall have the right to arrange for the deferment of payments (including the payment to be made to the General Partner referred to in paragraphs 3 and 4 hereof) for materials, rights and services in connection with the production of the Motion Pictures (either prior to or after the payment of distribution fees and expenses). Such arrangements are herein referred to as "Deferments."

C. The General Partner shall obtain limited contributions ("Limited Contributions") to the Partnership from Limited Partners to meet the production expenses of the Motion Pictures which have not been met by Loans and/or Deferments. The minimum amount of the Limited Contributions shall be the difference between (1) the Production requirements (which shall not be less than *$50,000* nor more than *$60,000)* and (2) the sum of the loans (referred to in sub-paragraph A above) and the value of the Deferments (referred to in sub-paragraph B above).

7. *Limited Contributions.* All Limited Contributions contributed by the Limited Partners shall be deposited in a special bank account to be opened by the General Partner under the name of the Partnership. The Limited Contributions contributed by the Limited Partners will, in the discretion of the General Partner, be expended for Partnership purposes without awaiting subscription of the entire Production Requirement.

8. *Filing of Certificate of Limited Partnership and Amended Certificate.* The Partnership shall commence on the day upon which, pursuant to *Pennsylvania Uniform Partnership Act, 1915, March 26, P.L. 18,* the Certificate of Limited Partnership is duly filed in *the office of the Recorder of Deeds, Allegheny County, Pennsylvania,* and shall continue until terminated as provided in this agreement. A notice containing the substance of the Certificate of Limited Partnership shall be published as required by the Pennsylvania Limited Partnership Law.

After the Certificate of Limited Partnership has been filed, the General Partner shall have the right to continue to obtain Limited Contributions to the Partnership from additional Limited Partners and to admit such additional Limited Partners to the Partnership, provided that the share of profits payable to such additional Limited Partners shall be paid from the General Partner's share of profits hereunder, without affecting the share of net profits payable to the original Limited Partners. In this connection the General Partner shall file amended Certificates of Limited Partnership.

9. *Excess Production Requirements.* If the cost of supplying the materials, rights and services to complete the Motion Pictures to Edited 16 Millimeter Workprint Stage, shall exceed the sum of the Loans, the Deferments and the Limited Contributions of all Limited Partners, then the General Partner agrees, either by making cash contributions itself as a Limited Partner, or by obtaining contributions from the other Limited Partners, or by making or obtaining additional Loans to the Partnership, to make available to the Partnership such sums as shall equal the excess. The foregoing to the contrary notwithstanding, the General Partner shall have the right to abandon production of the Motion Pictures before commencement of principal photography if, as a consequence of changes in economic conditions subsequent to the date of this agreement, the estimated costs of the production of the Motion Pictures should exceed the estimated Production Requirements by more than 10%. Further, the General Partner shall not be obligated to make or obtain additional contributions or additional Loans if the costs of the production shall be increased as a result of extraordinary events, such as enemy invasions, strikes, Acts of God (such as the death or incapacity of principal performers in the Motion Pictures) etc., or events beyond the control of the General Partner, whether such events occur before or after commencement of principal photography.

10. *Joint Ventures and Additional General Partners.* In connection with the obtaining of Loans, Deferments or Limited Contributions to the Limited Partnership, the General Partner shall have the right, in its sole discretion, to cause the Limited Partnership to enter into joint venture or co-production arrangements with respect to the Motion Pictures with any other person, firm or corporation on terms and conditions which shall be in the sole discretion of the General Partner.

Without impairing in any way its right and obligations, under statute or otherwise, as a General Partner of the Limited Partnership, the General Partner may enter into agreements with any persons, firms or corporations whereby the General Partner agrees to share its share, as a General Partner, of the net profits of the Partnership, and its power to make decisions in regard to any consents, approvals, or recommendations it might make in connection with the Motion Pictures.

11. *Return of Limited Contributions.* The contributions of the Limited Partners shall be returned to them as hereafter set forth in this paragraph 11.

At such time after the commencement of exhibition of the motion pictures and after the payment of all expenses incurred in connection with the production, distribution and exhibition of the Motion Pictures (including, without limitation, distribution fees and expenses) and establishment of a Sinking Fund reasonable to meet future expenses, all cash which (a) has not to that date been expended by the Partnership, and (b) is received from time to time by the Partnership as its share of the proceeds derived from the distribution of the Motion Pictures, pursuant to the agreements with distributors, or any other source, shall be distributed as follows and in the following order of priority:

A. *First,* to the repayment of all Loans (plus the interest thereon, but not in excess of 13% per annum) and to the payment of all Deferments.

B. *Second,* to the repayment to the Limited Partners of their Limited Contributions. Each Limited Partner shall receive that proportion of the proceeds available as his Limited Contribution to be repaid pursuant to this sub-paragraph B bears to the aggregate amount of all Limited Contributions to be repaid pursuant to this sub-paragraph B. The distributions to be made pursuant to this sub-paragraph B shall be made monthly until such time as the total Limited Contributions of all Limited Partners shall have been fully repaid.

12. *Definition of Net Profits.* The term "Net Profits" as used in this agreement shall be deemed to mean all of the proceeds derived from the distribution of the Motion Pictures and any other proceeds derived from any other source from the exploitation of any rights held by the Partnership in and to the Motion Pictures, after the deduction of:

A. All distribution fees and expenses (including without limitation, the cost of prints and advertising).

B. The total cost of the production of the Motion Pictures, including, without limitation, the following:

(I) The payments to be made to the General Partner, set forth in paragraph 3 hereof;

(II) Interest on Loans (but not in excess of 13% per annum);

(III) The value of all Deferments;

(IV) Any compensation measured by net profits of the Partnership payable to any actor, composer, editor, or cameraman who performs services with respect to the Motion Pictures.

C. Any amounts payable to the producer's representative engaged by the Partnership in connection with the Motion Pictures.

D. Any other expenses actually incurred by the General Partner in connection with the production, distribution or exhibition of the Motion Pictures (except compensation measured by net profits which is payable to any person, firm or corporation, other than an actor, composer, editor or cameraman for furnishing services or materials to the Partnership).

13. *Division of Net Profits.* The General Partner hereby agrees that it will not participate in any division of net profits made by the Partnership until such time as all of the Limited Partners in the Partnership have recouped a sum of money equal to that of their original Limited Contributions. Each Limited Partner of the Partnership shall receive *1%* of the net profits of the Partnership for each *$1,000* of Limited Contributions made by him to the Partnership. (If the amount of a Limited Partner's Limited Contribution shall not be a multiple of *$1,000,* then his share of net profits shall be appropriately prorated.) The remaining net profits of the Partnership shall be paid to the General Partner.

Net profits shall be distributed not less frequently than semi-annually unless the amount of net profits available for distribution shall be less than $5,000, in which event distribution may be deferred to the next semi-annual distribution date.

14. *Term of Partnership.* The partnership shall continue until the completion of all distribution of the Motion Pictures or until the termination of the Partnership's rights in the Motion Pictures. The General Partner shall have the right, in its sole discretion, to sell, or otherwise dispose of, any or all rights in the Motion Picture, and if all such rights shall be sold or otherwise disposed of, then the Partnership shall terminate. The Partnership shall also terminate in the event of dissolution of the General Partner. If a Lim-

ited Partner shall die, his executors, administrators, or, if he shall become insane, his committee or other representatives, shall have the same rights that the Limited Partner would have had if he had not died or become insane, and the share of such Limited Partner in the assets of the Partnership shall, until the termination of the Partnership, be subject to all the terms, provisions and conditions of this agreement as if such Limited Partner had not died or become insane.

15. *Limitation of Liability.* No Limited Partner shall be personally liable for any debts, obligations or loss of the Partnership beyond the amount of his Limited Contribution to the capital of the Partnership. If any sum by way of repayment of Limited Contribution or distribution of net profits shall have been paid prior or subsequent to the termination date of the Partnership and at any time subsequent to such repayment there shall be any unpaid debts, taxes, liabilities or obligations of the Partnership, and the Partnership shall not have sufficient assets to meet them, then each Limited Partner and the General Partner shall be obligated to repay to the Partnership up to the amount of profits distributed to him, and capital so returned to him, as the General Partner may need for such purpose.

16. *Termination.* Upon the termination of the Partnership, the assets of the Partnership shall be liquidated as promptly as possible and the cash proceeds shall be applied as set forth in paragraph 11 and thereafter as set forth in paragraph 13 above and in the same order of priority set forth therein. When there is a contingent debt, obligation or liability, a reserve shall be set up to meet it, and if and when said contingency shall cease to exist, the monies, if any, in said reserve shall be distributed as provided for in paragraph 11 and thereafter as set forth in paragraph 13.

17. *Obligations of General Partner.* The General Partner agrees:

A. To open and maintain a special bank account in which shall be deposited the Partnership funds.

B. To keep full and faithful books of account in which shall be entered fully and accurately each transaction of the Partnership.

C. To furnish each Limited Partner with a statement of expense within 90 days after the commencement of exhibition of the Motion Pictures, and a statement of income and expenses not less frequently than semi-annually following the commencement of exhibition of the Motion Pictures; to furnish each Limited Partner with all so-called "information returns" (prior to the filing thereof with the federal and state governments) showing the income of the Partnership and of each Partner received therefrom; to have all of such statements prepared by a Certified Public Accountant experienced in the motion picture business.

D. To render in connection with the Motion Pictures services customarily and usually rendered by motion picture producers, and to devote as much time thereto as may be necessary, it being understood and agreed, however, that the General Partner may engage in other businesses, including other motion picture productions, and the Limited Partners shall have no right to share in the proceeds therefrom.

18. *Control.* The General Partner shall have complete control of the production, distribution and exhibition of the Motion Pictures, and the exploitation and turning to account of all rights therein. Without limitation, the General Partner shall have the complete control over all business decisions with respect to the Motion Pictures; including the sale or other disposition of the Motion Pictures, distribution and exhibition arrangements, and any other marketing arrangements.

19. *Assignments.* No assignee of a Limited Partner shall have the right to become a substitute Limited Partner in the place of his assignor.

20. *No Right to Demand Property.* No Limited Partner shall have the right to demand and receive property other than cash in return for his Limited Contribution. In the repayment of Limited Contributions, the division of net profits or otherwise, no Limited Partner shall have any priority over any other Limited Partner.

21. *Counterparts.* This agreement may be executed in counterparts, all of which taken together shall be deemed one original.

22. *Additional General Partners.* At any time prior to the formation of the Partnership, the General Partner, in its sole discretion, may cause an additional person or persons to become General Partners of the Partnership by having such person or persons execute this agreement as General Partners provided that the Lim-

ited Partners' share in the net profits of the Partnership shall not be affected thereby.

23. *Power of Attorney.* Each partner does hereby make, constitute and appoint the General Partner his true and lawful attorney, and in his name, place and stead, to make, execute, sign, acknowledge and file (I) The Certificate of Limited Partnership of the Partnership, and to include therein all information required by the laws of the Commonwealth of Pennsylvania, (II) Any amended Certificate of Limited Partnership as may be required, and (III) All papers which may be required to effectuate the dissolution of the Partnership after its termination.

24. *Purchase of Limited Partnership Interest for Investment.* Each Limited Partner hereby represents to the General Partner that he is acquiring the limited partnership interests offered hereunder for purposes of investment only.

IN WITNESS WHEREOF, the parties have hereunto set their hands and seals to the Limited Partnership Agreement of *Contemporary-American Film Company* as of this _____.

AS GENERAL PARTNER

NAME   ADDRESS

_____   _____

BY _____   _____

                                       _____

AS LIMITED PARTNERS

Name and Soc. Sec. No.	Residence	Cash Amount Agreed to be Contributed	Percentage of Profits to be Received

_____
SIGNATURE OF LIMITED PARTNER

FREE LANCE PLAYERS CONTRACT

This agreement made this _____ day of _____
19 ____, between The Majorettes Inc. hereinafter
called "Producer" and _____
hereinafter called "Player", do hereby set forth and
intend to be legally bound by the following conditions.
These conditions extend also to the heirs and assigns
of both "Producer" and "Player".

WITNESSTH:

1) PHOTOPLAY, ROLE, SALARY AND GUARANTEE:
   Producer hereby engages Player to render services
as such in the role of _____ in a
photoplay, the working title of which is now The Majorettes Inc. at the salary of $_____ per day or $_____ per
week. Player accepts such engagement upon the terms
herein specified. Producer guarantees that it will
furnish Player not less than _____ day(s) or _____ week(s)
employment; however, Player's work days or weeks may
not be consecutive and player will only be paid for actual days or weeks on camera.

2) TERM:
   The term of employment hereunder shall begin on or
about _____
_____ and shall continue thereafter until
the completion of the photography and the recordation
of said role. If in the judgment of the Producer, for any
reason, the Player fails to perform his role satisfactorily, the Producer has the right to terminate employment of the Player at any time during the production of
the photoplay at which time wages will also terminate.

3) PLAYER'S ADDRESS:
   All notices which the Producer is required or may
wish to give to the Player may be given either by mailing
the same, addressed to the Player at _____,
_____
or such notice may be given to the Player personally,
either orally or in writing.

4) PLAYER'S TELEPHONE:
   The Player must keep the Producer advised as to
where the Player may be reached by telephone without

unreasonable delay. The current telephone number of
the Player is _____.

5) FURNISHING OF WARDROBE:
The Player agrees to furnish all modern wardrobe
and wearing apparel reasonably necessary for the por-
trayal of said role; it being agreed, however, that
should so-called "character" or "period" costumes be
required, the Producer shall supply the same.

6) PLAYER'S WORKWEEK:
The Player's workweek shall consist of five (5)
nine (9) hour days or a total of forty-five (45) hours.

7) PLAYER'S WORKDAY:
The Player's workday shall consist of nine (9)
hours.

8) TERMS OF WAGE PAYMENTS:
The Player agrees to defer _____% of wage payments
specified under Paragraph 1 of this FREE LANCE PLAYERS
CONTRACT. Such deferments shall be paid by the Producer
from first monies derived from the theatrical release
of said photoplay. The Producer may, at his discretion,
pay all or any portion of the deferred wages before release of the completed photoplay.

9) RIGHT TO USE PHOTOGRAPHS:
The Player grants all rights to the Producer to use
any photographs, still pictures or motion pictures
that may be taken in connection with the above mentioned photoplay. The Player agrees that the Producer's "right to use photographs" extends also to cover
any advertising, promotional or publicity purposes,
and also extends to the producer's heirs and assigns.

10 SCREEN CREDIT:
The Producer agrees that the Player will receive
full name screen credit on each release print which is
made.

11) PLAYER'S SOCIAL SECURITY NUMBER:
    The Player's Social Security Number is _____.

_____   _____
For the Producer   Player

_____   _____
Witness   Witness

THE MAJORETTES INC.
732 Filbert Street
Pittsburgh, PA. 15232
(412)621-6702

TALENT, SERVICES AND ADVERTISING RELEASE FORM

_____

City & State

_____

Date

For value received, I agree and consent that The Majorettes Inc. and its nominees and assigns may use any motion pictures, still photographs, videotape recordings, magnetic tape recordings, optical recordings,
taken of _____ on _____ or
any reproduction thereof, in any form, style or color,
together with any writing and/or other advertising
and/or publicity material in connection therewith,
including the use of my name, as they may select.

I understand that my talents and/or services and any
related advertising and publicity materials are to be
used in connection with The Majorettes Inc.

This consent and release is given by me without limitations upon any use for projection, playback, reprints,
rerun, broadcast, telecast, or publication of every
kind, including the advertising and publicity connected therewith. I also agree that the originals and
copies therefrom shall be and remain in the exclusive
property of The Majorettes Inc. or its nominees and assigns.

I am over eighteen (18) years of age. If subject is under 18, a parent or guardian must sign this form on behalf of the minor.

Name

Address

City and State

Social Security Number

Phone

Witness

MUSIC AGREEMENT

AGREEMENT made this _____ day of _____, _____
by and between _____ with its
place of business at _____
_____,
hereinafter referred to as "Film Producer," and the
following persons and/or entities, names and addresses as follows:

_____
_____
_____
_____
_____

hereinafter singly and/or collectively referred to as
"Music Producer," do hereby set forth and intend to be
legally bound by the following conditions. These conditions extend also to the heirs and assigns of both
"Film Producer" and "Music Producer."

WITNESSETH:

1. ENGAGEMENT:
   Film Producer has engaged Music Producer to render
services as such in creating, arranging, writing and
causing to be performed music selections for use within
the sound track of a Motion Picture entitled _____,
which Film Producer has or will have produced. Music
Producer understands and accepts that other entities
may be hired by Film Producer to contribute music to
said sound track, in addition to what Music Producer
contributes.

2. WAIVER OF PAYMENT FOR SOUND TRACK SYNCHRONIZATION
   USE.
   Music Producer agrees to forever waive any and all
claims of payment for use of the Music referred to in
paragraph one as part of the sound track of the Motion
Picture. Music Producer gives Film Producer, gratis,
the sole and exclusive right to use the Music on all
prints of the Motion Picture in all formats and all markets world-wide, including theatrical motion picture,
television, and any and all improvements thereon,
whether now known or hereafter devised, developed, invented or discovered, including but not limited to so-
called "free television" and so-called "pay" or
subscription television; non-theatrical (including

16mm, 8mm and all other gauges), cassette or cartridge uses, and any and all other forms of possible distribution or exploitation of said Motion Picture; also including the use of said Music on portions of the Motion Picture which may appear in preview trailers, television trailers or other forms of advertising and promotion in which portions of the Motion Picture are shown.

3. RIGHTS RETAINED BY MUSIC PRODUCER.
Music Producer will retain all rights in and to the Music, except for sound track synchronization use described in paragraph two above. Film Producer agrees to forever waive any and all claims of payment for use or sale of the Music for purposes other than sound track synchronization.

4. TITLES AND SELECTIONS.
The following titles and selections comprise the Music covered under this Agreement:

_____
_____
_____
_____
_____
_____
_____
_____
_____
_____
_____
_____
_____
_____
_____
_____

5. MUSIC PRODUCER'S WARRANTIES.
Music Producer hereby represents and warrants to the Film Producer as to the date hereof and forever:

a. That it has the full right, power and authority to enter into and perform this Agreement;

b. That it has not executed, done or permitted any document, act or thing which would or might preclude it from entering into and performing this Agreement and permitting the Music to be used and marketed by Film Producer as contemplated by this Agreement;

c. That there is not and will not be any contract, commitment or other arrangement which is in conflict with this Agreement or which might in any way limit, re-strict or impair Film Producer's rights hereunder;

d. That Music Producer has heretofore acquired ex-clusively all the rights for performance, production and sale of the Music, including without limitation the right to use the ideas, themes, lyrics, arrangements and all other matters and things upon which the music was based or which were or shall be used in its produc-tion or recording;

e. That all rights granted hereunto to the Film Pro-ducer are or shall be paid for and will be free and clear of liens and encumbrances of every kind and character;

f. That the performing rights in all the Music com-positions shall be (1) controlled by BMI or ASCAP or a foreign affiliate or counterpart of either thereof; (2) or in the public domain; (3) or controlled by Music Producer to the extent required for the purposes of this Agreement;

g. That Film Producer shall incur no liability for residual or other compensation or consideration for re-runs or subsequent runs of the Motion Picture on television or elsewhere to music composers, music pub-lishers, musicians or other parties in connection therewith;

h. That no part of the Music infringes or shall in-fringe the right of privacy of any person or constitute a libel or slander and no part of the Music shall violate the trademark, tradename, copyright, artistic, dra-matic, patent, personal, property or other rights of any third party.

6. SCREEN CREDITS.
The following credits shall be given on all prints of the Motion Picture which contain the Music herein dis-cussed:

_____

_____

_____

_____

_____

_____

_____

_____

_____

_____

_____

7. ALTERATIONS IN SCORE OR CREDITS.

Music Producer understands and agrees that it may become necessary, due to desires of the Motion Picture distributor or others, to change or eliminate some or all pieces of the Music which Music Producer has produced, in which case screen credits will change accordingly. Music Producer grants to Film Producer the right to make any and all changes which may become necessary in this regard.

8. ALTERATION OF AGREEMENT.

This Agreement may not be altered, changed or modified, nor any provision hereof be waived, except in writing signed by both parties hereto.

9. NOTICES.

All notices, statements, approvals, objections, etc., that either party may wish to serve or may be required to serve on the other hereunder shall be in writing and may be served by personal delivery or by U.S. First Class Mail, postage prepaid, addressed to the respective party at the address hereunder set forth. Either party may from time to time designate in writing a different address for such service.

10. CONSTRUCTION.

This Agreement shall be construed and interpreted pursuant to the laws of the Commonwealth of Pennsylvania, United States of America.

11. ENTIRE UNDERSTANDING.

This Agreement contains the entire understanding of the parties. There are no representations, warranties, promises, covenants or undertakings of any nature whatsoever, except as herein expressly set forth.

IN WITNESS WHEREOF, the parties have executed this Agreement on the day and the year first above written.

ATTEST FOR THE FILM PRODUCER:

_____

_____

_____

ATTEST FOR THE MUSIC PRODUCER:

_____

_____

_____

Notes

Page 1
Tom Bernard, Orion Classics. *In Motion* magazine. "The Future of Entertainment Films"

Newsweek. December 7, 1970

Pages 9–10
George A. Romero. *Cinefantastique* magazine. "Romero," by Tony Scott

Page 17
David Puttnam. *Newsweek.* "Hollywood Goes Independent" April 6, 1987

Newsweek. Same as above.

Page 29
George A. Romero—from my interview with him

Page 93
Tom Bernard, Orion Classics. *In Motion* magazine. "The Future of Entertainment Films"

Page 99
William Goldman, *Adventures in the Screen Trade.* Warner Books, 1983

Page 106
David Puttnam. *American Film* magazine. September 1987. "Power Kvetching" by Kate Bales

Page 107
James L. Brooks. *Premiere* magazine. February 1988. "Our Mr. Brooks" by Christopher Connelly

Page 135
Ingo Preminger. *Esquire.* August 1970

Joseph Gelmis. *The Film Director As Superstar.* Doubleday and Company, 1970

Page 179
Sam Goldwyn. Quoted by Don Simpson in *Premiere* magazine. July/August 1987. "The Emotion of Triumph" by Tony Schwartz

Jack Nicholson. *Newsweek.* December 7, 1970

Page 205
Robert M. Cheren, New World Pictures. *Boxoffice* magazine. May, 1987. "New World Means Independence"

Earl Owensby, E. O. Pictures. *Newsweek.* January 12, 1987. "A Down-Home Movie Mogul"

Page 237
Karen Arthur. *American Film* magazine. October 1987. "Dialogue on Film"

All other quotes are from my interviews.

Index

Note: Page numbers in italics refer to illustrations.